Co-Active Coaching

Co-Active

**New Skills for
Coaching People
Toward Success
in Work and Life**

Laura Whitworth
Henry Kimsey-House
Phil Sandahl

Davies-Black Publishing
Palo Alto, California

Published by Davies-Black Publishing, a division of CPP, Inc., 3803 East Bayshore Road, Palo Alto, CA 94303; 800-624-1765.

Special discounts on bulk quantities of Davies-Black books are available to corporations, professional associations, and other organizations. For details, contact the Director of Book Marketing and Sales at Davies-Black Publishing, 650-691-9123; fax 650-623-9271.

Visit the Davies-Black website at www.daviesblack.com.

06 05 04 03   13 12 11 10 9
Printed in the United States of America

Library of Congress Cataloging-in-Publication Data
Whitworth, Laura
    Co-active coaching : new skills for coaching people toward success in work
    and life / Laura Whitworth, Henry Kimsey-House, Phil Sandahl. —1st ed.
        p. cm.
    Includes bibliographical references and index.
    ISBN 0-89106-123-1
    1. Self-actualization (Psychology)   2. Mentoring.   3. Motivation
    (Psychology)   4. Success.   I. Kimsey-House, Henry.   II. Sandahl, Phil.
    III. Title.
    BF637.s4W484 1998
    158'.3—dc21   98–25924

FIRST EDITION
First printing 1998

This book is dedicated to the clients and coaches

whose lives we have touched

and whose lives have touched us . . .

and to the clients and coaches to come.

Many people have already heard the story of the starfish on the beach, but it bears repeating here because it illustrates the essence of co-active coaching and what it means to be a coach.

Early one morning a man was walking along the beach, watching the ocean waves breaking on the shore, and he saw a most unusual thing. He saw that the beach was littered with thousands of starfish that had been washed up on shore and were dying in the sun. Far down the beach in the distance, he could see a young woman picking up starfish and throwing them back in the ocean, one at a time. When he was close enough to her to be heard above the waves the man said, "You're wasting your time. There are *thousands* of starfish here. You can't possibly make any difference." The young woman reached down, picked up a starfish, and threw it as far as she could, back into the sea. "I made a difference to that one," she said, and she reached down to pick up another.

Contents

Foreword   ix

Preface   xi

Acknowledgments   xv

Introduction   xvii

one
Co-Active Coaching Fundamentals   1

1   The Co-Active Coaching Model   3

2   The Co-Active Coaching Relationship   13

two
Co-Active Coaching Skills   29

3   Listening   31

4   Intuition   49

5   Curiosity   63

6   Action/Learning   79

7   Self-Management   95

three

Co-Active Coaching Practices   113

8   Client Fulfillment   115

9   Client Balance   127

10   Client Process   143

11   Tips and Traps   157

12   A Vision for the Future   169

The Coach's Toolkit   177

Glossary   253

About the Authors   259

Index   261

Foreword

Laura Whitworth, Henry Kimsey-House, and Phil Sandahl have collaborated here to produce an important resource for all who aspire to coach—from parents to professionals. In *Co-Active Coaching* they have given a comprehensive structure to guide, inform, and expand our coaching, not constrict or constrain it as some textbooks do—but then this is much more than a textbook. To take the many abstract principles, terms, and concepts of coaching and make them accessible in concrete rational English is no easy task, but one in which they have excelled. I see myself referring to a variety of sections of this book often in the future.

Coaching is still a new skill or new way of being—or something in between, depending on one's perspective. The term's long association with sport is not helpful. What is all too often done on the sports field in the name of coaching gives coaching a bad name. Moreover, there are sports coaches who get great results and are well liked by their athletes, but who use methods very different from co-active coaching.

The new genre of coaching based on humanistic and transpersonal psychological principles rejects much of old discredited behaviorism. It was first applied to sport by Timothy Gallwey with his all-time coaching classic, *The Inner Game of Tennis*. My *Coaching for Performance* extended the application of these principles to business, the area of coaching development that predominates in Europe. *Co-Active Coaching* is an important stepping stone in the wider acceptance and professionalization of the role and value of the personal coach in the United States. I suspect that we will soon see the merging of these differing European and U.S. developments on both sides of the Atlantic.

To some people, counseling and psychotherapy carry the stigma of mental illness. The personal coach has no such connotations, however, and *Co-Active Coaching* will contribute much to maintaining that status. Not only do we live in a changing world, but the speed of change is ever on the increase and with it come stresses and confusion sometimes beyond our own apparent resources. A personal coach does not remove these problems, but goes two steps further. The coach can help us turn them into challenges and enable us to overcome them by drawing on resources within ourselves that we never knew we had. With our new-found confidence we can then face new challenges.

One line in the book says it all: "People come to coaching for lots of different reasons, but the bottom line is change." This reminds me of one of my favorite quotes, presumably from Confucius: "If we do not change direction, we are liable to end up where we are headed." Yes, the world is changing and we can choose to change ourselves or get left behind in a treacherous backwater. A personal coach may be one of our best investments for the future: a read of this book, whether you are a prospective coach or client, certainly will be.

John Whitmore
Author of *Coaching for Performance*

Preface

This book is about coaching. In fact, it is about a particular kind of coaching: professional/personal coaching. This is a field that has grown dramatically over the last five to ten years. You can trace its heritage to executive coaching in large organizations and to mentoring programs. There are traces of consulting and counseling in the coaching background, as well as the application of contemporary management theory.

What has emerged is a profession that works with individual clients to help them achieve results and sustain life-changing behavior in their lives and careers. Professional/personal coaching addresses the whole person—with an emphasis on producing action and uncovering learning that can lead to more fulfillment, more balance, and a more effective process for living.

A New Approach

This book is about a particular approach to professional/personal coaching—a style of coaching we call *co-active coaching* because it involves the active and collaborative participation of both the coach and the client.

There are a variety of different coaching models in the world today. Many of these models come out of management or organizational development and emphasize improved productivity, team building, and other organizational performance goals. Some coaching models are built on the premise that the coach is the expert who provides advice as well as support and motivation. These expert-coach models put a strong emphasis on the coach's background and expertise. And then there are content coaches with niche specialties: sales coach, speech coach, business coach, coaches to help you organize your files and office, and so on. There are coaching models that are essentially mentoring models with a new name, "coach." In today's horizontal and dispersed workplace, many traditional managers are now cast in the role of "coach" with a team that functions almost like independent operators. In this scenario, the coach's job is to provide a game plan and individual attention as necessary—like a basketball coach—so the team operates productively.

The co-active coaching model takes a different stand. A primary purpose of this book is to provide professional coaches (and those who want to be professional coaches) with a well-established model and set of skills that have proved effective with hundreds of different clients over a period of many years. It is a model of coaching that several hundred coaches have learned and now apply every day in their coaching practices. It is a model with specific techniques and a comprehensive way of organizing the components of coaching. This book describes the model in detail, defines the skills and techniques of coaching, and offers samples of coaching conversations as well as practical exercises that will enhance your understanding of coaching.

The design of the co-active coaching model comes from our experience as coaches. The model reflects the world of coaching—effective coaching—we have experienced. It's a model whose design has emerged from a wide variety of workshops and seminars we have conducted over the years on various topics that are directly and indirectly related to coaching. Most of that work in recent years has been the training of coaches through The Coaches Training Institute (CTI).

CTI was founded in 1992 by Laura Whitworth and Henry Kimsey-House and joined a year later by Karen Kimsey-House. Today CTI is the nation's largest nonprofit organization devoted exclusively to training coaches and teaching coaching skills and is internationally recognized as a leading coaching organization. Delivering courses in the United States and Canada, with participants from Europe and Asia, CTI offers a comprehensive training program for coaches as well as a highly regarded certification program, a unique leadership development program, and a strong presence as a visionary force in the field of coaching.

How to Use This Book

We recommend that you start by getting a feel for a co-active coaching relationship—by projecting yourself into a coaching setting as client. The Introduction is designed to create a strong sense of what it would be like as a client in a powerful co-active coaching relationship.

Part One presents an overview of the co-active coaching model. The first chapter outlines the five contexts of co-active coaching: listening, intuition, curiosity, action/learning, and self-management. The chapter also describes the three principles—fulfillment, balance, and process—that together form the client's agenda at the heart of the model. Part One also explains how to design the alliance between coach and client—the foundation on which the entire coaching relationship is built.

Part Two describes each of the five contexts in detail and presents descriptions and examples of the coaching skills in action. Here we provide sample coaching conversations as well as exercises that bring the skills to life.

Part Three covers the three core principles: how to coach the client's fulfillment, balance, and process. In real life, of course, these are rarely distinct and a half-hour coaching session may trigger coaching in all three areas. For the sake of learning they are separated here. This part of the book also describes the practice of coaching—What is it *like* to be a coach?—and presents our vision for the future presence of coaching in the world.

What a Book About Coaching Can Do

Our workshops create the experience of coaching in a way that a book simply can't. For years we have said that it's more effective to learn about coaching by doing it than talking about it or reading about it. That's one of the reasons why it took so long to get this book written. Another reason is that we've been busy expanding to meet the growing demand for coaches and training. As we've grown, however, and moved into new areas of the country, we've noticed that there is still a great deal of confusion about coaching and what it can do for people. The time was right, therefore, to take a stand for co-active coaching and present it to the widest possible audience. That's why the book is available today. The book won't replace the actual experience of coaching, but it will give you a picture of what is involved. The book is designed to shine a bright light on the field of coaching and, in particular, a model of coaching we believe in. It's a model that makes sense—and we have years of experience working with it to prove that's true. More than that, it's an approach to coaching that we have seen make a difference in hundreds of lives. We know it works because we have seen it and experienced it firsthand. We now invite you to be part of that world.

Acknowledgments

Many people made this book possible, but one person in particular deserves special attention. This book would not exist without the support and contributions of Karen Kimsey-House. One of the three directors of The Coaches Training Institute, together with Laura Whitworth and Henry Kimsey-House, she is the heart and soul of CTI and the person who managed its dramatic growth during the time that this book was written. Karen has been an integral part of the creative team since joining CTI in 1993. She developed and implemented the CTI certification program, which is recognized as a model for certifying professional coaches. Her commitment to the impact of coaching is visible throughout the work of CTI as it grows internationally; her dedication to the coaching profession helped inspire us to complete this book.

In addition, a number of others deserve to be recognized for their contributions or their influence in the creation of this book, including CJ Hayden, Judy Pike, Judith Cohen, John Vercelli, Thomas Leonard, John Whitmore, our own coaches, the CTI Leader body—a community of extraordinary workshop leaders—all of our clients, and our families.

Introduction

If you bought this book, it's because you want to be a coach or to improve your coaching skills. But before we get to that, we'd like you to step back and consider—from the client's perspective—what an ideal coaching relationship would be like.

Imagine a relationship where the total focus is on you, on what you want in your life, and on what will help you achieve it. The coaching relationship is like that. It's unique. There is no other relationship in our lives that consistently offers this extraordinary level of support and encouragement. That's especially true in the style of coaching we describe as co-active coaching. This relationship is like having your own personal navigator for the journey of your life: someone who will help you find your way and stay on course.

Coaching is a powerful relationship for people making important changes in their lives. The model of co-active coaching described in this book illustrates a framework for effective coaching relationships based on years of client experience. These clients represent the full spectrum of occupations: CEOs at top corporate offices, artists, managers, consultants, small business owners, entrepreneurs. Moreover, they represent people for whom the job was just a small part of their reason for seeking out coaching.

Imagine someone listening, not only to your words, but also to what's behind them—who even listens to the spaces between the words. Someone in tune with the nuances of your voice, your emotion, your energy—who is intent on receiving everything you communicate. Someone who listens to the very best in you, even when you can't hear it in yourself. Listening at this level is just one of the special coaching skills we focus on here. The skills of coaching are not only described but reinforced with practical exercises you can use for your own coaching development as well as exercises you can use with your clients.

Imagine someone who will hold you accountable and keep you moving forward toward your dreams and goals. The field of coaching has grown dramatically in recent years because it provides a powerful structure to help people focus on specific outcomes and stay on track. There is much more to the coaching relationship than just accountability, of course, and this book expands the perspective of coaching so you can see and apply its inherent strengths.

In fact, in today's marketplace, coaching includes a variety of specialists using the name "coaching" applied to a wide range of practices. There are coaching programs for executives, programs for managers, and programs with a specialized core of content delivered along with coaching—for example, programs to help people be better sales reps, better writers, be better organized, or give more persuasive presentations from the podium. This book is about co-active coaching—an approach that can be broadly applied to different occupations and coaching needs. It is an integrated approach to coaching because people live a whole life. They take their work frustrations home with them into their relationships. Their money worries influence their leisure time and their job. The effort they put into personal growth can affect their career and family. That's why the co-active coaching model not only emphasizes the big picture but focuses attention on specific action plans.

Imagine a relationship with someone who is totally curious about your dreams and aspirations, what makes you tick, what you value, what you are most passionate about in your life—a person who will help you clarify your goals and provide the tools for action and learning that lead to the results you want. This book will show you how to design an effective coaching relationship to help others make powerful changes in their lives and work. It's a relationship that can motivate clients and unstick the stuck. People come to coaching for lots of different reasons, but the bottom line is change. They no longer want things to stay the same and they see that coaching can make that change happen. The coach is there while they work on the mechanisms of their life—handing them the tools, holding the light, so they can see what needs to be done and have both hands free to do it.

Imagine a relationship in your life with a person who is sometimes even more committed to what you want in your life than you are. Imagine what it would be like if someone knew your values and life purpose and was holding you true to them—someone who would hold the flag at the top of the hill, encouraging you to press on, someone to celebrate your victories and help you learn from your setbacks. Coaching creates a context where people regularly work on the most important issues of their lives. In this book you will find specific techniques to clarify choices, create action plans, and monitor results. But coaching also functions on a process level to help people understand who and where they are in their lives. This book offers the means to help others find fulfillment, to clarify choices, and to be fully in the process of life, riding the waves through crest and trough to the destination.

Imagine a relationship with someone who will *absolutely* tell you the truth—the truth about where you are strong, for example, and where you sell yourself short—someone who knows you can handle it and knows that's what you want. Someone who sees how big you can be and constantly holds that big image for you—even when you can't hold it for yourself. Think of someone in your family or a close friend who is going through change. Imagine what a gift it would be for them to have a coach in their life—a professional trained to make maximum use of listening, communicating, and intuition skills to help people live full lives. The emphasis in this book is on providing information and exercises for professional coaching, especially the ongoing, one-on-one professional and personal coaching relationship. And yet the skills and insights you acquire from this book can be applied in your own life, in your work relationships, in your relationships with family and friends—because coaching skills and insights help people become more effective, resourceful, satisfied, and productive in their lives at many levels.

Imagine someone who listens to you without judgment and allows you to show emotion—in fact, accepts you without analyzing you. Imagine you get to talk to this person every week, even when you've just made a mess of things or when you've had great success. This is the place you visit regularly and consistently . . . to consolidate, to integrate, and to push on. Everybody does have conversations like this once in a while. The advantage of being in a coaching relationship is that it happens regularly. The coach is there, waiting for them, trained to make the most out of each interaction. In the process, the coaching relationship grows and develops and becomes more effective. The impact of coaching increases as coach and client get to know each other better and as the coach becomes more familiar with the client's strengths, weaknesses, dreams, and acts of sabotage.

In this book you'll learn how to discover and promote your client's agenda—and be almost invisible in the process so that the success and the learning belong to the client completely. You'll see effective ways to rigorously hold others to account and do it with a light hand. You'll learn the co-active coaching approach to values, setting goals, life balance, and self-management.

Imagine a relationship where you finally break free of those self-limiting conversations you've been having over the years—where now the voices of defeat and sabotage are simply noticed for what they are and the powerful part of you is always encouraged. You know what it's like to deal with these issues all by yourself because you have done so for years. In this book we present coaching strategies that address the self-limiting qualities that often show up strongest, just when people need the courage to take risks for the sake of change—proven strategies for staying on track and overcoming the self-administered sabotage that often holds them back.

This book offers a comprehensive approach to coaching and coaching skills. It provides a systematic structure reinforced with real-life examples and practical exercises to develop your coaching abilities. This is a book for those who want to expand their knowledge and develop their capacities in this new realm of coaching others using a unique model we call co-active coaching.

Co-Active Coaching Fundamentals

From the very beginning, coaching focuses on what *clients* want. People come to coaching because they want things to be different. They are looking for change or they have an important goal to reach. People come to coaching for lots of individual reasons. They are motivated to achieve specific goals: to write a book, to start a business, to have a healthier body. They come to coaching in order to be more effective or more satisfied at work. They hire a coach because they want to create more order and balance in their lives. Sometimes people want more from life—more peace of mind, more simplicity, more joy—and sometimes they want less: less confusion, less stress, less financial pressure. In general they come to coaching because they want a better quality of life: more fulfillment, better balance, or a different process to accomplish their life desires. Whatever the individual reason, it all starts with the client. Part One explains what the *coach* brings to coaching in response to the client and shows what the process looks like from a co-active coaching perspective. In this part of the book we outline the elements and convey a sense of how they fit together in a comprehensive model. In later chapters we expand on these major components to provide more depth and offer examples from coaching conversations.

The Co-Active Coaching Model

The term *co-active* refers to the fundamental nature of a coaching relationship in which the coach and client are active collaborators. In co-active coaching, this relationship is an alliance between two equals for the purpose of meeting the client's needs.

Four Cornerstones

There are four cornerstones that form the foundation of co-active coaching:

1. The client is naturally creative, resourceful, and whole.
2. Co-active coaching addresses the client's whole life.
3. The agenda comes from the client.
4. The relationship is a designed alliance.

The Client's Strengths

The primary building block for all co-active coaching is this: Clients have the answers or they can find the answers. From the co-active coach's point of view, nothing is wrong or broken, there is no need to fix the client. The coach does not have the answers; the coach has questions. Sometimes clients don't *think* they have the answers; sometimes they'd rather believe someone else—an expert—has the answers for them. Often there is a natural desire to buy the answers in a packaged program rather than do the work it takes to find a solution. All too often, what people end up with is an empty package.

In some cases people have a powerful sabotaging voice that tells them they don't have the answers. But co-active coaching stands on the certainty that clients really do know. When they look inside, with the help of a coach, they'll find they know themselves, their strengths, and their limitations. They'll also discover what they want, what they fear, what motivates them and what holds them back, their purpose and their vision, and where they sell out. They may never have sought the answer before the coach asks the question—the question that creates the channel for self-discovery—but the answer is there. Clients do know how to find their way, especially with the help of their coach. Years of experience using the co-active coaching model confirm it. This is why we say that the coach's job is to ask questions, not give answers. We have found that clients are more resourceful, more effective, and generally more satisfied when they find their own answers. And because they found the answers themselves, they are more likely to follow through with action.

Addressing the Client's Whole Life

Every day people make dozens, even hundreds, of decisions to do or not do certain things. The choices we make during the day, no matter how trivial they may seem, contribute to creating a life that is more (or less) fulfilling. The decisions we make move us toward better balance in our lives or they move us away. The choices contribute to a more effective life process or to a process that is less effective. Co-active coaching focuses on these three client principles: fulfillment, balance, and process.

The Client's Agenda

In a co-active coaching relationship the agenda comes from the client, not the coach. This is one of the most important distinctions of co-active coaching. The relationship is entirely focused on getting the results clients want. They set the agenda. The coach's job is to make sure the agenda doesn't get lost. So while the clients focus on the ongoing changes they are making in their lives, the coach holds onto the agenda. The coach ensures that the clients are always steering toward fulfillment and balance, and are able to engage in the process of their lives. "Holding the client's agenda" is such an important co-active coaching concept that you will see the phrase used over and over in this book.

This is different from consulting, for example, where the consultant brings specialized expertise and very often sets the agenda for the relationship. Co-active coaching is not about the coach's content, or the coach's expertise, or giving solutions. In co-active coaching the coach's expertise is confined to the coaching process. The coach's job is to help clients articulate their dreams, desires, and aspirations, help them clarify their mission, purpose, and goals, and help them achieve that outcome.

A Designed Alliance

In co-active coaching, power is granted to the coaching relationship—not to the coach. The client and coach work together to design an alliance that meets the client's needs. In fact, clients play an important role in declaring how they want to be coached. In co-active coaching, clients don't buy a packaged program. They are involved in creating a powerful relationship that fits their working and learning styles. The relationship is custom tailored to the communication approach that works best for them. The process of designing the alliance is a model of the mutual responsibility of client and coach. Clients learn that they are in control of the relationship and ultimately of the changes they make in their lives.

Coaching Means Action and Learning

The product of the work the client and coach do together is action and learning. These two forces, action and learning, combine to create change. Because the notion of *action* that moves the client forward is so central to the purpose of coaching, we make "forward" a verb and say that one of the purposes of coaching is to "forward the action" of the client. The other force at work in the human change process is *learning*. Learning is not simply a by-product of action, it is an equal and complementary force. The learning generates new resourcefulness, expanded possibilities, stronger muscles for change.

One of the common misunderstandings about coaching is that it's simply about getting things done. Because of this misunderstanding coaching has been compared to hiring a nagging parent to make sure your bed is made, your homework is done, and you create the life you

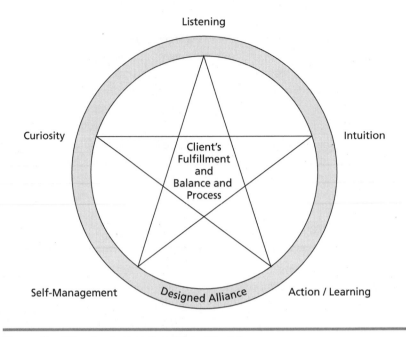

Listening

Curiosity

Intuition

Client's Fulfillment and Balance and Process

Self-Management

Designed Alliance

Action / Learning

Figure 1   The Co-Active Coaching Model

want for yourself. But coaching is not just about action; it is just as importantly about continuing to learn. So we say the other half of the coach's job is to "deepen the learning."

The action and learning take place within a container: the coaching model (Figure 1).

The Heart of the Model: The Client's Agenda

The client is the focus of the coaching. The client's wants and compelling desires are the topics. The ongoing relationship between coach and client exists only to address the client's agenda—and so the client's agenda is at the center of the diagram in Figure 1. The agenda addresses the three central aspects of the client's life: the three principles of fulfillment, balance, and process. They are principles because they are fundamental to the liveliness of life. In the same way that oxygen, fuel, and heat are necessary for fire, these three principles combine to create an ignited life.

Fulfillment

The definition of what fulfillment means to the client is always intensely personal. It may include, especially at first, outward measures of success: a great job, enough money, a certain lifestyle. In most cases the coaching will quickly progress to a deeper definition of fulfillment. It's not about having more—it's not about what fills the client's pockets or closets—it's about what fills the client's heart and soul. A fulfilling life is a valued life, and clients will have their own definition of what they truly value. If they value risk taking, is there enough adventure in their lives? If they value family, are they shortchanging themselves by caving in to the demands of work? What is the value they honor in their work? Sorting out values is a way of sorting out life choices because when the choices honor the client's values, life is more satisfying and seems almost effortless. Achieving a certain goal can be very fulfilling—especially as a benchmark—but most clients find that fulfillment is not the finish line. At its deepest level it is about finding and experiencing a life of purpose. It is about reaching one's full potential.

Balance

At today's pace of life, with so many responsibilities, attractive options, demands, and distractions, balance may feel like an impossible dream. It's especially elusive for most of the people who come to coaching. They tend to be dissatisfied functioning at some minimum standard of living: they want more from life and want to give more back. They can be passionate about the things that matter to them, focused in their commitment, and so intense that one corner of their lives is a model of excellence while the rest is in ruin. They understand the value of balance and have probably made numerous attempts to achieve it—with good intentions to exercise more, or take a little time off, or reconnect with friends—and found that weeks or months passed without any action.

Co-active coaching approaches the whole of a person's life. It is no service to help clients excel in one area of their lives without caring for the rest. It's one of the reasons why coaches almost always do a broad assessment at the very first session. It's a way to see where clients place their level of satisfaction in the significant areas of a balanced life: career, health, finances, relationships, personal growth, spirituality, and recreation. Because clients don't live their lives in discrete compartments, there are links between all of the pieces. Health affects career; finances and recreation are intertwined; relationships are interwoven throughout. It's hard to pull a thread out without bringing two or three other pieces with it.

"Out of balance" often has a resigned or helpless sound to it—as if that's the way life is. That's the real world. That's what my manager/my family/my business partner/my friends expect from me. There's just one way of looking at it, and it looks bad. Coaching for balance, however, focuses on widening the range of perspectives and, therefore, adding more choices. Ultimately balance is about making choices: saying yes to some things and no to others. This can be challenging. Clients often want to say yes to more in their lives without making room for the yes by saying no to something else. This impulse leads to an overwhelmed feeling in a hurry—and lives that are out of balance.

Balance is a fluid state, always in motion, because life itself is dynamic. Therefore, it makes more sense to look at whether a client is moving toward balance or away from balance—rather than offering the client "balance" as a goal to be achieved. Like the seasons of the year, balance is best viewed over the long haul. It is also a perennial issue: one that coaches will see, in some form or another, over and over in the course of a coaching relationship.

Process

We are always in process. Sometimes it looks frantic. Sometimes it looks graceful. Because coaching is effective at achieving results, both clients and coaches can get drawn into the "results" trap—focusing entirely on the destination ahead and losing sight of the flow of the journey. In fact, process is often compared to a river. As life flows there will be fast periods of onrushing, white-water progress. But there will also be times of going nowhere, being stuck in job eddies, relationship whirlpools, and backsliding into treacherous pools. There will be days of serene still water and days of terrifying rapids; there will be flooding and drought. The coach's job is to notice, point out, and be with clients wherever they are in their process. The coach is there to encourage and support, to provide companionship around the rocks and shoals, to escort the client through the dark waters of failure as well as to celebrate the client's skill and success at navigating the difficult passages. Coaching the client's process allows clients to live more fully in a deeper relationship with *all* of their life.

Co-active coaching, therefore, embraces this whole picture of the client: fulfillment, balance, and process. They are the core principles at the heart of the coaching model. Together they create the heat and light of a life that is fully alive.

The Five Contexts

Visually, the coaching model represents a five-pointed star as in Figure 1. Each point of the star is a context that the coach brings to the coaching. Each is a point of contact with the client. And each is also an underlying coaching talent and skill. The coach consistently draws from these skills in the practice of coaching. In time, and through training, the coach develops these talents the way a musician develops innate musical talent.

Listening

The coach listens to the words that come from the client, of course. But the real listening of coaching takes place on a deeper level. It is the listening for the meaning behind the story, for the underlying process, for the theme that will deepen the learning. The coach is listening for the appearance of the client's vision, values, purpose. The coach is also listening for resistance, fear, backtracking, and the voice of that internal saboteur—the Gremlin*—who is there to object to change, point out the client's weakness and failure, and cite reasons for holding back.

The coach is listening at many levels at once to hear where clients are in their process, to hear where they are out of balance, to hear their progress on the journey of fulfillment. The coach is listening for the nuance of hesitation, too, for the sour ring of something not quite true. Even in telephone coaching it is possible to hear much more than the words of the story. There's a great deal of information conveyed in a conversation's tone and pacing that the coach hears, especially after getting to know the client.

To understand this crucial listening context, imagine there are three levels of listening:

- In Level I the listening is internal. We hear the words of the other person, but the focus is on what it means to us. In a coaching relationship the client is at Level I: looking inside.
- Level II is focused listening. The attention is laser-focused over there: on the other person. The coach needs to be listening at Level II—and at Level III.
- Level III is a global range of listening: hearing that picks up emotion, body language, the environment itself.

Levels I and II listen primarily for words. Level III picks up everything else including all of the sensory data as well as mood, pace, energy. The

---

*There are many names for this internal saboteur. We gratefully acknowledge Richard Carson and his book *Taming Your Gremlin* for the image we use throughout this book.

most effective coaches operate easily at both Levels II and III, which gives them the broadest range of information to work with. This is true whether the coaching is one-on-one, group coaching, in person, or on the telephone. Effective coaching listens for much more than just the words of the story. And, while coaching in person adds the visual dimension of body language, it can also be a distraction. Those who practice telephone coaching develop over time a very strong ability to read the Level III nuances of tone and energy from clients. Telephone coaching has other advantages as well, such as convenience, which we will talk more about in Chapter 11.

Intuition

Listening at Levels II and III also gives coaches greater access to their intuition—that place just below the surface where the hard data and soft data merge. It's a kind of knowing that resides in the background and usually remains unspoken. It remains in the background because it's not easy to trust. Our culture doesn't validate it as a reliable means for drawing conclusions or making decisions, so we hesitate to say what our intuition tells us. We hold back because we don't want to appear foolish. And yet it is one of the most powerful gifts a coach brings to coaching.

A coach receives a great deal of information from the client and then, in the moment of coaching, combines it with previous information as well as experience not only in coaching but in operating in the world. Add to this one more factor: the unknown exponent of not knowing where some things come from. In the instant that it takes this whole process to happen, our intuition gives us a message. We may not call it intuition. We may call it a thought, or a hunch, or a gut feeling. But however it comes out, it emerges as a statement from our intuition. This is a skill that, for most coaches, needs practice and development. It is enormously valuable because time and again it synthesizes more impressions and information than we could ever analyze consciously.

Curiosity

One of the fundamental tenets of co-active coaching is that clients are capable and resourceful and they have the answers. The coach's job is to ask the questions. The context of curiosity gives a certain frame to the question-asking process. Curiosity is open, inviting, spacious, almost playful. And yet it is also enormously powerful. Like scientific curiosity that explores the deepest questions of matter, life, and the universe, curiosity in coaching allows coach and client to enter the deepest areas of the client's life, side by side, simply looking, curious about what they will find.

Because the coach is not an inquisitor, but really on the client's side in this search, the coach can ask powerful questions that break through old defenses. When clients learn to be curious about their lives, it reduces some of the pressure and lowers the risk. They become more willing to look in the dark places and try the hard things because they are curious too.

Action/Learning

The coaching conversation has a powerful purpose—or, to be more accurate, in co-active coaching it has two purposes: to forward the action and to deepen the learning. That's what makes this conversation different from all other conversations: it's not to explain, or inform, or entertain, or rectify; its purpose is to generate action and learning.

One of the things that attracts people to coaching is the emphasis on action and the built-in structure of accountability. It's a structure that works very well. When people of integrity make a promise to someone, they work much harder to follow through. It's part of the cultural contract. In coaching, clients account for their action and learning.

Accountability makes the process of change more tangible, more focused, more disciplined. Consequently, the process of change is also more successful. Accountability asks basic questions: "What will you do?" "When will you do it?" (or "For how long?") and "How will I know you've done it?" The coach and client often set up additional reporting structures for accountability. Reports might include daily phone calls, a fax, or e-mail. Accountability is unique in the coaching relationship because it is completely judgment free. There is no shame or blame attached to whatever the client does. The objective is action and learning, not specific results. The client can learn as much from failure as from accomplishment.

Self-Management

In order to truly hold the client's agenda, the coach must get out of the way—not always an easy thing to do. Self-management is the coach's ability to set aside his or her own personal opinions, preferences, pride, defensiveness, ego. The coach needs to be "over there" with the client, immersed in the client's situation and struggle, not "over here" dealing with the coach's judgments and thoughts. Self-management means giving up on the need to look good and the need to be right. For the coach, in this case, to manage one's self means to become nearly invisible.

Moreover, the coach also helps with the client's self-management—that is, the client's ability to manage the judgment and opinions of self and others. It also means recognizing the client's internal saboteur at work and helping the client work loose from this Gremlin's constraints.

The Coach's Place in the Model

By now you may have noticed one glaring omission. The coach doesn't appear in the model at all! This is precisely the point in the co-active coaching model. The coach's role is to create an environment in which clients focus entirely on their fulfillment, balance, and process. The coach and client work together to design the working alliance, and the coach uses the five contexts of coaching to make contact with the client and facilitate action and learning. The client is the star in this model and the coach is invisible. Or perhaps we should say: because this is a two-dimensional model, the coach appears in the third dimension—in the action of the coaching.

Following the Client's Lead in Co-Active Coaching

Because clients set the agenda in co-active coaching, when the coaching session begins, coaches need to be ready to respond to whatever clients have determined is most important. The issue clients bring is rarely a complete surprise; after all, this is an ongoing relationship and there is typically a major issue coach and client are working on, with some form of accountability. Even so, in co-active coaching the focus is on asking questions so that clients find their own answers, rather than superimposing a particular direction or giving answers. Since the coach doesn't have the answer, the coach is always on the edge, waiting to hear the client's response. The response will determine the direction of the coaching interaction. To be effective, co-active coaches must really be on their toes, ready to move gracefully into the next question or to employ a coaching skill—not knowing until that moment which skill is called for. This creates the unique dancelike quality of following the client's lead in co-active coaching. In fact, a phrase we use to describe the action of co-active coaching is "dancing in the moment."

The Co-Active Coaching Relationship

Surrounding the client's agenda, as shown in Figure 1, is the *designed alliance*. This is the container that holds the client during the coaching relationship.

The Designed Alliance

The design of the coaching relationship begins during the initial discovery session, also called an intake session. The relationship is "designed" because it is customized to meet the exclusive needs of the client. It is an "alliance" because both players are intimately involved in making it work. Clients realize they are not buying an off-the-shelf personal success program. They are committing themselves to an ongoing relationship.

The relationship is like a triangle: the coach at one point, the client at another point, and the relationship at the third point (Figure 2). In this model you can see that the client grants power to the relationship—not to the coach. But clients are in turn empowered by the relationship—empowered to take charge and change their lives, to be bold. The coach

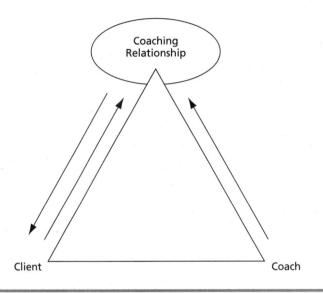

Figure 2   The Coaching Triangle

grants power to the relationship, as well, so that in this model all the power in the relationship goes to serve the client.

Although there is no arrow in Figure 2 showing power coming back to the coach, it's hard to imagine a single coach who isn't energized or empowered by the coaching relationship. Coaches clearly get something out of the relationship. It is powerful and energizing to be in the presence of personal change. It can be exhausting too—another sign of the emotional impact of being present in such a deep way in clients' lives. The diagram simply emphasizes the unique nature of the relationship—that it is mutually created and entirely focused on the client. Whatever the coach receives is a bonus—a reverberation of the energy.

In fact the co-active coach must make the shift from "I am powerful" to "the coaching relationship is powerful." Powerful coaching is not about being a powerful coach; it's about the power the *client* experiences. Imagine that the coaching relationship is a recharging place where clients tap into the source of energy they need to get over the hurdles in their lives. They can't get the work done if the energy level is low. The power is not coming directly from the coach, however, but from the relationship.

The coaching relationship is separate from the client and coach. What's more, it is more powerful than either the coach or the client. At times it will sustain them when they are unable to do it alone. It's easier to see how this happens for the client, who, after all, is experiencing the slings and arrows of battling change. The power in the relationship can sustain the client between regular meetings. It can also sustain the coach, who, being human, will have days when his or her reservoir of courage is low. Fortunately, the power of coaching doesn't depend solely on the energy level of the coach; the relationship itself is powerful.

What makes this relationship unique for clients is the significant role they get to play in its design. In fact, they are in charge of designing the relationship that will work best for them. This level of client involvement in creating the relationship is unique to co-active coaching, and it is one of the reasons co-active coaching is effective for clients in making and sustaining significant change. Instead of trying to fit themselves into a predetermined process of change, they create the conditions that will give them the best results.

The Coaching Environment

There are a variety of different ways to deliver coaching. The most common is the weekly phone call, often a thirty-minute conversation, with the client calling the coach. It is compact, efficient, convenient, and frequent enough, at weekly intervals, to maintain momentum. There are, however, other options for coaching, and some coaches prefer face-to-face sessions. Coaching even takes place in cyberspace. Each medium has its own inherent strengths and weaknesses. However it happens, the environment in which coaching takes place does not depend on the medium.

This coaching space is the environment in which the client is able to grow, change, fail, and rise again. What makes this space so unusual in people's lives is that it is designed exclusively for them. It is their own custom workshop focused entirely on their personal goals. They come to this place on a regular basis with no other purpose than their own growth. The first step in building an effective coaching relationship is to create a safe and courageous space for the client. We use the word *courageous* purposely here because, although as coaches we can be encouraging, clients need to find the courage in themselves to make significant change in their lives. After all, if what they want were easy to accomplish, they would already be doing it. They wouldn't need a coach or the coaching relationship. The environment that is created must be safe enough for clients to take the risks they need to take and be courageous. It is in this space that clients will be able to approach their lives with curiosity, interest, power, creativity, and choice. To be safe and courageous, this environment must meet certain conditions.

Confidentiality

The relationship starts on the bedrock of confidentiality. Clients come to coaching ready to take major life-changing action. The material that the coach and client will be working with is no less than the details of the client's life. If clients are going to risk making significant change, they must be able to risk talking freely about their lives. This disclosure is crucial because it leads to the personal discovery that is at the heart of the learning. The disclosure is also likely to be a little intimidating for clients—especially at first when they feel vulnerable and unaccustomed to the coaching relationship. The coach's job is to make the space safe for exploration. Coaches can build a sense of safety by creating a pattern of encouragement, nonjudgment, and acknowledging the client's honesty, effort, and success. Confidentiality plays a key role too. To give themselves wholly to the coaching relationship, clients need the assurance of confidentiality. The coach needs to address this issue as early as possible in the working relationship—certainly at the outset of the initial intake session. The agreement should be precise and explicit: "As your coach I will not disclose the details of our conversation without your permission."

Trust

Trust starts with the creation of a safe, confidential space, but trust is built gradually as both client and coach learn they can be counted on and the client learns that the relationship delivers results. Trust is built from small things like being on time for the phone call, following through on the assignments and promises. This is as important for the coach as it is for the client. The coach must be trustworthy in his or her action. The coach also needs to hold clients responsible for living up to what they say they want. Earlier we noted that coaching starts from the premise that clients are capable and resourceful. The coach demonstrates this belief by trusting that clients will be responsible. The experience of trust is enormously empowering for clients. They see that their coach is really on their side, respecting their dreams and willing to be honest and direct for their sake. They have a person in their life who totally believes they can do what they say they want to do, who believes they can be the person they say they want to be. The unqualified trust creates a powerful force for change.

Veracity

A safe and courageous space for change must be, by definition, a place where the truth can be told. It is a place where clients can tell the whole truth about what they have done (and not done) without worrying about looking good. This is an environment without judgment. And it is a place where the coach expects the truth from the client because there is no consequence of truth other than growth and learning. The client expects the truth because that is precisely the perspective for which the coach has been hired. But clients are often so close to their own situation, so wrapped up in their own history and patterns, they are unable to see the truth accurately. This may be one of the reasons why they sought out coaching. They are relying on the coach for the acuity that sees through the chaos and fog. This should be one relationship in which clients can count on being dealt with in a straightforward and honest way.

Truth telling doesn't need to be confrontational, although it may be confronting. Truth telling gets in the way of, stands in front of, the usual tacit acceptance of the client's explanations. Truth telling refuses to sidestep or overlook: it boldly points out when the emperor is not wearing clothes. There is no inherent judgment in telling the truth. The coach is merely stating what he or she sees. Withholding the truth serves neither the client nor the coaching relationship. A real relationship is not built on being nice; it's built on being real. When the coach has the courage to tell the truth, the client gets a model of the art of being straight. And in the process, more trust is built between coach and client.

Spaciousness

One of the qualities of this alliance that makes it work is its spaciousness. For one thing, it contains all of the client's life. That's a pretty spacious place to begin. Beyond that, it is a space without judgment or "shoulds." This is a place open to change and wide-ranging possibilities. This is a place where clients can breathe, experiment, fantasize, dream. It is another world—a different galaxy far from their present limitations. It is a space in which they can vent their anger, troubles, spites, injustices. It is a place where failure is acknowledged as a means for learning. It is a place where there are no absolutes and few rules.

For the coach, spaciousness also means complete detachment from any particular course of action or any results that the client achieves. The coach continues to care about the client, the client's agenda, the client's health and growth, but not the road the client takes to get there, the speed of travel, or the detours that might take place in the meantime—so long as the client continues to move toward the results the client wants. Ultimately, coaching is not about what the coach delivers but concerns what the client does with action and learning. A coach may propose a course of action to get the results the client desires. That is fine. Brainstorming is part of coaching and a valuable addition to the discussion. But the spaciousness of the relationship requires that the coach must not be attached to whether clients take suggestions or, if they do, whether they do it "right" or "wrong." Either way the client is right. It is a paradox that the coach often expects more of clients than they dare dream for themselves, and yet clients are unconditionally supported whatever they do. That is the breadth of the spaciousness in the relationship.

Five Aspects of the Intake Session

The design of the alliance is clearly the focus of the initial intake session. This is where most clients learn what to expect from coaching. It's also a time when they will clarify where they are, where they're headed, the strengths they will use to get there, and the obstacles that often get in the way.

The coach typically covers these five areas during the initial intake session, but not necessarily in this order:

- Permission
- Discovery
- Designing the future
- Logistics
- Providing the client with tools

The order will depend on the coach's preference and the flow of conversation during the intake. Clients may have a burning desire to cover logistics first, for example, or to declare their future goals and commitments. Figure 3 outlines the five elements of the intake session.

Permission

One of the unique qualities of the coaching relationship comes from the coach's asking for permission. That's why it's at the heart of the intake diagram depicted in Figure 3. At first it may seem awkward, yet it is an excellent example of honoring the fact that coaching exists solely to serve the client's needs and agenda. It isn't always necessary. Like any other coaching tool, experienced coaches will use it when they need to and will know when they don't need permission. This is a tool that is best used when the coach wishes to explore an area that might be especially sensitive or challenging. For example, the coach might ask: "May I tell you what I think? Yes? I think you're kidding yourself." Or: "May we brainstorm alternative courses of action?" In any case, the coach must be willing to accept no as an answer and take it from there.

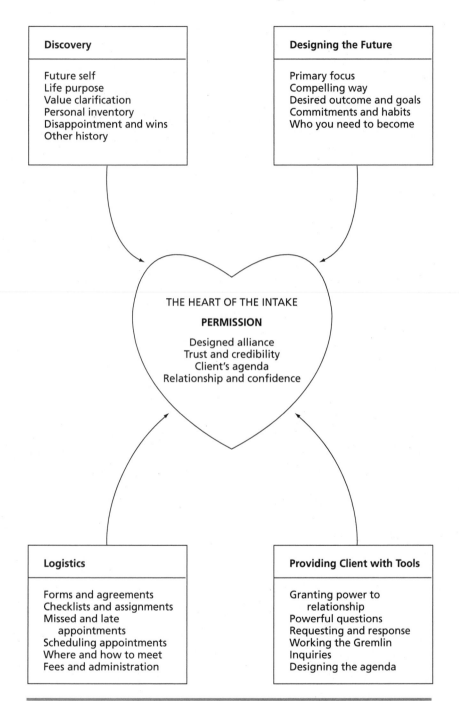

Figure 3   The Five Elements of the Initial Intake Session

Discovery

Discovery focuses on where the client is today and how he or she got there. It's a conversation about what makes them, what moves them, what blocks them. This portion of the intake session might address such issues as the client's life purpose or mission, values, principles, or personal beliefs. There is no "right" way to design the discovery process. Usually the coach will make an overall assessment of satisfaction in the significant areas of the client's life using a tool like the Wheel of Life (Figure 4) or some other personal inventory. (See the "Coach's Toolkit" for more information on using this and other tools for discovery.)

Client and coach might talk about previous disappointments and successes to get an idea of where the client is fulfilled and strategies the client uses to handle breakdowns and failures. The client may bring other experiences or personal background to the discovery process that will be relevant to the ongoing work together. Both client and coach are beginning the process of really getting to know this person, the client, from the inside out: the bright places, the dark places, the effective places, and the not so effective places.

The coach may use assessment tools or exercises, but the heart of the discovery process is asking simple, powerful questions: "Where do you

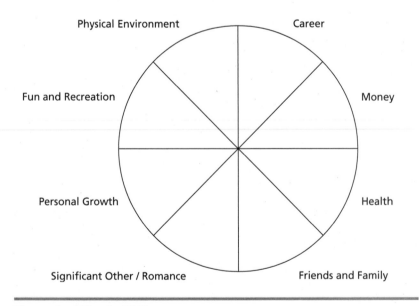

Figure 4   Wheel of Life

want to make a difference with your life?" "What do you value most in your relationship with others?" "What works for you when you are successful at making changes?" "Where do you usually get stuck?" "What motivates you when you get stuck?" "How do you deal with disappointment or failure?" "How are you about doing what you say you'll do?" The answers to such questions help the coach and client alike to really understand the client.

The answers also point very clearly to the design of the most effective coaching relationship. For example, the question "Where do you usually get stuck?" elicits a good indication of where the client becomes mired. The next question might be: "How would you like me to respond as your coach when you're stuck?" Questions that invite the client to define the coach's role will continue throughout the intake session and the coaching relationship. They are a periodic reminder of the client's role in designing the alliance.

Designing the Future

Another segment of the intake session focuses on the motivating purpose that brought the client to coaching in the first place. Here the focus is on having clients describe what they'd like to be different about their life. These future outcomes will be the result of achieving goals, fulfilling commitments, changing habits, and bringing a compelling vision to life. This conversation explores who the client will have to become to create a new future. There are a number of ways to approach this future design.

Primary Focus. The client is likely to open up a number of possible coaching directions during the intake session. Having decided to make changes, there can be an intoxicating euphoria and a wish to bring every issue of desire or dissatisfaction into the coaching relationship all at once. Success is more likely, however, when the coach can sort through all the possibilities with the client and settle on four or five issues. Using a form that lists these areas of focus can be very useful: it becomes the master plan; it establishes what is important; and it represents a way to get back on track when the unexpected takes the client off course. It's also enormously satisfying as a means to show how clients have succeeded in addressing the primary issues of their life. Naturally items will fall off the list during the coaching relationship as they are completed, or become less important, and as others more important are added. For a typical Primary Focus form, see the Coach's Toolkit at the back of the book.

Desired Outcome and Goals. Clients bring a desire for change to coaching. The outcome they have in mind may be muddy or crystal clear, but in either case they have not yet been able to reach it—which is often why they bring it to coaching. Desired outcomes may be as specific as a goal. Or clients may want to move toward a certain state of being such as "balanced" or "happy at work" or "more fulfilled in my time with family." Part of the intake session will be devoted to clarifying outcomes and, in many cases, creating specific goals from the broadly stated desires: What will happen? By when? And how will clients know they have reached their goal? Coach and client work together to clarify the goals as well as work out strategies to achieve them. Although goal setting seems fundamental to coaching, it's important to note that some clients rarely state specific goals. They prefer to identify general areas to work on in coaching. So long as there are ways for clients to recognize progress in the work they do, coaching can be an effective relationship even without the specific goals.

Compelling Way. We can be pushed down the road by deadlines and expectations and to-do lists. Or we can be driven by the desire for money, accomplishment, or the promises we make. We can also be pulled down the road by the gravitational force of a "compelling way." This image of what we are *drawn* to do has the power to overcome the bonds of lethargy and fear. The compelling way can take any goal, action, or outcome and invest it with new power. The job your client has today may be light-years short of her ideal—the job she will have someday that truly fulfills her life purpose. But today she is still struggling to get a clear picture of what that might be. It doesn't mean that work can't be fulfilling for her today. She needs to look at her current situation and design the compelling version of this job. In effect the coach is asking: "What would make this job so compelling that you would go to work eagerly?" Many people find exercise, for example, a tedious task. What would be the compelling way? One way to have clients create this compelling way is to tie it to their values or to the vision they have created of a fulfilling life. For example, if their vision includes more time for family, look for the compelling way they can organize their current work life—even if the work isn't ideal—so it includes more time for family. Or if learning is an important value, look for the way they can incorporate that value into their current work to create a more compelling way.

Commitments and Habits. There is a fundamental difference between goals and commitments. The goal is the outward, visible outcome; the commitment is the inner drive that produced the goal to begin with. Asking a client "What are you committed to?" causes the client to look deeper inside than asking "What is your goal?" In some cases, understanding the commitment is necessary before goals can be set. In some cases, clarifying the commitment changes the goals.

Daily or weekly habits are significant because they are small signs of a larger process of taking care of the things that are most important in life. In fact, until they are seen in that context, habits are just nagging items on an endless, unfinished to-do list. The client adopts these habits for their inherent benefit and because of their value as tools of self-care and discipline.

Who You Need to Become. The classic definition of crazy is continuing to do things the same way and expecting different results. The truth is: if nothing changes, nothing changes. Something new on the outside, like a new outcome, starts with something new on the inside. In order for the future to be different from the past, the client must change on the inside. In the process of learning and change, clients will become more empowered, more resourceful, and find strengths they didn't know they had. But to achieve the results they want, it's very likely they will need to change attitudes, paradigms, or underlying beliefs. The prospect of making this kind of interior change can be daunting. After all, if it were easy the client would already have done it. Looking at who they will have to become is particularly germane at the start of the coaching relationship.

Logistics

Certain ground rules and administrative procedures should be covered in the initial intake session. This is the time to discuss scheduling appointments, what happens if you're late or don't call, when to pay, how to pay, what's expected between calls, how to handle the coach's requests. This can also be an opportunity to look over the forms and checklists that might be of interest to the client (see the Coach's Toolkit at the back of the book).

The coach's level of preparation and straight delivery will establish his or her credibility in this relationship. The message the client receives is: "This coach knows what he's doing. He's professional, experienced, and reliable. I can trust this relationship."

Providing the Client with Tools

The intake session is also a good place to teach clients about the unique tools of coaching so they will know what to expect. The coaching relationship is different from other relationships. The client will discover this in time, but it's easier on the client to point out the differences at the start. For example, a coach is likely to intrude in the middle of a client's story to ask a pointed question. This intrusion might be considered rude in polite social conversation, but it is a powerful aspect of the coaching conversation. It's designed to cut to the heart of the matter. When clients understand this and expect it to happen, they simply answer the question without reacting to the intrusion.

Requesting is another special situation. At some point in the conversation the coach may request a certain course of action—such as "I request that you make twelve sales calls by Friday." This is not an ultimatum, it is a request. And as with all coaching requests, there are at least three responses: "Yes, I will," "No, I won't," or "Here is my counteroffer." A fourth response might be: "I need some time to consider your request. I'll let you know by Monday." Prepare clients for the notion that the request may not fit them—but before they simply turn it down, they should consider making a counteroffer. Likewise, the coach must be prepared to accept a client's no; otherwise it was never a true request but a demand. Requesting is not only a powerful coaching skill; it is also a powerful skill clients can learn to use in their everyday lives.

This is the time to discuss the client's need to grant power to the relationship and the ongoing nature of the designed alliance between coach and client. Moreover, the coach may talk about what to expect in terms of assignments (sometimes called "fieldwork" or "homework") between calls—as well as the role of the inquiry assignment as an open-ended question the client ponders for a period of time because it can deepen the learning.

The coach will also talk about what to expect when failure happens. Training the client for failure is one of the key early tasks. Having made the commitment to coaching and to change, clients have a lot invested in success. The first time they hit failure or disappointment, the first time the goal eludes their grasp, they may think the whole plan has collapsed. It's the coach's job to prepare the client for this moment with the knowledge that there is as much learning from failure as from success—often there's even more learning because the lessons are so poignant. Acknowledging failure is not something that comes naturally to most clients, but it's important to coaching and clients need to hear this early.

The intake session is also a good time to talk about what clients can expect over the course of the coaching relationship: ups and downs, plateaus, periods of great insight, everything happening at lightning speed, followed by the trough of the wave, drifting in the doldrums.

In particular, for most clients there's a slump between weeks three and eight. It happens because change is not happening fast enough or the initial euphoria of commitment has worn off. The client realizes that talking about action is one thing and actually taking action is quite another. One of the reasons coaching relationships typically have a minimum time agreement of three months is to help clients get past this initial slump period.

The Gremlin Effect

The slump can also be the sabotaging work of the client's Gremlin— that inner voice that abhors change and demands the status quo. It's the voice that says: "This is stupid, or too risky, or you're not ready, or you're not equipped, or . . ." Well, you probably know that voice yourself. As soon as the client's Gremlin catches a whiff of significant life change, it's likely to show up with lots of reasons why this program shouldn't go one step farther. The coach needs to point this out during the intake session so the client can be forewarned and forearmed.

The intent of the Gremlin is not malicious mischief. The intent is to preserve the status quo. A similar voice has kept us from doing stupid and dangerous things in the past. It's just that, at the point when people really *need* to take risks and make changes, the Gremlin shows up uninvited. And because clients come to you to help them make *significant* changes in their lives, the Gremlin will always be there.

The Gremlin has its favorite language set: "I should be stronger . . . I shouldn't be so needy . . . they won't like it if I do . . . I can't succeed on my own . . . I don't have the answers/don't have the talent/don't have the experience/don't have whatever they're looking for." The variations are endless. And at any point where the client is considering action that poses the least chance of risk, you will hear the Gremlin's familiar phrases: "What was I thinking of? This is stupid! This is too risky and I might get hurt. What will they think of me? I'm out of my league and way over my head!"

The Gremlin is scared most of the time. But it's even scarier when the Gremlin starts to sound almost reasonable: "I'll be more productive if I wait until Monday. . . . I have to earn a living after all. . . . I should give this more consideration—no need to be hasty." The Gremlin is always there to point out your weaknesses, your fear, your failure—to reinforce your self-limiting judgments. He's there to hold you back and hold you down.

Because this character is so persistent, creative, and elusive, the coach and client must address the Gremlin in the initial session. From the very beginning, you and the client must find a way to talk about self-sabotaging behavior. Even though the Gremlin's power is genuinely serious, addressing the subject works best when you handle it during the intake session with humor and commiseration. If you talk about it in a technical or psychological manner, clients tend to get tense, upset, or resistant.

The point to remember is this: The Gremlin does not care whether or not you honor your values. The Gremlin wants what it wants in the moment. About the only time the Gremlin cares about your values is when you're not honoring them the way you said you would. Then the Gremlin says: "See, you've got no spine. You've got no followthrough. Give it up." And remember that the Gremlin is with you for life. There is no killing it off. So it's important that the coach and the client become skilled at noticing the Gremlin. It's the first step to liberation.

Don't be deceived. It is not possible to coach the Gremlin. The client's Gremlin is too sharp, too fast, and too experienced at these games to be pinned down by coaching questions. And yet you can't ignore the Gremlin either. It won't go away on its own. One of the best strategies is to notice it, recognize it, name it. By bringing it out of the shadows, it begins to lose its power. It can't stand up to too much scrutiny.

It is possible, though, to coach the client *around* the Gremlin. Imagine this scenario. You and your client have focused for weeks on a major move: the client needs to talk to an employee about his lack of performance. But just as the client is about to embark on this new course of action, she says something like: "I'm not ready," "I can't do that," or "I should be much stronger." At this point you can sidestep the Gremlin's judgment and coach the client's original vision: "Remember your enthusiasm and commitment? Just tap into the desire and passion you have for that! You're already on your way!" Or you can confront the Gremlin directly: "Is that your Gremlin talking? Hello, Gremlin. Who invited you? What's that worn-out message you want to play again? We've done that—thanks very much."

Outcomes of the Intake Session

Certain results of the intake session are expected: goal setting, communicating the administrative process, getting to know each other, setting expectations. Just as important is the model of interaction that the client experiences in this session. Clients experience what it's like to be a full partner. They see that the coach believes they are healthy and resourceful and capable of creating their own solutions. They see, too, that the coach is committed to helping them create the life and work they want. It is empowering to have such confidence bestowed on the client. It is also extremely rare. The intake session often leaves clients on a tremendous high with a huge commitment of their own—a commitment to themselves and to the results that coaching can deliver. When was the last time someone spent two or three hours totally absorbed in discovering your goals and dreams, understanding your obstacles, encouraging your action, absorbed in the fulfillment of your vision for yourself?

There is no single formula for the intake session. So long as the five major components are covered—if not during the initial intake, then certainly in the first few coaching sessions—the process is complete. And while we discuss the various elements of the intake process in this chapter, we do not prescribe a rigid format. Both the client and coach are best served if coaches determine their own coaching style and process—and that includes designing the intake in a way that is adapted to their own talents and preferences.

The intake session is the bedrock for the ongoing coaching relationship. It is the place where clients first experience the designed alliance and the place where the designed alliance begins the work of coaching. Clients see that they are responsible partners in the relationship and fully responsible for their lives. The intake session lets clients know that although the coach is on their side and committed to their solutions, they themselves are responsible for creating the life they want. It is the only way they will be able to claim the results when they are done.

Clients come to coaching because they want better results or because they want results they can't achieve on their own. They say they want significant life change. If that's really true, it means the stakes are remarkably high. That's part of the fundamental understanding about what will take place in the alliance and what it will take to make the changes. This can be energizing, exciting, inspiring. But it will not be trivial. The coach is committed to the client's ultimate goals, which means that coaching will challenge, incite, motivate, encourage, and sometimes demand that the client be powerful. This is not weekly chitchat. Good coaching gets to the real heart of the matter. It pierces through social niceties and asks questions and calls for commitment in ways that will change people's lives.

Coaching takes place in an environment where clients are willing to make enormous investments of self, time, money, and energy. The very decision to play a big enough game to warrant coaching establishes a playing field of significance. When clients step into that space it is like crossing a threshold into a new world of possibility and higher challenge. In this space they know that the coach is fully committed to them and their quest to create a rich and fulfilling life.

Co-Active Coaching Skills

One of the easiest ways to see and understand the application of coaching skills is to view them within the five contexts of coaching:

- Listening
- Intuition
- Curiosity
- Action/Learning
- Self-Management

The following five chapters present detailed explanations of each of the contexts, as well as definitions of specific coaching skills. Each chapter also contains coaching conversations that illustrate the skills in action along with a number of exercises you can use to develop the skills.

Listening

To be listened to is a striking experience—partly because it is so rare. When another person is totally with you, leaning in, interested in every word, eager to empathize, you feel known and understood. People get bigger when they know they're being listened to; they have more presence. They feel safer and more secure, as well, and can begin to trust. It is why listening is so important to coaching and why it is the first of the five contexts we will discuss.

Listening is a talent that each of us is given in some measure. People who become coaches tend to be gifted listeners to begin with. But listening is also a skill that can be trained and developed. Masterful coaches have taken their abundant gift and brought it to a high level of proficiency. Indeed they use it with the same unconscious grace that an athlete uses in the midst of a game or a musician in a performance.

Most people do not listen at a very deep level. Their day-to-day occupations and preoccupations don't require more than a minimum level of listening—just as most of us never acquire more than an average level of physical fitness. We don't need the muscles because we are not world-class athletes. In everyday listening we listen mostly to the words. The focus is on what *you* said and what *I* said. Think of all the arguments you've been in where the crux of the fight was over the precise words that were used: "That's *not* what you said" . . . "it's what I meant" . . . "But it's *not* what you said." Or we hear the words and then disconnect from the conversation while we process the words internally. We start thinking about what we'll say next. We look for a comparable story—or one that's just a little more dramatic: "You *think* that was scary, let me tell you about the time I . . ." We get caught up in our own feelings; we take things personally; we listen at a superficial level as we evaluate and judge what we're listening to.

Most of us would say our friends are generally good listeners because they are willing to suspend their judgment of us and sometimes will even be quiet and listen. And yet, too often, when we really want just to be *listened* to, our family, friends, and co-workers, with the best intentions in the world, want to solve the problem or take care of the feelings. Masterful coaching requires masterful listening, attuned and adept, with the ability to maximize the listening interaction. Interaction is the right word, too, because listening is not simply passively hearing. There is action in listening.

Attention and Impact

There are two aspects of listening in coaching. One is attention, or awareness. It is the receiving of information through what we hear with our ears, of course, but it is also listening with all the senses and with our intuition. We hear, see, and experience sounds, words, images, feelings, energy. We are attentive to all the information we draw in from our senses. The attention is on the information coming in: the words, impressions, shifts of energy. We are multifaceted receivers with many receptors of various kinds, all of which are receiving information: we notice the breathing on the other end of the phone, the pace of the delivery, the modulation of the voice. We sense the pressure behind the words—the voice might be soft or hard edged, tentative or enraged. We not only listen to the person but, simultaneously, we listen to everything else that is happening in the environment. We see body language. Over the phone we sense emotion and can see the clenched jaw or the head bowed in sorrow. It's all information. We are attentive.

The second aspect is what we *do* with our listening. We call this the *impact* of our listening on others—specifically, the impact of the coach's listening on the client. As an experienced coach you need to be conscious not only of your listening but the impact you have when you act on your listening. Most of the time, this consciousness is just below the surface. Your attention is still on the other person. Imagine you're in a fencing match. All your attention is focused on the opponent as you instantaneously make choices and respond, parry, thrust. Your attention is not on the choices you are making—that would break your concentration with disastrous results. Once the match is over, you can recap the action and review the choices you made. When you listen like this, you are not thinking about your listening or about what you're going to do next. Your listening is hyperconscious and unconscious at the same time.

To understand the process of attention and impact, imagine you're in a crowded room and you smell smoke—could be a fire. Your attention is drawn to the smoke. You notice it. That's the first aspect of the awareness. Then you decide what to do with this information. You might yell "Fire!" or you might mention it casually to the host. You could grab a fire extinguisher and shoulder your way through the crowd to heroically fight the fire, or you could slip quietly out the side door. Each of these choices will have a different impact. At some level, you must be aware of that impact and recognize that you are responsible for it. Even if you appear to do nothing, there will be an impact. No doubt you've had this experience on a listening level. Think back to a time when you were in a shouting match with a loved one: fists on hips, veins bulging, words flying back and forth like napalm. In the midst of this your partner stops talking and gives you the silent treatment. You keep talking—perhaps even louder now. "You are so bleeping aggravating," you say. "Why," they respond coolly, "I'm not saying anything . . . I'm just listening." Did you feel the impact?

Clearly, listening is not passive, especially in the coaching relationship. You may have learned about "active listening" in the past, perhaps in a communications training program. These programs generally do an excellent job of expanding people's understanding of listening and providing more tools for listening. Active listening often involves clarifying what the other person says, noticing body language, increasing your awareness of the feelings behind the words, and sharpening your sensitivity to the context of the conversation. Listening as a coach includes all these components—which we'll cover a little later—and much more. In our listening model there are three levels of listening. These three levels give the coach an enormous range and, ultimately, a greater capacity for listening.

Level I: Internal Listening

At Level I our attention is on ourselves. We listen to the words of the other person but the focus is on what it means to us. At Level I the spotlight is on me: my thoughts, my judgments, my feelings, my conclusions about myself and others. Whatever is happening with the other person is coming back to me through a diode: a one-way energy trap that lets information in but not out. I'm absorbing information by listening but holding it in a trap that recycles it. At Level I there is only one question: What does this mean to me?

There are many times when this is entirely appropriate. Traveling alone to a different city, you are likely to be operating at Level I most of the time—thinking about where to check in, whether you remembered your ticket, how much time before the flight, the fact that you hate flying, your opinion of airline food, your awareness that the person in the seat behind you keeps kicking you. All your attention is on yourself, as it should be. Another indication that you are operating at Level I is a strong desire for more information. You want answers, explanations, details, data. The internal conversation might sound like this: The flight is delayed? But I'll be late. When will we leave? When will I eat? How can I let people know I might be delayed? Is there another flight? Did I bring enough to read? The purpose of the information gathering at Level I is to meet your own needs.

Another typical setting for Level I is a restaurant. Your awareness and attention are self-directed, and the impact of Level I listening is all about *you*. Do you want a beverage before ordering? What are the specials today? Is the chair comfortable? Is there a draft? Are you too close to the kitchen? How are the prices? Can you afford it? You are conscious of your thoughts and feelings. The decisions, choices, and judgments you make are all about you. You love certain kinds of fish—but not if they serve the whole fish with those dead blank eyes staring up from the plate. You think about the weight you want to lose—so you decide to order the low-fat dressing on the side. Your internal mind chatter is at maximum speed here. Even though you are sitting in the restaurant across the table from someone you are madly in love with, your attention may well be at Level I until you have ordered.

Level I informs us about ourselves and what's going on around us. It's where we figure it out and understand. It's very important. Clients are usually at Level I. That's their job: to look at themselves and their lives—to process, think about, understand. But it is definitely not appropriate for the coach to be operating at this self-absorbed level for any length of time. Coaching happens at Level II.

Level I Dialogue

Client: The new house is a mess. I've got boxes everywhere. I can hardly get from the front door to the bathroom.

COACH: How important is it to get settled at home? This is the most productive time you've had in your business since you started.

Client: I know. The business is booming. It's so exciting to see it take off! But living with the clutter—it's driving me nuts.

COACH: And the mess is temporary. Don't let it distract you from the real issue—maintaining momentum.

Client: But it *is* a distraction.

COACH: I've been in that situation myself before. Trust me—it's not a big deal. You'll find a way to take care of it. In the meantime, let's get back to your business plan.

Client: Okay. If you're sure . . .

Summary
Clearly the coach is listening at Level I—paying more attention to his own judgments and opinions and driving his own agenda.

Level II: Focused Listening

At Level II there is a sharp focus on the other person. You can see it in people's posture when they are communicating at Level II: probably both leaning forward, looking intently at each other. There is a great deal of attention on the other person and not much awareness of the outside world.

Let's go back to the restaurant scene and our two lovers. Their eyes are focused on each other and nothing else. Their desire is to be so close that they become one. They are so oblivious of the outside world that this scene of complete romantic isolation has become a caricature used in commercials. It's as if they're living in their own bubble.

For a coach, all the listening at Level II is directed at the client. Unlike the two lovers, the attention and impact are not about you. At Level II your awareness is totally on the other person. You listen for their words, their expression, their emotion, everything they bring. You notice what they say, how they say it. You notice what they don't say. You see how they smile or hear the tears in their voice. You listen for what they value. You listen for their vision and what makes them energetic. You listen for what makes them come alive in the coaching session and what makes them go dead or withdraw.

Energy and information come from the client and they are reflected back. At Level II the impact of listening is on the speaker. The coach is like a perfect mirror that absorbs none of the light; what comes from the client is returned. At Level II coaches are constantly aware of the impact their listening is having on the client—not always monitoring the impact, but aware.

Most coaching, as noted, happens at Level II. It is the level of empathy, creativity, clarification, collaboration, innovation. Now there is a conduit directly between coach and client. At this level coaches are unattached to self, their agenda, their thoughts, or their opinions. At Level II the coach is so focused on the client that the mind chatter virtually disappears and the coaching becomes almost spontaneous. As a coach you are no longer trying to figure out the next move. In fact, if your attention is on trying to figure out what to say next—what brilliant question to pose to the client—that should be a clue that you are listening at Level 1: inside your own experience.

As a coach listening at Level II you hear the client speak. You hear the words but you hear much more: the tone, the pace, the feeling expressed. You notice all that is coming to you in the form of information. Then you choose what to respond to and how you will respond. Then you notice the impact of your response on the client and receive that information as well. It's as though you listen twice before the client responds again. You listen for the client's initial conversation, and you listen for the client's reaction to your response. You receive information both times. This is listening at Level II.

Level II Dialogue

Client: The new house is a mess. I've got boxes everywhere. I can hardly get from the front door to the bathroom.

COACH: How important is it to get settled at home? This is the most productive time you've had in your business since you started.

Client: I know. The business is booming. It's so exciting to see it take off! But living with the clutter—it's driving me nuts.

COACH: How can you deal with the clutter—and still maintain your momentum with the new business?

Client: I just don't have the time to deal with it right now.

COACH: What do you have time for?

Client: I'd love to be able to devote a whole week just to moving in, but that's not practical.

COACH: So what can you do instead?

Client: I could do fifteen minutes or so when I get home at night.

Summary
Here the coach is listening at Level II—following the client's lead, actively listening, and checking.

Level III: Global Listening

At Level III, you listen at 360 degrees. In fact, you listen as though you and the client were at the center of the universe receiving information from everywhere at once. It's as though you're surrounded by a force field that contains you, the client, and a space of knowing. Level III includes everything you can observe with your senses: what you see, hear, smell, and feel—the tactile sensations as well as the emotional sensations. Level III includes the action and the inaction and the interaction.

If Level II is hardwired, then Level III is like a radio field. The radio waves are entirely invisible, yet we can trust they exist because we hear music coming from the radio. Level III is like the radio waves. They cross our antenna and they become information we can use. But it takes a special receiver to pick up Level III, and it takes practice for most people because they don't often need to make use of Level III listening the way a coach does. For many people this is a new realm of listening. But then imagine the surprise when people discovered Marconi was right: signals travel through the air on invisible waves, and they can be received by tuning an antenna and receiver.

One of the benefits of learning to listen at Level III is greater access to your intuition. From your intuition you receive information that is not directly observable, and you use that information just as you'd use words coming from the client's mouth. At Level III, intuition is simply more information. As a coach you take in the information and respond. Then you notice the impact. How did your response land? What did you notice about that?

Level III listening is sometimes described as environmental listening. You notice the temperature, the energy level, the lightness or darkness, both literally and figuratively. Is the client's energy sparking or flat? Is she cool, lightly present, or tightly controlled? You will know by listening at Level III. You'll learn to trust your senses about that and you can always just ask: "I get the sense that you're in a very dark place. Are you? What's that about?" Performers develop a strong sense of Level III listening. Stand-up comedians, musicians, actors, training presenters—all have the ability to instantly read the Level III in a room and monitor how it changes in response to what they do. This is a great example of noticing one's impact. The performer, the coach, the leader, the facilitator—anyone who is successful at influencing people is skilled at listening at Level III. They have an ability to read the impact they're having and to adjust their behavior accordingly.

To listen at Level III the coach must be very open and softly focused, sensitive to tiny stimuli, ready to receive information from all the senses—in your own sphere, in the world around you, in the world around your client. As you listen at this level, you also affect the world around you and your client, like ripples on a pond that move out and touch the shore in different ways. Level III will make sense to you even when you don't understand what the information means. The key to Level III listening is simply to take in the information and play with it and see what emerges.

Level III Dialogue

Client: The new house is a mess. I've got boxes everywhere. I can hardly get from the front door to the bathroom.

COACH: How important is it to get settled at home? This is the most productive time you've had in your business since you started.

Client: I know. The business is booming. It's so exciting to see it take off! But living with the clutter—it's driving me nuts.

COACH: What's that about? I get the sense that you're pretty agitated.

Client: It takes up so much room. It's really in the way.

COACH: Am I hearing that something has you blocked? I think I hear it in your voice—it's like a choking almost.

Client: I think there's more to this than boxes of dishes and books. I actually think it's about some unfinished business in the relationship. It's like clutter—like all the old boxes we've moved from place to place. It's in the way.

COACH: What do you want to do about that?

Client: What I've been *trying* to do is step around it, or over it, and that doesn't seem to be working. I guess it's time to sit down and work it out—unpack it all, so to speak.

Summary
In this case the coach was tuned to Level III: the nuances of the space between coach and client—beyond the words—including all the energy and emotion that was spoken and unspoken. Note that in the dialogue samples we've just seen, the conversation was crafted to illustrate the distinctions between the three levels. In a real conversation, of course, the coach is switching between Levels II and III constantly.

The Coach Is Listening

Everything in coaching hinges on listening—especially listening, with the client's agenda in mind: Is the client on track with his vision. Is he honoring his values? Where is he today? The coach is listening for signs of life, the choices clients are making, and how those choices move them toward balance or away. The coach is listening, too, for resistance and turbulence in the process.

Listening is the entry point for all of the coaching. In one sense, all the other contexts depend on listening at Levels II and III. Listening, then, is the gate through which all the coaching passes.

As the coach listens, he or she makes choices that change the direction and focus of coaching. That's what we mean by the impact of listening. One of the ways this impact shows up is in the spontaneous choice of which coaching skill to use next. All skills depend on listening first, of course, but certain skills are especially appropriate in the context of listening.

Coaching Skills

The following coaching skills are generally associated with the context of listening. Of course, effective listening is a prerequisite for the use of all the coaching skills. The skills we selected for this section are skills that seem particularly appropriate responses to a listening situation.

Articulating

With your listening skills at Levels II and III fully engaged, you have a heightened sense of attention and awareness. You have a picture of what is going on with the client at this moment. When you combine that sense of what is happening right now with what you know about this client, you have a tremendous amount of information. Articulation is the ability to succinctly describe what is going on. Often clients can't see for themselves what they are doing or saying. Or perhaps they can see the details but not the bigger picture of their life. With this skill you share your observations as clearly as possible but without judgment. You tell clients what you see them doing. Sometimes articulation takes the form of the hard truth and can be confrontive: "I see you're continuing to schedule evening and weekend time away from your family. You've said in the past that your family is a high priority and this overtime work doesn't jibe with that. What's up?" Another example might be: "So you didn't get the job done on time. It looks like you blew it." Not sidestepping the mess is part of the coaching alliance. And articulating—as in pointing out the mess in the road—is part of the coach's job. Cleaning up the mess is the client's job.

Articulating is also a component of active listening. It involves mirroring back to clients what they've just said to you. It's a summary of what they've said and the feeling behind it. For example: "I sense you really want to build this business and despite all the hours you're putting in, it's not growing the way you want" or "It sounds like you're really beginning to enjoy working out first thing in the morning."

Articulating is a skill that affirms the client. When clients tell you what it's like for them and you say it back, especially when you use their own words, it's very validating. They feel listened to and confirmed. There is a sense of corroboration and a sense of being known. Clients also get a stronger sense of what is going on when they hear themselves restated. Sometimes the coach will play back what clients have said just to have them hear their own experience again. It's like turning up the volume: it's stronger. After repeating what they've said, especially with the tone and feeling they expressed, you'll sometimes hear clients respond with surprise: "I said that?"

Sample Dialogue

Client: So I'm not sure if I should stay on or leave. It's like I'm stuck in the middle.

COACH: What I'm hearing you say is you feel a conflict between your loyalty to your employer—a person who helped you when you really needed it—and your desire to take a shot at starting your own business.

Client: It *is* a hard choice. But it's not a choice between loyalty and independence. I can still find ways to show gratitude for Dick's support.

Clarifying

Many of us have a tendency to operate from vague or incomplete thoughts and unresolved feelings. Often we leap to conclusions—or draw the wrong conclusions based on sketchy information—because we haven't thought matters through. And sometimes our best thinking happens when we're able to test our ideas and feelings on someone else. Coaches serve as a resource for their client's self-reflection to create greater clarity.

Clients may ramble. They get caught up in their own stories. They may be drifting in a fog trying to paddle their way out. They get stuck in fuzzy thinking and outdated ways of looking at their world. They may be reading old maps. In such situations, part of the coach's role is to help clients see what they can't see for themselves. The skill of clarifying is a combination of listening, asking, articulating, reframing—sometimes simply testing different perspectives: "Here's what I'm hearing. . . . Is that right? . . . It sounds like you are looking for . . ." Remember: it is still about the client figuring it out; it is not about the coach telling the client (as if the coach had the right answer). Clarifying is used to bring the image into sharp focus, add detail, hold it up for inspection, so the client can say: "Yes! That's it!" or "No—that's not it at all. It's this other thing over here." Sometimes you have to show clients blue before they realize it was green they had in mind all along.

Sample Dialogue

Client: I can't seem to come to a conclusion that feels right.

COACH: It's an issue you've been wrestling with for a few weeks. It sounds like you'd really like to make a decision but you're still on the fence.

Client: I'm too close to it right now to have the perspective I need.

COACH: I'd be willing to describe what I see from the outside. Would that be helpful?

Client: Absolutely.

COACH: Taking the part-time job will provide income. Money's tight. Income would be a good thing. And yet, that kind of security isn't a high value for you. You've taken big risks in the past and given up financial security.

Client: It's true. Sometimes my parents think I'm nuts.

COACH: Plus, taking the part-time job will virtually eliminate free time—no time to work on your art and little if any for friends or a new relationship. Creativity is a high value for you. I'm not lobbying for one choice over another. I'm just pointing out what you've said in the past about what is truly of value to you.

Client: Thanks. That helps put things in perspective for me.

Meta-View

Get in the hypothetical helicopter with the client, take it up to about 5,000 feet, and look down on the client's life. This is the coaching skill of meta-view. It is especially useful when the client is in a rut and can only see six inches of dirt on either side. Meta-view presents the big picture and opens up room for perspective. The coach might ask: "What do you see from up here? What's the truth you can see from this vantage point that you couldn't see down there?"

The meta-view reconnects clients to their vision of themselves and a fulfilling life. When they're struggling at the foot of the mountain, looking up at the daunting work to be done, meta-view allows them to float above it all to get a fresh perspective—a snapshot of the big picture when they're in the midst of a difficult period.

Another way to look at the meta-view is to see it as an elevated platform—a high place where coaches can stand to survey the client's life with all its circumstances and issues. The coach can see more than the client from this vantage point. In fact, that is the coach's job: to maintain clarity of perspective and hold the big picture. This platform allows the coach to speak from outside the details of the immediate conversation. If the client is struggling with a co-worker, for example, the coach might say: "This story reminds me of the conversation you had with your ex-boss and the situation with your sister. Is there a pattern here?" Another example might be the client who appears to be making a great effort but never gets anywhere. In this case the coach might say: "There seems to be a lot of struggle—what are you getting out of your suffering?" In this last example the meta-view is from a higher level that captures the underlying theme. Meta-view presents a panoramic view of the journey.

Coaches sometimes forget to get a meta-view of the client's situation because it's so easy to be pulled into the details of the moment. Suppose a client comes to the coaching session worried about the flak she expects over the upcoming firing of a staff member. The coach asks her to look at the situation from the meta-view—from the point of view of building a work culture—rather than focusing on hurt feelings or upsets. What are the costs to the organization of *not* firing that person? How will the firing affect communication and trust among co-workers in the long run?

Metaphor

The skill of using metaphor is a way to draw on imagery and experience to help the client comprehend faster and more easily. The question "Are you drifting in a fog?" addresses the client at a more effective emotional level than the question "Are you confused?" which merely addresses the client's intellect. Clients can step into a picture of drifting in a fog. They know what it looks like and feels like. It's a whole experience. Often the truth for clients is not in their mind but in their heart or their gut. Metaphor tends to bypass the analysis and target those powerful places. And when the metaphor doesn't land in a way that bursts into insight, you try something else. The best way to become adept at this skill is the same way we encourage all learning in coaching: try it a lot, fail at it a lot, don't be attached to being right, and keep learning.

Acknowledging

The coaching skill of acknowledgment strengthens the client's foundation. The client can stand straighter after a true acknowledgment. This skill addresses who the client *is*. Praise and compliments highlight what people do: "Good job on that report, Janet." Or they highlight the opinion of the person giving the praise, or the impact on the person giving the compliment: "Your presentation was thoughtful and inspiring to me." Acknowledgment recognizes the inner character of the person it is addressed to. More than what they did, or what it means to the sender, acknowledgment highlights who they are: "Janet, you really showed your commitment to learning." "You took a big risk." "I can see your love of beauty in it." Acknowledgment often highlights a value that clients honored in the action they took: "You made it really fun for yourself. Congratulations. I know you had to take a risk to do that." The client values fun. Or: "Great job. You took a stand for honesty and authenticity. It wasn't easy." The client values honesty.

Acknowledgment is almost a context of coaching. At some level we are always supporting who clients must be in order to make the changes they want. The client had to be courageous, or had to be a person willing to stand up to the fear, or had to be tenacious for the sake of a relationship. The skill of acknowledgment celebrates their internal strengths. Acknowledgment helps clients see what they sometimes dismiss in themselves from a distorted sense of humility or simply don't see at all. By acknowledging that strength you give your client access to it. Clients will know when the acknowledgment is honest and true. They will be more resourceful in the future because they recognize the truth you illuminated. Acknowledgment might take this form: "Look at what you were able to tell your boss. Think about how far you've come in the last four months. Your ability to be clear and ask for what you want is so much stronger today. You've really shown you can stand up to the fear and speak your own truth." Acknowledgment goes right to the heart of where the client is growing and getting stronger (and, often, feeling the need of validation). When you acknowledge this, you empower the client to keep growing.

There are actually two parts to every acknowledgment in co-active coaching. The first part we've already covered: delivering the acknowledgment. The second part is noticing the impact on the client. This is a way for the coach to test, to make sure that the acknowledgment was truly on target. Notice the client's reaction. At Level III you will know if you found the right description of who the client had to be in that situation. The acknowledgment will definitely land in a way you can hear, sense, and see. It is enormously moving for clients to be seen and known in this way, and it is rare. That's the power of acknowledgment.

Sample Dialogue

Client: Maybe I should have kept my mouth shut. I ended up looking like a fool.

COACH: You could have handled that situation lots of different ways. What you did was take a stand for your own learning and growth— even though you knew it would come at a cost. At that moment, you had to be more committed to your own learning than to looking good. That's who you are.

Client: Thanks. After the embarrassment wears off, in the end it's the learning that will serve me.

What It Means to Be Heard

Personal growth is a self-creative process. It's like cutting your own hair. Listening provides the mirror: the reflection in which the work can be done. Whether it's going well or poorly for the client, whether it's coiffure or chop job, one of the most powerful aspects of the relationship is the listening. There is no other place in their lives where clients are heard like they're heard when they talk with you.

Exercises

1. Listening at Levels I and II

The goal of this exercise is to listen completely at Level I—that is, focused entirely on your own thoughts and opinions. To do this exercise, ask a friend or colleague to take a half hour or so to play the Level I and Level II listening games with you.

Level I

Describe Level I listening to your partner and ask that person to describe a trip they took, including stories about things that went well and things that didn't go so well. As your partner tells the story of the trip, your job is to listen to the words and interpret the story entirely in terms of your own experience. Comment frequently to your partner with your own opinion. How would you have done the trip differently? What's going on in you while this other person is talking? What does this story remind you of in your own life? What advice would you give your partner? How can you improve on their story?

After fifteen minutes or so, tell each other what it was like to listen at Level I and what it was like to be listened to at Level I.

Level II

Work with the same friend—and the same story—again for about fifteen minutes. But this time without describing Level II be curious. Ask questions, clarify, and articulate what you see. Be alert for your partner's values as they are expressed in the story. Stay completely focused on the partner by listening and responding at Level II.

This time tell each other what it was like to listen at Level II and what it was like to be listened to at Level II. How was it different from the Level I listening?

2. Listening at Level III

Take a field trip or two to venues where the Level III activity is likely to be noticeable. For example: a library, a hotel lobby, the waiting area in an emergency room, an airport bar. Pay attention to simply gathering your Level III awareness of how people are feeling: angry, frustrated, joyful, bored, at peace, anxious? What else do you notice about the environment? What is the "buzz" or "hum" in the room? Notice where the energy is in the room and how it shifts as people arrive or depart. Write down your impressions. Then try listening at Level III with your eyes closed. How is it different? What do you note that you didn't notice with your eyes open?

Variation: Have a friend enter the room clearly annoyed and angry. Notice how the room reacts at Level III. Or have two friends enter the room and start a loud, rude conversation. Notice how the Level III energy changes.

3. Meta-View

A meta-view is the big picture. It is part theme, part positioning statement, and part vision. Examples of meta-views:

Launching a new life

Being in transition

Struggling with change

Drifting at sea

High-speed action machine

Peaceful unfolding

What is the meta-view for your own life today?

Write down the names of ten close friends or relatives. What is the meta-view for them at this time?

4. Metaphor

Create a metaphor for each of the following client situations:

Stuck between two appealing choices

About to enter an exciting new period with a lot of unknowns

After a long period of inaction, everything happening at once

Chaotic work environment

Two new romantic relationships

Money losses because of mismanagement

From too little exercise to overdoing it

Making great progress building the business until the interruption

Success

Sadness

Series of windfalls

Exhaustion

Denial

5. Acknowledging

List five friends. Write an acknowledgment of who they are being or who they have been to get to where they are today. Write an acknowledgment for yourself.

Intuition

Maybe you've had an experience like this. You're driving in the country on back roads that aren't marked very well. You come to an intersection of two roads and instinctively turn to the right. Or this may have happened. You're having dinner with a friend. Everything is normal. The conversation has its usual flow. And you suddenly ask your friend, "What's wrong? Is there something you need to tell me?"

Maybe you've made an unexpected phone call to someone or spontaneously dropped them a card. You weren't sure quite why you did it at that particular time—then found out later the timing was important for some reason. Some people get great hunches about investments. Some people get a sense of the answer to a question even when it doesn't seem to make much sense. They'd rather trust their instincts about some things because the feeling is so much stronger than the data. These are all examples of intuition at work. They are examples of gathering nonempirical information—usually in response to a question, spoken or unspoken. Which way to turn? What's going on with her? Which investment to choose? Which job is better suited to me? Why did the client just disappear in our conversation? Intuition comes up with an answer.

Speaking from your intuition is extraordinarily valuable in coaching. It's right alongside the ability to listen deeply and deftly. And even though we can put words in a definition, the *experience* of intuition is sometimes hard to explain—which also makes it difficult for some people to accept. The trouble for many people starts with the fact that intuition can be difficult to verify. Sometimes there's no observable evidence for the conclusion. In some cases the conclusions people derive from their intuition are actually contrary to the observable evidence. People who operate out of their intuition will say things like: "I know because my intuition is usually right about these things."

Many times, those who have trouble believing in intuition treat it as guessing or getting lucky. They just don't understand, trust, or believe in intuition. Facts that can be measured, recorded, repeated, recalled—that's what people frequently say they want when they're making decisions. It's certainly the scientific model and the stance taken by a majority of the population. People often make fun of intuition when they say, for example, "She relied on her feminine intuition." (We won't even go into the politics of that statement.) People are shy about admitting that they have used their intuition. Even those who have the talent of intuition in abundance are often reluctant to use it, or admit it, and so this ability atrophies in all of us. That's too bad, because it's a powerful asset in coaching.

The Known vs. the Unknown Universe

Most of us have come to believe that the known universe is within hand's reach. It is a world that is within your field of vision, your range of hearing, the susceptibility of your five senses. A thing is known when others corroborate it and come up with the same results. Intuition, however, is not directly observable—although sometimes its effects are. Like the wind in the trees, it may not be visible, but we can see and hear its effects. That's why it is sometimes called the "sixth sense." It is a sensitivity that goes beyond the physical world.

Suppose someone says, "It's going to rain today." You ask, "How do you know?" The answers might be:

"I heard the National Weather Service report on the radio."

"There was a red sky this morning."

"The barometer on the wall has been dropping fast all morning."

"The wind is from the east and clouds are building in the west."

"I feel it in my bones."

"I just know."

Of course, some people really do feel approaching rain in their bones. The point is that there are many ways of knowing. One of those ways is by scientifically verifiable evidence, but there is also "just knowing." When you look at this list of possible answers, you might want to ask: Which source is right? A different question would be: Which one do I trust? Many people would say there's a direct relationship between what they can observe directly and their confidence in knowing. For these people, their trust is in the direct experience. They would also say that intuition is way down on the trust scale—maybe even 0% for reliability.

But instead of one scale, let's suppose there are two. Imagine that intuition is simply a different dimension of the same space. It's a different plane. Imagine that conventional knowing is on one plane (the X-Y axis) and intuition is on a connected but different plane (the X-Z axis). Now we can see that our knowing is in three dimensions. In this graphic picture, we still have different degrees of trusting the intuition but we see that everyone has access to intuition as a way of knowing. And it is a sense that can be developed with practice. It's not down at the bottom of a truth scale. It's within mind's reach—even closer than empirical information sometimes.

But Is It Right?

Part of the difficulty of describing intuition as a way of knowing starts with the definition of knowing. One way of looking at intuition says it is neither right nor wrong—it's more like a nudge we receive. For example, answer these questions: What day of the week is tomorrow? What is tomorrow's date? What season is tomorrow in? What will the weather be like during this particular season in this particular year? What's your theme during this season of your life in this particular year? Notice that the answer to each question is found in a different place. One of the places is your memory, another place is your logical mind, another place is your history. And perhaps another place is your intuition. What if intuition were a place—not a place we are used to going, perhaps, but simply a place that we go to, like memory, that provides us with an answer. We take the nudge and give it expression.

In order to express our intuition in words, we make an interpretation. It's our *interpretation* of the intuitive nudge that can be off target. The intuitive impulse itself was neither right nor wrong. Imagine this scenario. Your client is in the midst of a report about the action she took last week. It's a great report with one success after another. She's followed through on everything she said she would. But your intuition tells you she's holding something back. So despite the overwhelming evidence of accomplishment, you say: "My intuition tells me there is something you're not saying about last week. Is that true?" Your intuition gave you a nudge. Your interpretation is that the client is holding back, so that's what you say. It doesn't matter whether you are right or wrong about your interpretation. If the client is holding back—great, you opened a door to talk about that. If the client says she isn't holding anything back—great, you reinforce the success story. The great thing about intuition and coaching is that intuition always forwards the action and deepens the learning, even when it lands with a clang instead of a melodious ping.

Intuition often shows up in the coaching conversation in unexpected ways as a hunch. Sometimes it appears as a visual image, or it might be an unexplained shift in emotion or energy. The important thing to remember in coaching is to be open to intuition—trusting it, aware of it, and completely unattached to the interpretation. In the end, intuition is valuable when it moves the client to action or deeper learning. It's irrelevant, really, whether your intuition was "correct."

Sample Dialogues

Client: It's like I've run out of options and I'm worn out. Doing the same things over and over, talking to the same people, showing the same old résumé. Even when the faces and names change, it's all a repeat performance.

COACH: My intuition tells me there's something else—something that's been overlooked. Like it's right there in a place you've been before. What could that be?

Client: I don't know. It's like I've been down this road before and I'm in a deep rut.

COACH: The road's a good image; let's work with that. Imagine there's a fence running along this road, and there's a gate in the fence. What's the gate?

Client: It's like the road not taken.

COACH: And what might be on the other side of that gate? If you were going to make something up, what would that be?

Client: Actually it reminds me of my grandparents' home in Connecticut. My grandfather is the only person in our family who worked for himself. I thought he was about the smartest man alive to be able to do that. I really admired his independence.

COACH: What does the gate mean to you in your own life?

Client: That gate's always been there. And I've always walked past, looking for security and maybe camaraderie in a large organization. I think it's time I stopped and took a serious look at what's behind the gate for me.

Intuitive Intelligence

Another way to think of intuition is to regard it as a kind of intelligence, like musical intelligence or visual intelligence. All of us who are not blind or color-blind can identify colors. We start this in preschool: red, blue, green. Many of us add to our color vocabulary over the years and become more adept at recognizing colors. Artists learn to identify many shades of colors and give them names. In their minds they can picture the subtle differences between hundreds of shades. Intuition is like that. It is an intelligence everyone has been given in some measure, and we can develop it the way artists or musicians develop their talents.

One of the interesting things about intuition is its elusive quality. It's almost as if trying hard makes it harder to grasp. Looking too intently for it makes it more difficult to find. The key seems to be to take a soft focus, be open, like looking at those colored, patterned pictures. The image of the clipper ship is in there, but you have to relax your focus to see it. Your intuition is there, giving you messages or clues, but just below the level of direct observation. This is the paradox of intuition: an open hand will hold it; it will slip through a fist.

Your Interpretation, Not Your Judgment

What you express from your intuition is your *interpretation*. It is an observation from your intuition, not a judgment, and it's important that you not be attached to its being right. When you say, "My intuition tells me there's something you are not saying about last week," that's an observation. It's an interpretation based on certain signals and nudges. Some of the interpretation is based on direct observation—Level III listening, for example—and some is pure inspiration. To your client, the observation might sound like a judgment—as if you're telling him that he's deliberately trying to hide something from you. You may think he is in fact hiding something, but the message you deliver is simply your intuitive observation. Of course, if you jump to conclusions and bypass observation, your client is much more likely to feel judged. If you ask, "What are you hiding from your report?" there's a built-in accusation. You didn't really give your client the benefit of your intuition. You were right to trust your intuition, but now you need to work on your phrasing because you came to a conclusion and expressed *that* instead of the intuitive observation.

If you're going to use your intuition effectively, you can't be attached to the interpretation. Being unattached to an interpretation can be a challenge, and it's one reason people don't express their intuition. People sometimes hold back because they're afraid of being wrong or appearing foolish. People also hold back because they're attached to their own interpretations and haven't made room for the possibility that they don't understand. They are attached to being right. So be prepared. When you express your intuition, clients may disagree. Even so, they will learn as much as if your intuition were somehow "correct." What was correct was the intuition to say something. What was correct was whatever the client learned. What's more, clients count on your intuition. When you hold back, you shortchange them.

Finding Your Own Access Point

We develop our access to intuition in the same way we develop other talents or muscles. Intuitive fitness is just as possible as physical fitness. Fortunately, coaching is an intuition fitness center. On the practical side, the question is: How do you find access to your intuition, especially if you're not accustomed to looking for it? It isn't easy at first. Compared to the triceps muscle, which is in pretty much the same place for all of us, each of us finds our intuition in a different place.

Many people find their intuition in the body—in their chest or stomach. It's no wonder people talk of intuition as a "gut response" or a feeling "in my gut." Some feel a burning in the forehead or tingle in the fingers. For others intuition is not felt in the body at all. It may be above you, or it may be a bubble that surrounds you. Take some time to find out where you sense your intuition. Stop, pay attention, listen to your body or your experience at that point in order to determine where the communication is coming from.

You may "see" your intuition in a visual way or feel it kinesthetically. Some people find that they're better able to access their intuition by standing up. For some people the connection is definitely verbal. Whatever your access point, eventually you'll need to verbalize the nudge from your intuition. You make sense out of the sensation by giving words to it. Let's be absolutely clear about this: Your responsibility as a coach is to *speak* what your intuition gives you. Having intuition and not using it in the coaching relationship is giving only part of the service the client wants from coaching.

The Intuitive On/Off Switch

Accessing your intuition may be new to you, especially at the deep level of intuitive access we are describing. Until it becomes a familiar and easy tool to use, you may need a way to remember it in your coaching: posting a reminder note over your phone, wearing your wristwatch on the opposite wrist, standing up if you usually sit down, whatever works for you. Then use the device until you find you use your intuition automatically. Your intuition is always on tap. You don't have to *generate* it any more than you have to generate the electricity to run the lights in your home. You simply have to remember to turn it on.

Blurting It Out

The natural tendency is to hold back at first, to analyze the intuition, to make sure it's viable. It doesn't really work that way. By the time you've performed a set of validation tests on your intuition the client has moved on to an entirely different phase of the conversation. Your moment is lost. Intuition is like a small flash of light that is already beginning to fade as soon as it appears. The most powerful moment is the first. Fear and timidity, hesitation, will pass it by.

Getting the Intuitive Hit

Sometimes intuition comes in the form of words, but it could just as easily be shapes or sounds or tingles. Your intuition might communicate to you through a sense of heaviness, an ache, a mood. Sometimes the intuitive hint arises from the conversation itself. Sometimes it is out there in the environment. A scene outside your office window might inspire an intuitive hit. The scene creates an image . . . which your intuition signals to you . . . and you share with your client . . . and then you see what the impact is. For example: Your client is describing a sense of confusion about a change in her work situation. She is trying to figure out which way to turn and wondering what the right course of action is. You look out your window and notice it is a crisp fall day, one of the first. It's a strong impression and you mention it: "I have this image of a fall day, the leaves changing color, the air cooler. What does that bring up for you?" It might suggest a sense of the changing seasons in her life and give her the means for sorting out the changes before her. Or it could remind her of chores that need to be done to get ready for winter. The source of the intuition is irrelevant. What is relevant is what happens to the client.

Intuition isn't supposed to be reasonable. It is not based on logic or evidence and doesn't need corroboration. It stands on its own. In fact some of the most powerful intuitions are the most unreasonable. It may take some courage at first to trust the power of your intuition, but gradually you will learn to use it by using it and gaining a little more confidence each time.

Phrasing It

This is a crib sheet for those who feel uneasy about expressing their intuition. Use any of the following phrases to open your intuitive expression. In fact it's good practice to simply begin one of these phrases with no idea what will come out of your mouth, trusting that your intuition will fill in the blanks as you go:

"I have a sense . . ."

"May I tell you a gut feeling I have?"

"I have a hunch that . . ."

"Can I check something out with you?"

"I wonder if . . ."

"See how this fits for you . . ."

And perhaps the best of all is also the simplest and most direct: "My intuition tells me . . ."

Remember: Intuition is not magic, though sometimes we may think so, especially when we're delighted with the results. Intuition is like listening. It is a powerful talent that can be used to help clients move into action or deepen their learning.

Coaching Skills

The following coaching skills are associated with intuition, although they are not exclusive to the context of intuition. We chose these skills for this section because they naturally come from a place of intuition or they help give intuition an opening for expression. We listed metaphor under the listening context, but it could just as easily be included here since metaphor is often drawn from one's intuition.

Intruding

Because of the brevity of most coaching calls, intruding in the client's report or storytelling may be necessary to get to the bottom line quicker. As the coach you use your Level III awareness to decide when it's time to do that. Rather than wait for a socially polite break in the conversation, you interrupt and redirect the conversation or ask a question. Often your intuition urges you to intrude.

Note that it isn't necessary to be rude in order to intrude, although your interruption may be perceived by some as rude, especially in parts of the country where direct conversation is considered a cultural faux pas. Remember, too, that clients usually know when they're droning on and on. If you don't redirect this type of rambling activity, clients begin to think of the coaching session as a place to tell stories and before long get dissatisfied and are ready to abandon the coaching relationship. Clients do not want to use up all their time in a coaching session with "and then I . . ." or "and she said . . ."

In general, it's best if you prepare your client for intrusions at the initial intake session. Explain that you'll sometimes interrupt the conversation in a way that may surprise them. Let them know that a coaching conversation is different from having chitchat with a friend over coffee. Sometimes you may need to interrupt, and you ask that they not take it personally. Ask them to let you know if they feel offended so the two of you can talk about it again if necessary. This should be all the permission you need, as coach, to intrude whenever you have to.

Maybe you're still reluctant to intrude, thinking that it's not your style. Here's the real point. You're not intruding on *them*. You're intruding on the story that gets in the way of getting to the truth. You are intruding on the distraction, the smoke screen, the confusion. Would you really rather be perceived as polite, or nice, than intrude to give your clients access to a fuller life? Remember that coaching is about the client, not the coach. Coaching is therefore not for the faint of heart.

Your job as coach is to work with whatever comes up and to leave your agenda and ego out of the conversation. In fact the coach doesn't even appear in the coaching model illustrated in Chapter 1. But there are times when you need to take charge. Your experience and training in coaching give you some authority that you can use to serve the client. Holding back, being nice at this point, does not serve the client's best interests. There will be times when you'll have to jump in to clarify, make a strong request or a powerful challenge, or tell the hard truth. Since there is no hard-and-fast rule, this is a good place to trust your intuition to know when to intrude.

Beginning coaches often suppose that they need more information, need to listen to more of the story, before they can inject coaching. They say they feel the need for more background or context. But in most cases, they let the story go on far longer than necessary. The skill of intruding helps cut off unnecessary storytelling—which is frequently a smoke screen put up by the client to avoid getting to the heart of the issue. Intruding accelerates the process of getting to the core: the action and learning.

Sample Dialogue

Example A: Poor Use of the Skill

Client: Mary's the one I told you about, the one who seems so contrary. If I say I think we should go east, she says no, we should head west. If I say the only way to meet the deadline is to hire outside help, she says no, it's up to us, it just means we need better teamwork. Teamwork! What could be more hypocritical? Over and over I've asked her to be a more involved member of the team. And it's always, "I don't have the time" or "this is your team to run." You know, just excuse after excuse. She's the one that's constantly undermining the team.

COACH: She's the one that's constantly undermining the team. It's got to be frustrating trying to work with someone like that.

Client: Well, yeah. Did I tell you her latest?

COACH: More of the same, I'm sure.

Client: Of course. It doesn't end . . . blah, blah, blah, blah, blah, blah, blah, blah.

Example B: Good Use of the Skill

Client: Mary's the one I told you about, the one who seems so contrary. If I say I think we should go east, she says no, we should head west. If I say the only way to meet the deadline is to hire outside help, she says no, it's up to us . . .

COACH: What do you need to do about that?

Client: Do about it?

COACH: Right. What do you need to do about it?

Client: Well . . . I could have a talk with her, I suppose, about how disruptive that is, the fact that it undermines the team . . .

COACH: When do you want to have that conversation?

Client: Soon, I guess. This week, maybe Thursday or Friday.

Blurting

Odd as it may sound, blurting is actually a skill worth developing. Most of us spend so much time trying to analyze and figure things out we miss the opportunity to jump into action. In coaching, it actually serves the client to go right into the messiness without sorting it out first. It's better to dive in and be willing to look a little clumsy. Ironically, it often builds more trust than appearing to be the authority, always in control. Being clumsy or messy, and therefore more human, is also more authentic. And if *you* don't have to look good, your *clients* don't have to look good. For example, as coach you might say, "I'm not sure what the right words are here, but it's something like . . ." or "Let me just talk out loud for a minute. I'm not sure exactly what I want to say here. . . ."

Clients and Their Intuition

It's worth noting that watching the coach work with intuition allows clients to experiment and take risks with their own intuition. In fact, learning the coaching principles, contexts, and skills can benefit clients a lot. Clients who become proficient at listening at Levels II and III, for example, have a chance to be much more effective in their relationships at work and at home. Learning to clarify, or to keep the meta-view, in their personal lives would be a tremendous advantage too.

In teaching clients to work with intuition, begin by asking them simply to spend some time noticing their intuition and playing with it. You might ask them to investigate how they access their intuition, for instance, and urge them to free themselves from any attachment to doing it "right." Prepare them for the appearance of their internal skeptic—in addition to the external skeptics they are likely to encounter. When clients practice with their intuition, it's normal to compare their intuitive interpretations with whatever conclusions come up from their logical mind. For most people, especially as they begin to play with their intuition, the rational mind usually wins out. They should expect that to happen—and should be encouraged to keep exploring this unfamiliar terrain.

Exercises

1. Intuition

Intuition is that sixth sense that responds to a question. Sometimes the question is explicit and posed; sometimes it's part of the background of the conversation. In coaching, there is always a question in the air about the client's life.

To practice your intuition, meet with a friend or colleague in a quiet place where the two of you can be undisturbed for a while. Have the person write down a series of open-ended questions about their life. Ask them to choose one question from the list and have them repeat the question out loud, reading it more than once, with a brief space of quiet in between each repetition of the question. The two of you will then concentrate on the question for three to five minutes with no conversation. Your goal is simply to increase your concentration on the question and open yourself to whatever your intuition offers. At the end of the time period, simply tell the person everything that occurred: the random thoughts, the feelings, anything your senses noticed in terms of visual images, sounds, smells, touch, along with anything else you may have noticed or anything that distracted you. Some of what you report from your intuition is sure to connect for the person. As soon as there is a "hit," ask what the connection is and explore that area for greater awareness.

You can double the intrigue in this exercise by having the person write the questions on slips of paper and folding the paper so the questions can't be read. Pick a random question from the pile. Then the two of you spend three to five minutes concentrating on the question even though you don't know what it will say. Again report whatever comes up from your intuition. Then read the question and ask the person for comments. Where were the connections? Where does this lead?

2. Intruding

Sit down with a friend and let them know that, to practice the skill of intruding, you are going to interrupt them as they talk. Have them tell a story from a significant period of their life. It could be a learning experience when they were in school. It could be the story of how they met their best friend. Ask them to pick a story they can stretch; let them know you need them to go on and on. As they are telling you the story, your job is to interrupt the speaker and change the course of the storytelling by using a coaching skill:

Ask them to summarize: "What did that mean to you?"

Interrupt with a provocative question (not a question for more information) such as: "What did you learn from that?"

Interrupt by articulating what is going on in the story at that moment.

Interrupt with a request.

Intrude by announcing your intention to interrupt: "I'm going to interrupt here."

Sample language for interrupting: "Excuse me, you just . . ." "Let me ask . . ."

chapter five

Curiosity

As a context for coaching, curiosity presents a paradox: on the one hand it has a wonderful quality of playfulness; and yet, in practice, the coach's curiosity is a powerful way of opening doors that the client has closed, locked, and forgotten. Curiosity is therefore disarming but also engaging. Curiosity is not a context of dark significance, but it can lead to unexpectedly significant discoveries.

A Different Way of Asking

Curiosity starts with a question: I wonder . . . ? The interesting thing about the question is that it automatically causes us to go looking. For example: Is it cold outside or hot? Chances are you instantly considered the weather in your town. We have this Pavlovian response to a question. It nearly always throws us in the direction of the question, looking for an answer. Simply posing the question shifts the focus of the conversation. Being curious has the same effect. We naturally draw the client's attention to those things the coach and client become curious about—like the client's life purpose, values, passion, Gremlin. And yet being curious about these aspects of the client's life is not the same as gathering information. Curiosity is a different way of discovering.

Our experience in school trained us to gather information by asking specific questions that deduce answers. We learned that questions have specific answers—in fact, right answers. Even essay questions have right ways of answering that are specific, concrete, and measurable. We learned that questions are used to narrow the possibilities. This is the deductive, scientific method. We learned to fill in the blanks and we learned about being scored on our ability to get the right answers.

There is a big difference between conventional questions that elicit information and curious questions that evoke personal exploration. For example:

Information Gathering	Curious
What topics will you include in the report?	What will finishing the report give you?
How much exercise do you need each week?	What would "being fit" look like for you?
What are the training options available?	What do you want to know that you don't know today?

And the deadliest questions of all in this information gathering style are the questions that ask for yes or no. They simply erect a huge stop sign in the middle of the conversation. The road ends abruptly and the coach has to start all over again. Curious questions, however, are open-ended. They take the client on a journey and are easily phrased to avoid sudden stops:

Closed	Open
Is this an effective strategy for you?	What makes this an effective strategy for you?
Is there more to be learned here?	How can you double the learning in this experience?
It sounds like you're stuck between those two choices—is that true?	What's another choice you could make besides the two in front of you?

Another form of questioning we've learned over the years is the leading question. The leading question implies that there is a right answer, a conclusion, built into the question itself. But the leading question leaves little choice. It pretty much forces the learner to come up with the answer the teacher is looking for.

Another thing we've learned from our earliest years is that curiosity is dangerous. It kills the cat and does nothing for Curious George but get him into trouble. Being curious is often viewed as silly and immature and intrusive in conversation, so we learn to be careful about the questions we ask and not let our curiosity get the better of us.

The Value of Curiosity

In coaching, asking curious questions with a curious frame of mind is ideal. The curious coach doesn't have all the answers. When you are curious, you are no longer in the role of expert. Instead, you are joining clients in a quest to find out what's there. You are exploring their world with them, not superimposing your world on theirs.

As a consultant, you gather information so you can come up with appropriate recommendations. You have the expertise and you are casting for information to determine where to go. It's as if you're the general contractor and are hired to come in and build something with the materials you bring to the relationship. In co-active coaching, by contrast, you are curious. You come in as a collaborator with building experience and expertise and build from what is there. The information is inside the client. Your curiosity allows the client to explore and discover. It opens a wider range of possibility by being more flexible. Curiosity invites the client to look for answers. We presume the client knows the appropriate answers and has the resources to come up with them.

By finding the answers in themselves—rather than in you the coach—clients become even more resourceful. The effect of finding the answers is also very energizing because important learning takes place. Curiosity generates the search, defines and directs it, but it is the exploring that creates learning. And it is learning that lasts because it comes from within. It is learning that comes from experience, not just analysis. This kind of learning in the bones is important in coaching because it leads to sustainable change and growth.

Building the Relationship

Authentic curiosity is also a powerful builder of relationships—an aspect of curiosity that is very valuable in coaching. Imagine yourself at a dinner party seated next to a stranger who seems infinitely curious about you: your life, your work, your interests, what makes you tick, what ticks you off. This kind of curiosity is not only flattering but encouraging. It allows you to reveal a lot about yourself in an unchallenged way, and so you build a connection effortlessly. Now imagine the same dinner party and the same stranger asking questions, but this time imagine that the person is not simply curious. Instead, it's your prospective mother-in-law and the questions are put like an inquisition. The questions might be exactly the same, but the context is vastly different. Curiosity builds relationships; interrogation builds defenses. In the coaching relationship, curiosity invites the client to search and reveal in a way that permits safe exploration.

Steering Through Curiosity

The coach's question proposes a direction for looking. The client's attention is naturally drawn in that direction. With each new question, the coach encourages additional looking along a path—or shifts the path, allowing the curiosity to steer the looking. It is an example of intuition and curiosity guiding the coaching conversation. Being curious in coaching is two things: not being attached to a particular path or destination and yet always being intentional about moving toward the light—to seek out meaning, uncover values, discover learning. This is not aimless meandering.

Developing the Muscle

Like listening and intuition, curiosity is a talent. Some people are endowed with a stronger sense of curiosity than others. And like listening and intuition, curiosity can be developed, like other muscles, by exercising.

The first step is awareness: simply paying attention to being curious. We are so accustomed to feeling we have to know the answer before we ask the question, we sometimes find it nearly impossible to ask without knowing. In coaching, however, you have to learn to stop asking questions as the expert—with the intention of sorting, analyzing, and categorizing the information for later use—and simply ask out of curiosity.

Clients know when the coach is asking a question with the "correct answer" in mind. Their antennae tell them there is a correct response that leaves them two choices: either resist or try to discern the answer the coach is looking for. When the question is asked out of curiosity, they will sense this too. They'll know they are being asked to find their own answers from within.

One technique for developing the curiosity muscle is to use the phrase "I'm curious . . ." before asking a question. Notice how it changes the nature of the looking. Notice how it shifts the process of looking to the client but at the same time lowers the risk that usually accompanies coming up with the answer. Clients seem more willing to say, "I don't know" and then come up with an answer anyway. With curiosity there is both a playfulness and an unconditional sense that the answer that emerges is always the right answer because it's the client's. This doesn't mean it can't be challenged, however. It's a right answer because it's the client's, not the coach's, but it is an answer that is open to further coaching. When you ask the client, "How are you doing with making cold calls?" and the client says, "I'm doing fine at four calls a day," you can still ask: "Your initial plan was for eight calls a day. How does the change to four affect your goal?"

Another technique is to simply blurt questions. The goal is to combine your listening levels, your intuition, and your curiosity, and practice not knowing the answers yourself. Just ask the first question that comes to mind, trusting completely that the client has the answers, because the client always has the answers.

One more application of curiosity is to notice the energy shifts in the client's responses. If your sensing radar picks up hesitation, be curious about that. If you pick up anger or resistance, ask about that. Be curious about a change in pace in the client's conversation—or a more energetic spirit, more jokes, more laughter. Use these clues as signals to pursue your curiosity and turn on your intuition.

How Curiosity Fits in Coaching

At some level, curiosity is one of those tools common to all helping professions. Curiosity is especially important in coaching because it gets at sources of information that bypass the head. Asking questions for data will yield analysis, reasons, rationale, explanation. Asking questions out of curiosity will yield deeper—often more authentic—information about feelings and motivation. The information revealed through curiosity is likely to be less censored, less carefully crafted, messier. It will be more real.

The coach demonstrates curiosity in the very first meeting. Almost nothing is more engaging for prospective clients than a coach's genuine curiosity in them. Curiosity makes them feel special, their lives worth exploring, their issues worthy of work. Curiosity is abundant during the intake session as the coach becomes curious about everything in the client's life: why she wants a coach, which areas of her life are exciting and which need more excitement, what she values and clings to, what she desperately wants to be rid of, and more. Curiosity is always present in the ongoing coaching calls, of course. It is the means for uncovering new answers and new areas to explore. Knowing that lasting change will happen simply by being curious, the coach needs to make room for this kind of curiosity.

Curiosity is like picking up a string and following it to see where it leads. As the coach, you don't need to know where the string leads; the client is a full participant in this quest, and ultimately the client knows. It's one of the founding premises for co-active coaching: Clients know the answers. Coaches don't need to know. But coaches do need to be curious.

Sample Dialogue

COACH: I know you keep saying you want to exercise and lose weight—you just brought it up again—but week after week you don't do anything about it. What's going on?

Client: I really am tired of looking dumpy and feeling exhausted all the time. I think I am committed to getting in shape. It's just . . . obviously I'm not doing that.

COACH: What's stopping you?

Client: Clearly time is a big issue—that's what we focus on most weeks.

COACH: What does not exercising mean to you?

Client: My Gremlin says I'm a failure at follow through. It's a really old pattern of starting something and then dropping it without giving it a chance to succeed.

COACH: When you do exercise, what does that mean to you?

Client: It means I care about myself. I know if I don't start losing weight and getting healthier, I'm really putting myself in danger. It also means I care about my family. They want me to be healthy enough to stay around a few more years.

COACH: What kinds of things do you say to yourself when it's time to exercise?

Client: Mostly I say "I don't wanna"—like a six-year-old being told he has to take a bath.

COACH: What do you want?

Client: I want the discipline to stick with the program.

COACH: What works for you?

Client: What *really* works for me—at least it did once before—is having a workout buddy, somebody to do it with.

COACH: How can you make that happen?

Client: I'll bet I could find somebody at work who would be interested in exercising on the lunch hour. I could put a notice on the bulletin board.

Coaching Skills

The skills in this section are ideal examples of the context of curiosity. They are both examples of asking provocative, open-ended questions that send clients into the realm of discovery. The skills reinforce what is at the core of curiosity: it is not about gathering more information, it is about inviting clients to look—not just with their brains, but with their heart, soul, and intuition, into places that are familiar but seen with new eyes, and places they may not have looked before.

Powerful Questions

A particular kind of curiosity takes the form of what we call powerful questions. Asking rather than telling is at the foundation of co-active coaching, and the powerful question is a cornerstone. You can see why when you understand what makes questions powerful to begin with. When a person asks you a question, especially a personal question, it sends you looking for an answer in a particular direction. Let's say your coach asks: "When you work on an important project, what do you consistently do that can jeopardize its successful completion?" The question invites you to look in a particular direction. Or let's say someone asks: "What is a rationale for protecting the redwood trees in California?" Some people may recall seeing a map of California. Others may see groves of redwood trees against a blue sky. Some people's thoughts may consider an environmental viewpoint or return to the woods they remember from their childhood. It's likely that this simple question will take everyone somewhere.

Think of questions as caves and tunnels. Asking a powerful question is like sending the client into a vast and intricate tunnel system that leads to other tunnels, discoveries, and mysteries. A powerful question is expansive and opens up further vistas for the client. The closed-ended question creates a narrow tunnel that usually dead-ends abruptly with a "yes" or "no" or with data—there's no depth for further exploration.

Powerful questions invite introspection, present additional solutions, and lead to greater creativity and insight. They invite clients to look inside ("What do you really want?") or into the future ("Put yourself six months into the future. Standing there, what decisions would you make today?"). The way the question is framed determines where the client looks for the answer.

Some questions are not particularly powerful: those that narrow the looking, for example, or steer the client to a dead end. This happens with "why" questions because they invite the client to look for explanations or analyses—as in "Why did you decide to move to Delaware?" A more powerful question based on the same situation might be: "What are you moving toward?" Sometimes clients get defensive about answering because the Gremlin was provoked; sometimes it's because the question put them on the spot for justification rather than opening them up to exploration. For example: "How did you propose to launch a business with so little cash flow to back you up?" (versus "What risks were you willing to take?"). Such questions often imply right or wrong or are really questions for some third party—usually an authority figure, as in "What would your mother say?" Such questions ask for insignificant data or ask the client to provide more details or more storytelling than is necessary. Most of the time, asking for more information doesn't improve the coaching. It just takes more time. You don't need to know the whole story or understand all the dynamics in order to coach.

It is possible, in fact, to conduct an entire coaching session with powerful questions. Beginning coaches report time and again how amazed they are at the effectiveness of this aspect of coaching. Although they are tempted to give the client answers or advice, they see that clients really do have the answers even when coaches don't think so. In the Coach's Toolkit at the back of the book, there is an extensive sample of powerful questions that will give you a sense of the form.

The more direct the powerful question, the better. The object is to make the impact as powerful as possible. Compound or complex questions just force clients to be analytical, and they can get lost trying to figure it out. The powerful question is powerful because it makes the client stop and respond from the heart. Short is good. You can stop a well-practiced Gremlin conversation with a very simple query: "So what?" All of those reasons the client has built up over the years—rationales to explain why things are the way they are—are shattered by these two powerful words in the form of a question: "So what?"

Here are some especially powerful questions:

What is your desired outcome?

What makes it so scary?

What do you want?

Where do we go from here?

How will you know?

What will that get you?

What is the truth?

What do you need to say no to?

Powerful questions stop people in their tracks. So you should expect a moment of silence and allow time for the client to respond. After a moment there is a temptation to fill the space—maybe even ask another powerful question. Resist this temptation. Just listen and wait. Clients are not accustomed to having people confront them with strong, provocative questions that ask for the real truth. They are accustomed to nice, soft questions and a polite convention that says: if you won't ask any hard questions, I won't either. In coaching, powerful questions knock people off their automatic pilot program and make them fly the airplane.

Sample Dialogue

Client: I'm just not very happy at work.

COACH: What do you want?

Client: What I want is to *love* what I do. I don't feel that way. I thought I did—maybe I did once, but I don't now.

COACH: What would it be like to really love what you do?

Client: I'd wake up in the morning excited about the day. I'd be singing in the shower. I'd go through the day pumped up. The little stuff wouldn't get me down. Life would be a breeze and I'd come home tired but excited.

COACH: Great. What would it take to make that happen?

Client: It feels like I'd have to change my job.

COACH: What would you be willing to give up in order to have work that you love?

Client: I'd have to give up some security, or maybe I'd just have to give up complaining about not having work I love.

COACH: What would happen if you gave up complaining?

Using Powerful Questions Powerful questions fit anywhere and everywhere in coaching—from the original intake session to the last clearing and completion session between coach and client. To use powerful questions powerfully, the coach must be able to intrude—a skill we discussed earlier. You can't wait for an opening, you need to wedge your way in, often suddenly. Let's say your client is just getting into the groove of complaining—once again—about how impossible her work situation is and how helpless she is to change anything. You instantly recognize this "groove" as a rut, so just as she takes a breath you ask: "What are you tolerating?" Or: "What is the payoff for you in all of this?" Or: "What's another way this could be?" To ask powerful questions, the coach must be very curious and very courageous on the client's behalf. The coach needs to assume the client has the wherewithal to handle the really big questions and not hold back.

Powerful Questions vs. Dumb Questions Sometimes the most powerful questions are the ones that sound the dumbest. It's as if the client's defensive structure is designed specifically to handle the complex attack—especially the intellectual questions that pick at the justifications. The dumb question just lands like a bomb in all that. Imagine this situation: Your client has a tightly constructed set of reasons why he needs to keep doing what he's doing, with lots of explanations about the limiting factors for success, and the difficulty of getting cooperation from this person and that person, and . . . In the middle of this you ask: "What do you want?" Boom. You could have tested the rationale or looked for ways to expand perspectives or in some other way chipped the surface. But the simplest question, the dumb question, gets to the core.

Sometimes coaches get a little too clever in forming their powerful questions. It's a Level I weakness: a desire to gain more attention for the brilliance of their question than for a simple question, asked out of curiosity, that will help the client see a new path. This desire to sound especially intelligent or clever in the asking of questions has a tendency to annoy clients. It's a familiar trap for the intelligent coach. It's better for coach and client if the coach can simplify the question and have more impact.

Here are eight "dumb questions" that often prove useful:

What do you want?

Where are we?

What's next?

Where do you want to go from here?

What do you see?

What did you learn?

What will you do and when will you do it?

What do *you* think?

There are times when you may think the question is too dumb to ask. Go ahead and ask it and surprise yourself. Even if you get the answer you expect, remember that the reason for asking is not so you can hear the answer, but so the client can hear the answer and learn from it. The reason for asking the dumb question is to lock in the learning. Clients get to hear the answer: the truth, or the Gremlin, or the lie they keep telling themselves. It's like underlining. Asking the questions reinforces the learning before moving on.

Inquiry

An inquiry is another special kind of question. In fact, in its phrasing it can be identical to a powerful question. The difference is that the inquiry is typically used as a homework assignment in order to give the client time to thoroughly explore multiple answers and perspectives. Like all powerful questions, an inquiry is a tunnel—but it is the tunnel of tunnels.

An inquiry is often posed at the end of the coaching session to continue the exploration. Let's say the client is struggling with money issues—especially working more and consequently having less family time—but is hounded by a lifelong determination to be rich someday. So your inquiry for the week is: "What is it to be rich?" An inquiry may also be completely unrelated to that session's material or issues in the client's life at the moment. Because it appears to be coming out of the blue, this kind of inquiry can produce unexpected and profound results. For example, at the end of the call you ask the client: "What is your prevalent mood?" The following week, after discussing what the client describes as his prevalent mood, you pose the inquiry: "How is this mood habitual and how does it serve you?"

The inquiry is a thought-provoking question for the purpose of introspection and reflection. As with any powerful question there is no right answer to an inquiry. It is not a question to be resolved. What sets the inquiry apart is the quality of investigation from many angles and the fact that the inquiry is pondered for a length of time. Because of the natural tendency to view all questions as if they should have a single right answer, you may need to remind your client that the goal is to be curious with the inquiry. In time the inquiry leads to deeper understanding, new ways of looking at the issue, and more possibilities for action.

Here are some examples of inquiries:

What is it to have a rich, full life?

What is present when I'm at my best?

What am I resisting?

What am I unwilling to change?

How can I have this be easy?

The inquiry is a potent tool of coaching because it takes the coaching out of the session and integrates it into the client's life. Yes, coaching happens in the thirty minutes or sixty minutes once a week. But action and learning take place throughout the rest of the week, and the inquiry is a way of guiding the learning that will lead to action. Some coaches work from a list of inquiries, picking an appropriate one that fits the client's situation; or they may use one inquiry for all clients that week. (See the examples in the Coach's Toolkit at the back of the book.)

And to help clients stick with the question, there may be action attached to the inquiry. Action might include posting the inquiry question in strategic places so they keep noticing the question throughout the week. It's there in their daily calendar, stuck to the dashboard, posted above their computer, taped to the bathroom mirror, or written on a card they carry in their wallet. The key is to look at the inquiry in a new way each time and to keep engaging it every day and at different times of day for fresh perspectives. Other action steps might include processing the question by writing in a journal, drawing pictures, talking to a friend, going for a walk. You can build accountability into the inquiry by asking clients to fax, phone, or mail you their responses to the inquiry before your next session.

The inquiry is a valuable tool because it gets below the surface and looks at what is really going on. This is not an easy place for most clients to go. It's often challenging enough just to wrestle with the hard questions when they are on the coaching call with you—let alone keep wrestling when they are alone. But part of their becoming more resourceful includes learning to spend time with challenging questions. Don't let them off the hook. At the next coaching session be sure to discuss the inquiry. Explore the learning. And if the client ignored it, coach that too. Teach the client about the value of the inquiry by making it important. When clients do spend time on the inquiry, there's an opportunity for powerful learning and a great opportunity for acknowledgment.

Sample Dialogue

At the end of the coaching session last week, the coach left the client with an inquiry to ponder—a question that can have many different answers at different levels. In this case, the inquiry was: Where are you giving up your power?

Client: Well, at first I didn't see anything. And then I started realizing my helplessness around my calendar—how I never seem to have enough time because other people are filling up my calendar with appointments.

COACH: Giving up your power in the sense of giving away your time to other people. What's it like when you give away your time?

Client: I noticed I had this habit of saying "I can't do anything because my calendar is full"—until I finally realized that it's *my* calendar. I get to choose what I put in *my* calendar.

COACH: That's a great insight. Where else are you giving up your power?

Client: I also noticed it in my relationship. When my partner gets upset with me, I get defensive—I just abdicate all my power—and I don't have to do that.

COACH: You really did some great work on this. What else?

Client: Well, I just kept looking at it. I also noticed where other people give away *their* power.

COACH: Where was that?

Client: I could see that when a bigwig came along, certain people in the company all of a sudden would become like little kids. You know, they just lost their self-confidence. It was fascinating.

COACH: Was that true for you too?

Client: More than I'd like to admit. I thought I was more beyond that than I guess I am.

COACH: Anything else we have to do on this inquiry?

Client: No, I think that covers it. Thanks.

COACH: So here's your inquiry for next week. What do you need to do to step into your power?

Client: Okay. I'll chew on that one.

The Power of Being Curious

As a coach your curiosity leads you to know the client from the inside out. You learn, you are curious about what you learn, and so you keep asking. The client in turn keeps responding to your curiosity by going inside too—looking for his own answers, trying to understand his own world and the way he operates, what stirs him and what stops him. In time you get to know the client's interior workings until ultimately you become the client's voice asking the questions the client himself would ask. The coach is in a better position to ask these questions because the coach isn't distracted by Gremlins, or history, or colleagues' opinions, or loved one's feelings, or anything else. The inquiries become more intriguing; the powerful questions become more potent. And in the process the client adopts some of the strengths of the coaching—like building internal capabilities. Clients learn what it's like to be curious about themselves and less judgmental.

Exercises

1. Curiosity

Spend a half hour in a coffee shop being curious about everyone in the place. Without actually talking to anyone at first, let your curiosity wander and pose the questions to yourself: I wonder where they are out of balance in their lives. . . . I wonder what they value. . . . I'm curious about what they are missing in their lives, what makes them laugh, where they have constructed self-imposed limits. What do they like about the day? What are their life dreams? What empowers them? What do they like about the people they're sitting with? At the end of the half hour, find one person you can spend a little more time with and actually ask her or him the curious questions. As you ask the curious questions, be aware of what is happening with the other person. How does this person respond to you when you are curious? Then look at your own role in the conversation. What is happening at Level I? At Level II? At Level III? Afterward, be curious about your own curiosity. What did you learn about being curious? What was easy? What was hard? What made it easy or hard? How could you be more curious? What would that give you?

Here's another curiosity exercise. Go to a store where you don't normally shop and be totally curious. See how many curious questions you can ask.

Remember: Curious questions do not ask for more data. With curious questions, one question almost always leads to another, as if you were traveling down a tunnel.

2. Powerful Questions

One of the simplest ways to experience the power of powerful questions is also one of the most challenging. In this exercise, the goal is to have a thirty-minute conversation with another person in which you are only allowed to ask powerful questions: no statements, no summarizing, no advice or storytelling of your own, no drawing conclusions. Your role is to ask powerful questions and nothing more. (You may want to review the list of powerful questions in the Coach's Toolkit.) Afterward, ask the person for feedback. What was it like when all you did was ask questions? Then tell the person what it was like for you to be confined to questions. What worked for you about that? What made it difficult?

3. Inquiry

An inquiry is an open-ended, powerful question that is given to clients to help them explore an important area of their life for a whole week or more. To do this exercise, start by reviewing the inquiries in the Coach's Toolkit. Then go back to the list of ten friends or acquaintances for whom you wrote a meta-view statement. Using the meta-view and what you know about that person, write an inquiry for each person.

Action/Learning

Coaching works for many reasons that overlap and intertwine, but one of the strongest threads in this weave is action. In fact, it's the cycle of action and learning, over time, that leads to sustained and effective change. Clients take action and learn, which leads to more action based on what they learned, which leads to more learning, etc. Coaching is ideal for this process because the relationship is ongoing and is designed to focus on this interrelated pair. All of the coaching skills are used to forward the action and deepen the client's learning. The action component is the most visible and is often what draws clients to coaching. They may be competent and successful in many phases of their life, but there is one area where they can't seem to make the changes they want. By themselves they're just not getting it done, and they want the structure of a partnership to help them get into action and stay in action toward their goal. But it's the learning that makes change possible and sustainable.

Coaching works because it's not easy maintaining momentum alone. You've probably had your own experience of this at some time in your life. We all do. You start something with great enthusiasm—it might be an exercise program in January after the holidays, or renewed enthusiasm to get out and socialize more, or determination to pick up a hobby. And then, a few months later, nothing's happening. How many times in your life have you said you were going to do something and then not done it because nobody else would know the difference? Just the simple act of telling your plan to another person raises the stakes. Making your commitment public draws your attention to it and reinforces its importance. Most of us place a high value on doing what we say we'll do. There is something almost sacred about taking our commitments seriously when we profess them to another or when we join in a pact to reach a common goal. On a freezing January morning you might pull the covers back over your head rather than go to the health club alone. But if you've promised to meet someone there at seven, there's a much better chance you'll actually get out of bed and go. The relationship adds a significant measure of motivation.

This is especially true of a regular commitment and ongoing action. Athletes know it, musicians know it, so do others from other professions. A regular commitment provides discipline and focus and the support people need to stay on track. Thousands of people in weight reduction programs have had this experience of mutual support on an ongoing basis. It really does create focus and discipline. Coaching uses this power to keep the client on track, remain in action, and focus on the learning.

Still, even though there's little doubt that this support structure works, many people think of it as a crutch instead of a strength. They say that grown-ups shouldn't need to depend on others to get things done or stay on task. After all, being a mature adult means having the ability to be responsible for oneself. There is something needy and dependent, they say, about relying on someone else. This notion can be a powerful one, and sometimes it creates ambivalence in clients. They want the change the coaching relationship can deliver, but they don't want to depend on others. Just be aware as coach that this concern will appear in some clients.

The Coaching Perspective

One of the defining qualities of coaching is that it creates accountability: a measuring tool for action and a means to report on learning. Accountability is essential to forwarding the action and deepening the learning in co-active coaching because the coaching session is more than just conversation: it is conversation that leads to some form of action. In co-active coaching, accountability is more than simply a tally of tasks done or not done. The practice of accountability is so important that we have devoted a special section in this chapter to this skill.

Accountability as Feedback

Coaching has been compared unfavorably, by the uninformed, to hiring a professional nag. You can see where they get the idea. As you were growing up you were "held accountable" for homework, piano lessons, getting your chores done. It wasn't a matter of choice. So the other person in the accountability relationship was hardly an endearing figure for this structure, and it's unlikely they were concerned about your agenda. Consequently parents, teachers, tyrannical bosses, even athletic coaches and others in authority have created this tainted view of accountability as nagging, pestering, badgering.

The good news is: professional coaching is not like that—principally because the coach is holding the client's agenda. The accomplishments that clients are accountable for are those they design for themselves. In professional coaching, accountability does not include blame, scolding, punishment, or judgment. Accountability is a tool for the client's action and learning. To be accountable means simply that: to give an account. What worked? What didn't work? What happened? What would you do differently next time?

Another definitive difference between parents or bosses and co-active coaches is that co-active coaches are not attached to the results clients achieve. Parents and bosses definitely have an agenda and are *very* attached to the results. Coaches want their clients to excel, of course, and have fulfilled lives, but the results belong to the client.

Clients are moving into new territory, stretching their boundaries, finding new resourcefulness. They're coming up with new ways of operating and overcoming old resistance. Accountability gives structure to this growth and the by-product is measurable results in the client's life. As coaches, we hold clients accountable—not to see them perform, or measure how well they perform, but to empower the change they want to make. Accountability can provide the means for change and creates a great opportunity to acknowledge how they succeed. This is ultimately what clients are accountable for: their own lives, their own agenda. If you did nothing else as their coach but hold them accountable for this, you would be a powerful coach.

Accountability in Practice

Early in the coaching relationship, it's important to set the expectation that clients will do what they say they'll do. They need to know they're in charge. You will not "make them" do anything. But when they don't do what they say they will do, you will notice and ask. Note that to be nonjudgmental about their performance is not the same as giving them carte blanche not to do what they say they'll do. You both know the difference between following through on a commitment and not following through. And as coach, you won't be ignoring this lack of action. You'll point it out and ask about it. "What does it mean to you? This looks like resistance. What is the resistance? What would be a different way?"

Early in your relationship, clients are likely to test the accountability bond and your resolve as coach. They want to see how much latitude you'll give them. They'll be looking for how much slack you'll permit before you react and whether you're strict or lenient. Most of us have been practicing this tactic since we were teenagers. Consciously or unconsciously, we've tested accountability boundaries with authority figures for years. It's not much of a leap from "I wonder what will happen if my history report is late" to "I wonder what will happen if my marketing plan is late." Because clients are still operating out of that old paradigm, you'll have to explain how accountability is different in the coaching relationship. For example, the first time they don't follow through on an assignment you ask: "I notice you didn't do what you said you'd do. How do you want to handle being accountable in this relationship?" You're not a coach cast in the role of headmaster about to whack their knuckles. Instead, they find themselves in a designed alliance looking at what works best for them.

Coaching Sessions

The most common application of accountability occurs in the daily or weekly actions between sessions—sometimes called homework or field-work. Coaching creates an ideal structure for initiating action and measuring action. The level of detail, as well as the form the action takes, will depend on the client.

Some clients are very self-directed on the details: they know what needs to be accomplished and are adept at planning and implementing their action. Other clients are vague when it comes to action. One of the coach's tasks is to clarify action steps. Be careful, though, that this mutual clarification doesn't become a ploy by clients to have you tell them what to do next. In the process, such clients simply transfer responsibility for their accomplishments or lack of accomplishment to you and disconnect themselves from being in charge of their lives.

The client's situation also dictates the level of detail. Clients can be held accountable for personal reflection as well as for a detailed manifest of multiple action steps. Your job as coach is to sense which action will move clients forward or deepen their learning, but the actual details come primarily from the client. Remember that your clients are resourceful: they know what action they need to take and what will work. You, as coach, need to be ready to probe and push and raise the bar, but you don't have to create the task list for clients. They will learn more by doing it themselves. One of the most effective ways to handle accountability is also the simplest. Merely ask the client: "What do you want to be accountable for this week?" Often you'll be surprised at what clients are willing to ask of themselves. Sometimes you will need to challenge them to do more.

But accountability in the coaching relationship is about more than tasks. The designed alliance exists for the client's vision, life purpose, and balance. Many clients come to coaching with a desire to change their attitude, their approach, or possibly their facility with life itself. In that case the coach and client are designing actions around the process of the client's life. You'll need to hold your client accountable for that too. It's easy to get focused on the details in the action—and it's rewarding because it is specific and measurable and you can both see progress in the details. But as coach you need to keep in mind that you hold the client accountable for the vision as well as the action. And the action must lead to fulfilling the vision.

Tracking for Accountability

For accountability to exist in the coaching relationship, there needs to be a mutual understanding between the two of you on what to expect. There are three questions that nail this down:

What will you do?

When will you do it?

How will I know?

Let's say you and your client agree that she will make six sales calls by Thursday and call your voice mail each day with an update until all six are done. Or she agrees to write the first draft of the business plan by next Friday and will fax pages to you as they are completed.

The best accountability agreements embody the SMART acronym. Items on the accountability list should be Specific, Measurable, Attainable, Realistic, and Time-oriented. While this may seem simplistic, you would be surprised, even after months of coaching, by the number of clients who are still vague and nonspecific. As a coach you provide a service of great value when you ask clients to spell out exactly what they will do.

Some clients, however, do not thrive under the greenhouse approach. They need a more free flowing, more reflective way to account for what is happening. Simply asking, on a regular basis, "How's it going with your book project?" is an example of accountability in its most gentle form.

Rewards and Consequences

Usually the accountability of the coaching relationship is strong enough by itself to motivate action. After all, at stake is the client's life, his fulfillment, balance, and process. That should be consequence enough. What could be bigger than your whole life? Still, clients don't always operate from that perspective, so there are times when introducing consequences can raise the level of accountability. And "consequence" isn't limited to negative consequences, although that's often how it is used. Consequences can be positive—a great reward for completing a series of odious tasks. There can also be a negative cost for not following through—no TV or computer privileges or whatever the equivalent is for this client. Using consequences helps to reinforce, in a vivid way, the ultimate rewards and costs for following through. It's a mini-lesson for their lives—especially when the payoff is a long way off and in the meantime they're slogging through thick mud to get there. A periodic reward can lift the spirits. Alternatively, agreeing on costs for not following through can quickly bring home the *personal* cost of not following through in life.

Let's imagine that *you* are the client and you've told your coach you are really committed to giving up smoking. You've tried before, but this time you mean it. Over the last few weeks you've had mixed success with your attempts to quit smoking, and today when you call your coach you admit you actually bought a pack of cigarettes this afternoon. In your coaching session you agree not to smoke again—and you also agree that for every day you fail at this challenge you'll give $10 to cancer research. Would you play this game? If the answer is yes, is it because you can afford the $10? Then let's raise the payment to $100 per day when you fail. Now that is a different story.

As a coach you have no attachment to whether the client chooses to play this game. But if $100 is what it takes for the client to put on the brakes, then the real focus of the coaching is the level of commitment. Is this desire to quit smoking simply a $10 wish or is it a $100 commitment? For some people a $10 consequence may be enough to wake them up when they're tempted. For others the fee may need to be $500.

This technique of extensive consequences is one you will use only rarely—usually when you sense the client's strong commitment and an equally strong fear of succumbing to temptation. The consequence is designed to provide additional incentive. This technique can also be used when it takes a really big consequence to get past a persistent Gremlin. And of course the consequence doesn't have to be a money transaction—it can be time, for example. It's also important for the coach to be sure that clients actually pay up if they fail—ask for copies of receipts if necessary—otherwise you lead them to believe they can lie to themselves with only moderate concern from their coach.

Trapped in Accountability

Accountability works. People really can get into action. That is the strength, but it is also the trap. Accountability can be overused and overemphasized. Both client and coach can come to believe that it's everything that coaching is about—instead of one powerful tool. For clients who are stuck or overwhelmed, more emphasis on getting into action or more pressure for accountability may not be the answer. (You will have to use your coaching sense to know what is right.) For the resisting client, it may be time for process coaching.

Different clients have different needs. They even have different needs for accountability at different times in their lives. Figuring out the accountability relationship is a key part of the designed alliance—not only when you first start working with a client but later on, too, as the situation shifts. Just keep asking clients how they want you to hold them accountable.

Coaching Skills

Each of the following skills is designed to forward the action and deepen the learning. They range in effect from tame and collaborative to powerful and assertive; all are designed to help clients address the issues of their lives. The skillful coach will know when it is time to encourage the exploratory breadth of brainstorming and when it's time to light the dynamite of challenging.

Brainstorming

Brainstorming is a skill designed to create more ideas than clients can generate on their own. Brainstorming involves the equal participation by both coach and client to create possibilities and new perspectives: it relies on the expertise and experience of both to create more ideas. It also helps clients to see the resources they can bring to their lives and to the discussion: new ideas, new ways of operating, new choices. Because you, as coach, will be participating in the process directly—which is not your usual mode—it's a good idea to ask permission to brainstorm. You might say something like: "Shall we brainstorm some options?" Or: "Would you like me to talk over a few ideas with you?" Once again, nonattachment is key for coaches. Propose all the brilliant ideas you want—just don't get attached to any of them.

Sample Dialogue

Client: I'm a little stuck here. I haven't been on an actual date in fifteen years. What do people do?

COACH: What would *you* like to do?

Client: I don't know. Have you got any ideas? You're single.

COACH: Want to do a little brainstorming?

Client: Sure. I'm desperate.

COACH: Okay. You go first.

Client: I used to go to bars when I was in college. I don't think I want to do that anymore.

COACH: So maybe you won't choose it—but it's an option. Okay. What do you like to do for recreation? Skiing? Roller blading?

Client: Birding.

COACH: Great. You could join a birding group or even start one. Singles only. What's another option?

Client: A personals ad, I suppose. It just makes me feel awkward.

COACH: We're brainstorming here. There are no bad or unworkable ideas. Just options. So you said a personals ad. I'll say: volunteer at your kids' school.

Client: And I say: find out where the Parents Without Partners meeting is.

Planning/Goal Setting

As we'll see in the discussion of balance in Chapter 9, there's a seven-step method for moving from perspective to action. Some clients, however, get stuck in this sequence at the planning and goal setting stage. There is definitely a skill involved in clarifying the appropriate action steps—a skill some clients have not acquired on their own. They may have a general sense of the destination but little experience in being precise, looking at what's required in terms of time and money, and seeing how their goals will affect the relationships around them. Just the simple act of writing down their goals is sometimes a step they leave out or avoid because it makes the commitment to the goal real—as if, no kidding, they are taking a stand.

Many clients associate goal setting with New Year's resolutions, and it gives them a hangover just thinking about it. They've stopped making dramatic New Year's resolutions because all they did was set themselves up for failure. They need to see that this time the goal setting is different because they are working with a coach. You may have to coach the plan and goal setting to help clients create powerful, attainable action that helps them grow, safely but consistently. Splitting the goal into manageable pieces is often the first breakthrough for some clients. All they could see was the continent they had to cross. Now they see many short excursions. Helping clients do the basics can make a big difference in their success. Goals should be specific, measurable, action-oriented ("What will you actually do?"), realistic, and have a time line attached.

Sample Dialogue

Coaching provides a powerful structure for helping clients get into action, stay in action, and learn from their action as they do. But sometimes the action they crave is inaction.

COACH: I got your fax. You took the afternoon off. That's great.

Client: It was weird.

COACH: The whole afternoon?

Client: Yeah. I almost called in for my messages, but I didn't.

COACH: That's great. What did you learn?

Client: That the world doesn't collapse if I'm gone for four hours.

COACH: What else?

Client: That I hired competent people—people I can trust.

COACH: Anything else?

Client: It felt wonderful—once I got over being anxious.

COACH: Great. What's the next level?

Client: Raise the bar?

COACH: Right. Now that you've had a taste, what's the ultimate step?

Client: I actually know what it is. I want to start planning a vacation for July.

COACH: Radical. Congratulations. What will you do by next week?

Client: I'm planning to visit a travel agent in our building this afternoon and pick up brochures for Bali and Alaska.

Requesting

Over and over we've emphasized that this is the client's agenda, that the client is resourceful, that the client knows the answers. Still, there are appropriate times when you, the coach, will request certain actions. Based on your training, your experience, and your knowledge of the client, you'll have a sense of what direction clients might take for maximum learning from their action. You have a little more distance than they from their Gremlin. It's a perspective that gives you a different and valuable point of view. So there are times when you'll say to your client: "My request is that this week you create a detailed monthly budget for personal and household expenses. Will you do that?" Note that the language of a request takes a somewhat specific form: there is the request itself stated in a way that is specific and measurable—the client can actually be accountable for something—and there is the question at the end that asks for commitment. This is more powerful than simply asking a client to work on her finances this week. The language draws a line in the sand and puts the client on notice that this is important business. In time, using this format, clients learn that taking on a request is an act of personal commitment, not just the acceptance of an assignment from their coach.

The key to making a successful request is being detached from it. The moment you become attached to the brilliance of your own idea and start thinking it's the right way for the client to get results, then it's your agenda, not the client's. Always give the client the same three choices: the client can agree to your request, turn down your request, or make a counteroffer. If you're turned down, feel free to defend your idea a little. Go ahead and describe why you think it works and the value it would have. Maybe the client was distracted and didn't hear you correctly the first time. You might even probe to make sure it was the client who turned down the request and not the client's Gremlin.

If the client turns down your request, simply ask, "What will you do?" As far as you are concerned as the coach, the whole point is some form of action or learning—and so long as that happens, it doesn't matter who comes up with the request. There is always more for the client to do and more to learn. And maybe he'll come back to your great idea later anyway.

Sample Dialogue

Client: I suppose I'm like everyone else with a ten-year reunion. I'd love to lose about ten pounds.

COACH: How's your workout program going?

Client: I get to the club about once a week. I know it's not enough.

COACH: What kind of exercise do you enjoy the most?

Client: Swimming. I love the water.

COACH: Great. My request is that you swim a minimum of thirty minutes four times a week. Will you do that?

Client: You know what? I'd rather do forty minutes three times a week. That saves me one trip to the club, and it's the same amount of time.

COACH: How will I know you've done it?

Client: I'll make it a weekly check-in statistic—right when we start.

COACH: Anything else you want to add?

Client: Go for a walk or bike ride with my family on Sunday—my wife or son.

Challenging

A challenge asks clients to extend themselves beyond their self-imposed limits—way out to the edge of improbability. If the challenge is powerful enough, it should cause the client to sit up straight and exclaim: "No way." If that's the response, you know you're in the right territory. Your idea of their potential is much bigger than the picture they hold for themselves. Often clients respond with a dual reaction: exasperation when confronted by the enormity of your request but also a sense of being emboldened because someone believes in them that much. Most clients will flatly turn down your challenge but then make a counter-offer—at a level higher than they would have considered initially.

As coach you say to your client: "I challenge you to say no twenty times a day this week—make it thirty." Your client says: "No way. . . . That's impossible. I'd be fired and divorced in a week. I'll do ten a day, but that's my limit." So instead of not being able to say no at work or home, your client is now practicing this essential skill ten times a day. Such is the power of the challenge.

Sample Dialogue

Client: It's like a dark cloud that's been hanging over me for the last six months!

COACH: The way you've talked about it, it feels like much more than a cloud. You've been in this dark mood for weeks. You said you felt listless and you're not eating well . . . all because of this manuscript you have to finish.

Client: Research paper. Actually the research is done. All I need to do is write it up.

COACH: When will you get it done?

Client: At this rate I don't know.

COACH: How many hours will it take? What's your best estimate?

Client: Hard to say. Maybe thirty hours—a little more, a little less.

COACH: I have a challenge for you. My challenge is that you finish the paper before we talk next week.

Client: Next week! That's crazy.

COACH: Could you do it in a week?

Client: Well, yeah. If that's all I did.

COACH: What *will* you do?

Client: I'll do a rough draft.

COACH: That's terrific! And I want you to understand you're stepping into a huge challenge. Way to go!

Client: I could actually finish this thing in this lifetime.

Putting Structures to Work

We know that accountability in the coaching relationship is a structure. It's a means by which we create focus and discipline. In fact, a structure is any device that reminds the client to be in action. Setting an alarm to wake up is a structure. Turning your wristwatch over or wearing it on the other arm is a structure that reminds you to do something. There are millions of structures, an endless variation of creative ways to sharpen focus and discipline. They appeal to different senses: tactile, auditory, visual, behavioral. Putting fifteen minutes a day for meditation into your day planner is a structure. The physical act of writing it in plus the visual reminder in the calendar create a structure for this important activity in your life.

Here are some further examples of structures:

- Posting affirmations or reminders throughout the house
- Cutting out pictures of a dream home
- Choosing a particular piece of music for cleaning the office
- Listening to a meditation tape
- Wearing the same sweater—magic armor—when making cold calls
- Lighting a candle or burning incense
- Putting a reminder rock in your pocket
- Changing the lighting in the room by making it lighter or darker—or changing the color
- Throwing parties or having guests over twice a month to motivate housecleaning
- Establishing creative consequences or rewards
- Finding an exercise partner or personal trainer

Structures are a way to sustain the action and learning throughout the week in between coaching calls. Each client will be somewhat more sensitive in different sense areas. Experiment with structures to find out what works and keep playing with structures—the key word is "play." The reason for the structure is to provide discipline and focus in an area where it's hard for the client to stay on track. By making the structure playful, you increase the chances that the client will follow through and have some fun with it.

Accountability is only part of the coaching relationship, not the whole. Even so, it is a central aspect of coaching and one of the best ways to forward the action and deepen the learning.

Exercises

1. Requesting

Complaints are often uncommunicated requests. In a restaurant, if you've got a nagging complaint about the draft blowing down on you from the overhead air conditioner, you can sit with your complaint or you can make a request. When the appropriate request is made, action often happens and the complaint goes away. So the exercise works like this: make a list of twenty-five complaints in your life—things that just aren't going your way. They don't have to be reasonable. If you have a complaint about the weather, write it down. Acts of God are not off limits for complaints or requests. When you have your list of twenty-five complaints, compose a request that will address the complaint. Target your request to a specific person wherever possible, someone who has the power and the ability to do something about your request. Then, for as many as possible on your list, actually follow through and make the request. And remember—there are always three legitimate responses to your request: yes, no, or a counteroffer.

2. Challenging

Go back, once again, to the meta-view list of ten friends or colleagues you made in Chapter 3. In this exercise your goal is to write a challenge for them that addresses their meta-view in a way that dramatically raises the bar: an action step that will move them forward and provide extraordinary learning. Make sure it is a true challenge—that it asks them to go further than you know they will go—so they end up making a significant counteroffer.

3. Structures

Here is a simple and somewhat typical situation. Your client is much too busy to keep his house clean, yet the chaos that results is seriously distracting him. It has reached the point of no return. Something must be done. Here are several structures that might help this person stay in action long enough to actually get his house clean:

1. Invite guests over for dinner. There's nothing like having to face scandal and shame to move a person to action. Make the invitations before you start cleaning.
2. Hire a cleaning service—even if you can't afford it. You're already paying a terrible emotional cost for the chaos—up the ante by seeing it in dollars and cents.
3. Set aside cleaning time in your daily planner. Use a kitchen timer set for fifteen minutes to give yourself fifteen minutes of cleaning alternated with fifteen minutes of some pleasant activity.
4. Invite two or three friends over to help, and offer to share their house-cleaning too.

Your job is to come up with sixteen more structures.

Self-Management

As we noted in Chapter 1, the co-active coaching model has no coach in it. The coach is intentionally missing—invisible in the relationship. All of the coaching effort in the model is focused on the client. Yet, of course, as coach you not only play a significant role in the relationship but are 100 percent present for the client. Except when you're not—when you are distracted by the events and worries of your own life, when you are hit by a case of the coaching blues or ennui, when you are captivated by a new love, when you are bored with a client's Gremlin whining and making excuses.

But this is a professional relationship and you are being paid good money to submerge your own problems and attend to the client. The context of self-management is about how coaches manage the distractions and still succeed in being effective coaches. By paying attention to your own self-management, you learn more about how to help clients with *their* self-management and, moreover, you model good self-management for them. We all have times when we need to get a good grasp on ourselves. It's a classic case of "physician, heal thyself."

Getting a Grip

The professional coaching relationship demands that the client's fulfill-ment, balance, and process receive your full attention as coach as well as your client's attention. That's a complete job right there. There's really no room to deal with your own feelings, opinions, and judgments without taking something away from the client. And your stuff, frankly, just isn't on the bill of lading.

So what do you do? It's natural to have opinions and feelings. It's vir-tually impossible to live without them. Your job, then, is to monitor them and keep them under control. You need to be physically grounded, emotionally steady, and mentally present—which means, for starters, that you need to be taking care of the significant areas of your own life: your own fulfillment, balance, and process. Coaching is a demanding profession. What are you doing to ensure you have the mental sharpness, the physical stamina, and the emotional stability the job demands? This is fundamental. The client is counting on you to give 100 percent of what you are able. Part of your self-management is to make sure you've set high standards for yourself and show up for each call sharply focused. And if you are going to be an effective coach, it is a great idea to have a coach for yourself. How committed to the value of coaching can you be if you don't value it enough to include it in your own life?

As you listen to your client's report and conversation, as you attend to the client's agenda, certain things may trigger a memory of a similar experience you've had or even set off an emotional response in you. You need to be aware when that's happening and be able to distinguish between your emotions and those of your client. Let's say your client is describing a conflict she's having with a business partner over money. You may have had a similar experience with a business partner in the past. Or you may have had unhappy and unresolved problems about money with a friend, co-worker, or spouse. These memories, your emo-tional state, the action you took—all this can come suddenly flooding back. As it does, you need to decide if this is one of those times when it might be appropriate to share your experience and tell what you learned. Certainly there will be times when describing your personal experience is valuable for the client. You might be able to use such lessons to help the client deepen her learning . . . or move her forward into action. There are times when sharing your story can create trust and a stronger relationship with this client. The question is: Will telling your story be important for the client's learning? Or is it your own internal distraction that leads you to want to share it? You need to be aware of the issue and decide accordingly. This is an example of your Level III awareness of what's going on and the impact you have on the client.

Inevitably you'll have differences of opinion. You may even disagree with a direction your client wants to take. Just because your job is to promote the client's agenda doesn't mean you have to agree with it 100 percent of the time. You do need to honor it as theirs—theirs to work with, to change as necessary, to fail at completely, or to succeed at gloriously—even if you weren't initially convinced of its viability. It is possible to be completely committed to the client and have reservations about the means and an obligation to share your reservations for the sake of honesty in the relationship. And if for some reason you find the agenda morally repugnant or somehow dangerous, you may need to have a candid conversation with your client. While it's extremely rare, the two of you may not be suited for a coaching relationship, and this is an opportunity to refer the client to someone else.

Sample Dialogue

Last week, after several months of lingering illness, your mother died at the age of eighty-three. The phone calls and letters from friends and relatives are still coming in and you are still grieving. You are back to receiving coaching calls, though, when this call comes in.

COACH: Thanks, Michael, for being flexible about the time last week. I appreciate it. How is the plan coming?

Client: It's incredibly ironic. Not the plan—I'll get back to that later, maybe. Right after you called to reschedule, I got a call from my brother. My mom had a stroke. They had her in ICU for four days. She died last night.

COACH: Michael, I'm sorry. What would you like to talk about?

Client: I just want to talk for a few minutes about what I'll miss. The missed opportunities—the opportunities I don't want to miss with my own kids.

COACH: Tell me what you'll miss.

Additional Coaching Questions

What will you remember?

What is the truth you want to hold on to?

What do you want to let go of, as you let go of your mother?

Note: Obviously this is an emotionally charged coaching call. There are lots of ways for the coach to self-manage in this situation. For example:

1. The coach could work through this call and then call his or her own coach for clearing and processing.

2. "Michael, could I put you on hold for one minute?" (Coach screams, cries, pounds the sofa, or otherwise vents emotion for a minute, then returns to the call.)

3. It could simply be too emotional and the coach might decide to admit it honestly: "Michael, I just buried my own mother less than a week ago. This is too much for me."

Dealing with Your Level I Reactions

There will be times when you will react at Level I. Your client says something about welfare mothers, or divorced men, or makes an ethnic comment. It's bound to happen that, somewhere in the material clients bring you, your own pet peeves will get triggered. You might become judgmental, ungrounded, even opinionated. This is known as being "hooked." All of a sudden you are driven to Level I—recycling your own thoughts and opinions and no longer focused on the client.

There are many ways this can happen. Let's say your client is learning the skill of saying no: no to working long overtime hours without being paid, no to snacking on high-sugar treats, no to a particularly toxic relationship. This week he says he has tried everything, but to keep his job he has to work one or two evenings a week. And although he can see a day when he'll no longer be saddled with this demanding job, in the meantime he needs to be there. He says he is honoring his values of commitment and dedication. You've addressed this Gremlin many times before with this client. You can feel the steam building up under your collar, your heart beating faster, the poisonous words forming on your lips. You've had it with this crap!

Whoa. You may be totally convinced that the client is lying, dodging, unwilling to deal with his own behavior. "Why can't he see that?" you want to know. But what is going on inside you this minute—this steam, this frustration, this temper—is not about the client, but about *you*. For whatever reason—a bad night's sleep, an unexpected bill in the mail, a former spouse who talked like this—you have disconnected from the present and detached from the client.

Or maybe your Gremlin shows up. You've been working with a client for three months and nothing of consequence has happened. She is no closer to her goals today than she was the day of the intake session. She keeps droning on with the same reasons why she can't take action. You've tried all the tricks you think should work, but it's like pushing water up a straw. And today your Gremlin—who has always said you were weak in process coaching—has a field day with your tattered job of coaching this client. You have failed, you are inadequate, you are over your head, you've done nothing in three months to help this deserving soul who is counting on you. And now you don't even have the courage to admit it and help her get the help she needs from some other coach or a therapist. You miserable worm. Meanwhile, while you are into self-flagellation, your client is floundering.

The signals are there to see. When you find yourself trapped in self-analysis—defending, judging, feeling annoyed—the alarm bells are going off. You are at Level I. You are trapped in the squirrel cage, racing in that little exercise wheel going nowhere. During the coaching session, your job is to get yourself unhooked. You've got to push all of that internal confusion out of the way and return to Level II and III listening. You can't deny that the problems are there inside you—you've trained yourself to recognize them when they show up—but now is not the time to deal with them. You need to be meeting the client's needs. Just notice your internal reaction and judgment, freeze-frame it, and put it on hold temporarily while you put your attention back on the client.

When the coaching session is over, take a step back. Use whatever method works for you to get unhooked and reground yourself. It might be deep breathing, it might be yelling, it might be meditating or physical exercise—whatever it takes. It might take a few seconds, a couple of minutes, or longer. The self-management goal at the moment you notice you are at Level I is to return to being grounded—to that frame of mind where you are stable, resourceful, and ready.

Another option is to call another coach. Who could be better? Call a coach who will understand what just happened to you and will not want to jump in and fix you, but will be willing to wait while you ventilate all of it—or enough of it so that you can move on. Before you can really breathe again, deeply, cleanly, you need to clear the air. This has nothing to do with analysis or problem solving. This isn't the time to analyze what went wrong here. There will be time for analysis later. The immediate self-management task is to vent the bad air.

Where'd You Go?

Let's be honest. Despite your best intentions to always be present, there will be times when you disconnect from your client. It can happen for lots of reasons—some significant, some trivial. You happen to glance at your desk and notice a bill that's overdue . . . somebody is knocking on the door and the dog is barking . . . something your client just said reminded you of a very sad conversation in your own past. One of the most powerful things you can do at that moment is admit it: "I'm sorry, I just went blank for a moment. Would you repeat what you just said? I missed that."

Admitting that you disappeared actually creates trust. You may think you hide your vanishing act from clients, but often they sense your disappearance even if they don't articulate it. More than that, you model the veracity that builds a strong relationship between you and the client. Clients respect the fact that you were honest about what happened—didn't try to cover it up—and that your admission is a way of saying you are really committed to the client, not to pretending.

Fresh Air Strategies

Another occasion to practice clearing and grounding is before each coaching session. Many coaches have a ritual they use before the start of the day or before each appointment. It is a structure for orienting themselves to the coaching—preparing for clients in physical, emotional, mental, even spiritual ways. This kind of preparation is especially important when your personal life is getting the best of you. You are a human being as well as a coach. Periodically things will happen in your personal life that can cause your attention to focus on yourself rather than the client. Let's say you get stuck in traffic on your way back to the office and are rushing, harried, anxious about being on time, when you sit down and the phone rings. Your mind is still out there in frantic space. You need to clear your feelings before speaking with your client so your attention can be concentrated fully on the client and not on your troubles.

Apart from the everyday stumbles that knock us off balance before a coaching call, there is also the punch in the solar plexus. You just received bad news about a friend: the biopsy is back and the lump is cancer. You just walked out on a devastating argument with your partner over an issue that won't go away. Clearing and grounding allow you to be fully present in coaching without burying your own feelings. It's not easy. Sometimes it's not even possible, and you need to tell clients that you need to reschedule the appointment. Yes, you need to be strong for your clients. Gritting your teeth and persevering when the going is tough is admirable—but only up to a point. Self-management is about knowing where the point is.

Forbidden Territory

Self-management is also about where you stop your coaching. It would be wonderful if all great coaching could happen within the coach's comfort zone. But coaches have places they don't want to go, where they are afraid of the consequences. Maybe you sometimes find yourself holding back from telling the hard truth because you don't want to make waves or get the client upset—especially upset with you. Maybe you hold back because you don't want to lose the client. Coaches can hold back because they don't want to risk offending. What they risk instead is a less resourceful life for the client. Is it possible that the client will get upset and will leave? Yes, it's possible. That's a price the coach must be ready to pay on every call. Repeat: on every call. The risks we sometimes don't want to take are the same risks that clients don't want to take. They're the very things that keep clients from living full lives. And often they represent part of the reason that clients come to coaching.

Take a hard look at the areas in your own life where you are uncomfortable and where you have held back in the past. Chances are these are the same areas you are unwilling to probe with your client, whether they are risky areas for your client or not. For you they are blind spots: habits of defense. They are probably invisible to you most of the time. Maybe one day you'll work through what holds you back in your life. But you can't wait for that to happen before you explore those places with your clients. Maybe loneliness is unbearable for you. So when your client raises the issue of loneliness, you take a different tunnel and find something else to talk about. Because of the emotional charge it has for you, you didn't explore the issue that would have benefited your client.

Or maybe it's the issue of telling the truth, or the fear of taking risks, or not wanting to disappoint people, or awkwardness around money or intimacy. Delving into these areas may be crucial to your clients' action and learning. Self-management is about recognizing painful issues but exploring them for the sake of your clients anyway. You must be willing to coach outside your own comfort zone.

Controlling the Gremlin

You can be certain you have a Gremlin nearby who is ready to talk incessantly about your limitations and lack of success. This saboteur is never going to disappear completely. Even when you think you've got him fairly well chained, all of a sudden he pops up again. You get off the call with a client and feel like a miserable incompetent. You were lost and fumbling.

Or were you? Self-management is about recognizing the self-judgment that is going on inside your brain and knowing the difference between constructive analysis and the Gremlin's self-destructive chatter. The key for you as a coach is the same key you give your clients about the Gremlin. First, notice. Make sure you record it well in your mind. What was the Gremlin's criticism or observation, precisely? Be clear, be descriptive, be attentive to the experience. Notice and notice you've noticed. Then play with the alternatives that come up. Ask yourself a couple of questions: What is the truth in that for me? What's in that for me to learn? Something happened in there that hooked you, and it's something worth paying attention to. The Gremlin, of course, has the worst possible interpretation of the sign. You, on the other hand, recognize that these disruptive experiences are part of learning and growing stronger as a coach and person. The more adept you become at recognizing and working with your own Gremlin boldly and effectively, the more you'll be able to help clients work with theirs.

Self-management is also about knowing when it wasn't the Gremlin— when you really are in over your head. When that realization strikes, be gentle with yourself just as you'd ask your clients to be gentle with themselves. In such a situation the most constructive thing you can do for your clients—and for yourself, by the way—is to refer them to another coach or to another resource for help. No one wants to feel like they've failed. But the best course of action—and the most professional—in some cases is to end the relationship for the client's sake. The client may be better off with a career counselor or a therapist or a more detached coach. The client may not be ready to take control of his own life and live it responsibly. If the alliance won't work, you can't hold it together on your own. So if you truly feel you cannot work with this client, the two of you are best served by moving on.

Coaching Skills

There are a number of coaching skills generally associated with self-management. These skills underscore the dynamics in the relationship and help both coach and client maintain their individual strengths.

Asking Permission

One of the most important ways the coach reminds clients that they themselves are in charge is by asking permission: "May we work with this issue?" "Can I tell you what I see?" "Would you like some feedback on that?" When the coach asks permission, it demonstrates that the client has power in the relationship. It demonstrates, too, that the coach knows the limits of his or her power in the relationship. Asking permission is a sign of self-management on the coach's part and allows the client to take responsibility for managing the relationship and his or her work. Clients are honored when you ask permission; their boundaries are respected. This is especially important when the issue you'd like to work on is unusually intimate or potentially uncomfortable for the client. "May I tell you what I see about the way you've been handling this?"

Sample Dialogue

Client: I guess the point is that I realized the plan we worked out just wasn't going to work. I had to improvise on the spot . . . tap dance my way through it. It was like old times, making it up as I went.

COACH: First of all, there's nothing sacred about the plans we work out. You still get to choose the best course of action for you. I trust that you know what's right and you'll move forward and learn from whatever you decide. So what did you decide?

Client: That's basically what I did. I took action. Just a different course of action.

COACH: But before we move on, I'd like your permission to give you some feedback on the action you took. Would that be okay?

Client: I have a feeling I may not like what I hear. But yes—give me the bad news, coach.

Bottom Lining

There are times when a client's telling of the story begins to expand and take over the coaching session. Or times when the client begins wandering tangentially through story after story. Sometimes it's the client's style of conversing; many times it's a way of avoiding difficult or direct conversation. The client is out there circling in the fog. Bottom lining is the skill of getting to the point and asking the client to get to the point. What is the essence of the conversation? What is the question? What is your conclusion?

This is the skill of succinct communication. It is helpful to cover this skill during the intake session so clients are not caught unaware the first time you ask them to get to the bottom line. It's not that the story isn't interesting. In fact it may be fascinating. But the story is the background, and in the coaching relationship the background is quite secondary. Bottom lining is especially valuable—even necessary—in the half-hour coaching call. There simply isn't time for long-winded, detailed stories. You need to coach the essence, and asking clients to get to the bottom line helps them discover the heart of the matter. It helps them determine the key issue that can unlock the gate to where they go next.

Bottom lining is also an important skill for the coach. As coach, you should not be talking much. Your conversation should be bottom lined. Clients do the talking.

Sample Dialogue

Client: I know I'm starting to sound like a broken record on this, but there just wasn't time this week. Really, I'm not just spinning a story here. I'm out of town one or two days a week . . . I'm still carrying the one evening class . . . I need to spend *some* time with my family. . . .

COACH: So what's the bottom line here, Tom?

Client: I'm committed to my health. I just can't live up to the time commitment to make it happen.

COACH: What *will* you commit to about your health?

Client: I'm still committed to eating right and working out. I just don't see how I'm going to fit it all into my schedule—especially now . . .

COACH: Bottom line, Tom. What will you commit to?

Client: I'll commit to eliminating snacks between meals and three days of exercise every week.

Championing

We talked about acknowledgment earlier. Acknowledgment means recognizing who clients had to be in order to do what they have done. To champion a client is somewhat similar, but here the focus is on supporting the client rather than identifying traits. When you champion clients, you stand up for them when they question their abilities. It is not empty cheerleading. As the coach you champion what you know is true; clients will know if you aren't sincere. When you're not sincere, you not only destroy the effect of the championing but you put your own credibility at risk. But when you point out your clients' ability, their strength, their resourcefulness, and let them know you believe in them, you give them access to a little more of themselves. Perhaps it was a capacity they didn't realize they had or strengths their Gremlin denied were available. You champion when the road is steep and the client weary. That's when you recharge the client's enthusiasm: "You are so committed to this. I know you can do it!" Or: "You've shown over and over how you can be caring *and* firm. You can do it again." Or: "You have the creative gifts—in superabundance. You can do this!"

Sample Dialogue

Client: It's a great opportunity, but it's also a huge risk. I could be a hero and I could be the world's biggest goat.

COACH: To paraphrase the Olympic slogan, I say: "Go for the goat!" What will it take to be a gold medal winner?

Client: You've got to be kidding.

COACH: Maybe kidding you to take some of the pressure off. Mary, I know you can do this. It's a perfect match with your heart's desire and the path you laid out for yourself. You've got the skills to do it— and the panache to pull it off. Of course it's risky. That's where the adrenaline comes from and that's why the Gremlin is after you. I just know you can do this.

Client: I know you do. And it gives me confidence when I've lost my own.

Clearing

Earlier in the chapter we described clearing in some detail as a skill and structure for the coach. Clearing is a valuable exercise for clients as well—often for some of the same reasons we discussed for coaches. Clients call when they've just been fired, when their best friend has been diagnosed with cancer, when they just got off the phone with a bill collector, when they lost the big account to the hated competition. Or alternatively, when they are just back from vacation and their mind is still fogged with piña coladas or the euphoria of a newfound love. When clients are preoccupied with a situation, it interferes with their ability to take action.

The signals may be muted—you don't always hear huge klaxon alarms going off. The client may seem slightly miffed; perhaps you sense a minor disturbance in the energy field. Initially clients may not even want to discuss this "little thing." But when you notice that their normal creative expression is blocked or constrained, you may need to push for clearing. Let's say your client is annoyed about some injustice; there's a mood about her that just hangs there. You might say: "You seem really blocked. Let's take three minutes to get this out. . . . Really complain, whine, feel sorry for yourself. Exaggerate." The best thing you can do at this point is to help the client clear. In fact it is imperative that the coach recognize the volume of clearing necessary. Often clients feel awkward just venting and want to quit before they're completely clear. So you must really push until the last gasp of bad air is out. Make it a game and keep pressing for more: "Turn up the volume. What else happened? And then what? How did that feel? What a jerk! Tell me more."

Sample Dialogue

COACH: You seem distracted—like we're having to work too hard to stay on track this morning.

Client: I *am* distracted. I lost $2,500 yesterday in a stupid stock deal. I feel like an idiot.

COACH: It sounds like you need to clear the emotion before we can move on. What's your sense of that?

Client: I think you're right. I feel like a chump. Worse than that—I convinced two of my friends that this was the sweetest deal in a century and they both lost money too.

COACH: Ouch. What else? Let's turn up the volume.

Client: Okay. I'm mad at myself for getting sucked into an "easy money" scheme. I'm ashamed about looking like an easy mark. . . .

COACH: Go for it. What else?

Client: I'm afraid my wife's going to shoot me. . . . I let her down and the kids. . . . Where am I going to come up with another $2,500 for vacation this summer?

COACH: You feel like you let your family down. . . . What else?

Client: I should have seen this one coming.

COACH: So you've got a judgment—"should have seen this coming"— or your Gremlin does. What else?

Client: It's a pretty empty feeling.

COACH: Deep sadness and regret.

Client: Exactly.

COACH: What's next?

Client: I think I need to get past the sour feeling.

COACH: How will you do that?

Client: This clearing is a good start. I think working out tonight will help. I can sweat off some of the anger and sadness.

Reframing

Frequently clients get stuck with a certain way of looking at a situation or experience. Their perspective, moreover, has a message that is in some way disabling. Your ability to reframe the experience in a new way provides a fresh perspective and a sense of renewed possibility. Let's say your client had her hopes set on landing a major consulting contract and she just found out it has been put on hold for at least six months. Naturally she is focused on the disappointment. As her coach, you point out that it gives her the time she has been seeking to write a series of articles that can help her land new business. Thus you are able to recast this experience in terms of her ultimate goals. Using much the same data, you interpret the experience in a way that includes more of the client's life: the big picture.

Reframing is looking on the bright side of things, true enough, but it is more than just being perky for the client. Reframing offers more than cliché comfort—as in "There's plenty of fish in the sea" or "Tomorrow's another day." Reframing takes real pieces of the client's life and shifts the perspective to show opportunity or a pathway that didn't appear there minutes before. Let's say your client is struggling with credit card debt and tells you that it's hard to make progress, especially when major appliances keep breaking down and needing repair. You point out that she has managed to change her buying habits and has regularly paid down her outstanding balance for several months. The reframing doesn't change the fact that it is a struggle. The reframing shows the client how she is resourceful and committed—and making progress. Reframing changes the theme from "credit cards have control of my life" to "I have control of my life."

Sample Dialogue

In this case the client starts with a certain perspective: he has wasted six weeks of time developing a business plan that ended in a dead end. Still, the client learned a lot that will help with new business plans and met several good contacts. In short, there is plenty that is positive in this experience. And that's where the coach is headed: to reinforce the action and learning that accompanied this effort.

Client: Absolutely a dead end. Nada. Six weeks shot to hell.

COACH: You followed a path that looked very promising six weeks ago. I remember you were pretty excited.

Client: I *was* excited.

COACH: What did you learn in that six weeks?

Client: I learned how to write a business plan. Not that it did me much good.

COACH: What else did you learn?

Client: I learned how to present my business to people outside my field.

COACH: Nontechnical people?

Client: Yeah. Bankers and venture capitalists.

COACH: What else did you learn?

Client: I guess I learned that this is something I can do—even though I don't enjoy it as much as I do the engineering.

COACH: In that case, what's your assessment of the last six weeks?

Client: I wish I could have had the same learning in half the time. And now that I've got all these stupid overheads made, I might as well keep making the presentation until somebody sees the opportunity and gives me the money.

COACH: Great. What do you want to do about that this week?

Separating the Interpretations

Reframing is one way to help clients see a situation from a fresh perspective. Another way is to help them disentangle the interpretations. This is a special case in which two facts have been mushed together into one disempowering belief. The belief appears to be a fact of life and it's not. For example, let's say a client believes—because she's the mom and the wife—she needs to be the one that manages the household cleaning. She's stuck and frustrated because she believes she is responsible and she can't seem to get it all managed. The separate facts are that she is the wife and that there is housework to do. Or let's say the husband and father believes he has to work overtime because his family needs the money and he's the breadwinner. These are classic examples of interpretations that need to be separated in order for the client to become more resourceful about selecting options.

Sample Dialogue

Client: I plan every week. I use a planner. I take the time on Sunday nights to plan my week. None of it helps. By Tuesday my week is in shambles.

COACH: What happens when you try to stick to your plan?

Client: People make requests. They've got urgent things they need from me—things I didn't necessarily have in my plan—so wham, it's all out of kilter.

COACH: What happens if you say no?

Client: Not in this organization. It doesn't work that way. If you're going to succeed around here, you have to move fast, be flexible, respond to the fire that's burning. That's what they mean by "teamwork" in this company.

COACH: Sounds like you end up paying a pretty high price for that. It also sounds like you've got a couple of things tangled together. What if we tried to separate them?

Client: Like what? I'm not following you.

COACH: You seem to be saying: "When people make requests of me, I need to abandon my plan."

Client: I'd say that's true in this organization.

COACH: So . . . would you be willing to play along with me here? I'd like to find an alternative point of view, just to give you some additional perspective.

Client: Sure.

COACH: Here are the two facts: people make requests, and you have a plan. In the past, you've said yes to the requests automatically. What would be another way to deal with requests?

Client: I could postpone saying yes by telling people I have to check my calendar first.

COACH: Good. What would be another way?

Client: I suppose I could learn to say no sometimes.

When All Else Fails

Self-management is often the context in coaching when things seem to be coming apart. The lug nuts are loose and it feels like the wheels might be coming off. The need for self-management often shows up when there is failure—on the part of the coach or the client—which makes this an appropriate time to talk about failure as a means for learning. As painful as it can be ("Don't touch the stove. It's hot!"), failure is amazingly fast as a teaching aid. In fact life could be described as a failure-rich learning environment. Unfortunately one of the early lessons we learn in life is that failure is bad, even shameful. We learn to hide our failures, make excuses for them, or ignore them—and thereby lose the learning value of finding out what went wrong. Clients will fail early in the coaching relationship, and you as their coach will learn how they handle failure. One of the most powerful things you can do for your clients is to explore their failures and turn them into serious lessons about their lives, how they handle adversity, how they manage their learning.

In co-active coaching we encourage clients to look at what they call their "failures." We emphasize the difference between failing at something and being a failure. They are not the same. People are naturally creative, resourceful and whole. They are not failures, even if they fail sometimes. In fact, in order to make significant changes in their lives, clients often have to go to the edge of their ability or capacity. Sometimes they go too far and fail; sometimes they don't go far enough and fail by missing the opportunity. Whether you fail or succeed, one of the underlying goals is always to look at the learning that results from the experience. That's why we believe that failing is valuable. It is something to honor in clients because it takes courage and commitment to risk and to fail. We celebrate failure in the sense that we have reverence for what it means—in the same use of the word as in "celebrate mass" or "celebrate an important milestone." We have a high regard for failing because so few people are willing to put themselves in that position. It's worth celebrating when it happens.

Exercises

1. Self-Management
Where are you likely to get hooked in the midst of a coaching conversation? Where are you most likely to need self-management?

> List ten things your client might say that would pull you to Level I. For example: "I don't think you're listening to me."

> Next list ten things you can do to return to the coaching conversation and stay detached.

Now here are suggestions for managing your own Gremlin—and by the way, try giving the same exercise to your clients:

> Get to know your coaching Gremlin intimately. Draw a picture of your Gremlin and give this character a name.

> List the most common Gremlin statements? What is the Gremlin's tone of voice?

In what situations does your Gremlin show up most often?

Count the number of times your Gremlin shows up this week.

2. Championing

Pull out that list of ten friends or colleagues one more time. Call, write, or e-mail them as their champion. Let them know they can do the thing they need to do. Be specific.

3. Clearing

Train a friend or colleague in the skill of clearing so they can clear you. Their job is to encourage you to go deeper, to turn up the volume until you reach the bottom of whatever it is you are trying to clear. They don't need to understand what's going on with you; the job is to prompt you to vent, like cheering an athlete to the finish line. Then select an area of your life where you need clearing, and process the clearing exercise with your friend. When it is over, talk with your friend or make notes about what happened as you became clear. What happened to the "charge" when you allowed yourself to express it completely?

Co-Active Coaching Practices

The practice of coaching, as we have said, focuses on the client's agenda. Indeed the client's fulfillment, balance, and process constitute the three core principles of coaching. In this section of the book we describe each of these principles and provide exercises and examples for coaches. Part Three concludes with a chapter on the nuts and bolts of coaching and a vision of what coaching can contribute.

Client Fulfillment

Think about your own life for a moment. What would a fulfilling life be like for you? Whatever answer comes to mind, notice that the question takes you deeper than simply asking "What do you want?" This depth is the reason that fulfillment is one of the three core principles in co-active coaching. People who come to coaching often have a general sense of what a fulfilling life might look like. It is rich, full, and satisfying. It is a life of choice and quality, balanced the way they like. People often have ways to create a fulfilling life, especially in certain areas of their lives. Just as often, they get stuck on the question of what they want, or they can't see the broader question of what would make life fulfilling for them, or they're struggling with how to make it happen. One of the main reasons people come to coaching is a search for answers about personal fulfillment.

The Hunger for Fulfillment

Part of the difficulty in finding a fulfilling life starts with where clients are looking. They are looking for ways to *have* a fulfilling life. So they look at what they have . . . and what they don't have . . . and see a gap . . .

and then look for things to fill the gap. Clients often come to coaching in a search for something they need to have in their life. That "something" can be the obvious: a higher-paying job, a vacation home, a successful business. The search can also focus on getting things that are less tangible: a wonderful marriage or a promotion. Unfortunately, *having* things is momentary and the satisfaction is fleeting. You know that from your own life. Think of something you really wanted to have. Think about the moment of ecstasy when you acquired it and how soon the glow began to fade: six months after the new boat, or the new promotion, or the new relationship. So long as we continue to look for ways to *have* a fulfilling life, we are likely to be temporarily filled and constantly hungry.

To Be Fulfilled

Co-active coaching creates a different frame for fulfillment. It asks clients to look at what it would take to *be* fulfilled. There is an underlying implication that the possibility for fulfillment is available not just for today but for the rest of our lives. Imagine you are on the road called fulfillment. You don't have to reach a destination—a place where you'll finally have fulfillment. Instead, fulfillment is possible today.

Part of the confusion about fulfillment is in the language. We know what it means to be "full" and think fulfillment is a state we will eventually get to: filled full, capped off, finished. Instead there is this paradox about fulfillment that we can be filled today and still be filled again tomorrow, maybe even in a different way, and then be filled again the next day, and the day after that. It is disillusioning to think we can capture fulfillment. To "have" fulfillment is like trying to bottle daylight.

This doesn't mean that your clients will stop wanting to have things in their lives. Clients will still want to have things: a successful business, more money, romantic relationships. The difference is, these things are the expressions of their fulfillment. They are not the means to fulfillment.

Feeling Good Is Not a Sign

We often confuse being fulfilled with feeling good. The two conditions may coexist, but they need not. In a state of fulfillment, there's often a sense of effortlessness—of harmony and congruence with the great laws of the universe. But fulfillment can also exist when life is difficult, challenging, or uncomfortable. Some people will say the times when they felt most fulfilled were times when they had the least, when life was a struggle. They were doing what was important to them—what they were passionate about and committed to. It was not about having things or even *not* having things. Even in the midst of scarcity, life was abundant. Perhaps the simplicity of the time gave them a clearer picture of what was truly valuable and fulfilling for them, but it was not about feeling good all the time. Learning and growth can be difficult, even painful, but enormously fulfilling nevertheless. It is possible to have both a sense of inner peace and outer struggle at the same time. Sometimes we need to take action that doesn't feel good in order to experience a sense of fulfillment, such as leaving an unpleasant but high-paying job or getting up at 5:30 in the morning to exercise.

To Be Alive

The lesson is that life can be fulfilling even though there is struggle—sometimes the struggle is a sign of moving toward fulfillment. In fact it might be as simple as this: fulfillment is about being fully alive. Fulfillment is the state of being the full expression of who we are. Clients have a sense of that feeling. They describe it as wholeness, satisfaction, a sense of rightness and harmony. It is an experience of being complete. What it means to be fully alive not only is different for each person but changes over time. Coaching on fulfillment looks for strong signs of life in the client.

Questions about fulfillment start at the initial intake session, but it's unlikely you will completely uncover the client's perspective on fulfillment in that one session. The questions and issues represent such a wide range of discovery that you will continue to address them in ongoing coaching sessions. It will take time for clients to let go of some of the old definitions of fulfillment. Over the course of your coaching relationship the answers will come out of the client's life experience because it is there you will be looking for what is truly fulfilling.

Discovering a Personal Definition

Fulfillment is intensely personal and constantly evolving. What was fulfilling at age twenty-five may have lost its fascination by thirty-five; the empire-building passion of thirty-five may give way to a search for inner serenity by forty-five. As a coach there are a number of practical ways you can help people clarify their personal definition of fulfillment. It may take a variety of different methods, and it may involve asking the client several times in different ways. It's important, though, because the choices clients make will serve them best when they're based on an understanding of what fulfillment means to them.

One place to look is a familiar one: the Wheel of Life (Figure 5). Looking at each of the areas in the wheel, you and the client discuss, on a scale of 1 to 10, the state of the client's fulfillment: "How fulfilled are you in the area of money, or relationships, or health and wellness? What would a fulfilled life be like in the area of career?" Notice that you are not asking: "What do you need to *have* in order to be fulfilled in your career?" The question is: "What would it take to be fulfilled?" Then keep probing in that direction. Whatever comes up, follow it with: "What else?" or "Tell me more." The idea is to uncover deeper and deeper levels of meaning and, from time to time, clarifying what you hear and playing it back to the clients so they can hear what they're saying. For example: "I heard you say you'd like a sense of security when it comes to money—a sense that there will be enough in an emergency. Is that right?"

Using the Wheel of Life, clients will see for themselves, in a graphic way, the parts of their lives where they are unfulfilled. Together you have a process that will allow clients to define what fulfillment means to them. For example: "In health and wellness, you say your sense of

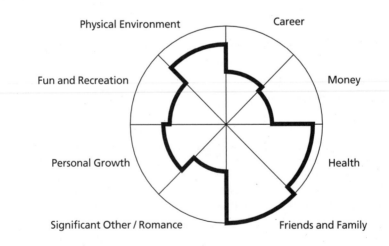

Figure 5   Wheel of Life: Fulfillment

fulfillment is 6. What would it take to raise that 6 to 8? What will you do to make it fulfilling?"

Fulfillment and Values

Imagine you could do what brings you the greatest joy: be with the people you love, use your natural talents, exploit your gifts to their fullest. That would indeed be fulfilling. It is a picture of a person living according to what he or she values most.

The link between values and fulfillment is so obvious it may be invisible. Helping clients discover and clarify their values is a way to create a map that will guide them through the decision paths of their lives. When you clarify values with the client you learn more about what makes the client tick: what's important and what's not. Clients discover what is truly essential to them in their lives. It helps them take a stand and make choices based on what is fulfilling to them.

Honoring our values is inherently fulfilling even when it is hard. If authenticity is a very high value for your clients, they may find there are times when they must suffer discomfort in order to live according to that value. The discomfort will pass and a sense of integrity or congruency with their values will remain. When that value is not being honored, however, the client feels internal tension or dissonance. Because human beings are flexible and resilient, it is possible to absorb a tremendous amount of discord and keep going. But there is a very high price to pay—a sense of selling out on oneself—and the result is an unfulfilling life—a life of toleration rather than fulfillment.

Values Are Not Morals or Principles

Values are not morals. There is no sense of morally right or wrong behavior here. Values are not about moral character or even ethical behavior, though living in a highly ethical way may be a value. Your client's value of receiving recognition is neither positive nor negative. It is either being honored in his life or not. Values are not principles, either, like self-government or a code of moral standards. There is nothing inherently virtuous in your client's values. What is to be admired is not the value itself but your client's ability to live that value fully in his life. Values are who we are. When we honor our values, there's a sense of internal "rightness" that has nothing to do with morality. It's as if each value produced its own special tone. When we live out our values, the various tones create a unique and blended harmony. When we are not living out our values, there is dissonance. The discord can get so out of tune, so jarring, that it can literally become unhealthy.

Because our language is imprecise, it's often easier to cluster values than to try to invest all the meaning in a single word. Thus we might separate a series of value attributes by slash marks to indicate a grouping of values that communicates a more distinct understanding. For example, freedom/risk taking/adventure, which is different from freedom/independence/choice. Just as the placement of our ears and eyes and so forth gives us our unique appearance, the articulation, priority, and clarity of our values determine who we are individually. It's important that each word in this cluster be as accurate as possible, so that clients can describe what the value really means to them. Then when they find they're off track, the precise wording of their values can help bring them back on course. As coach, you're not simply nitpicking the choice of words here or trying to press for some indisputable dictionary accuracy. You want to know what's in the client's heart. You are much less concerned about Webster's definition than the client's definition. The wording must work for the client.

Values are intangible. They are not something we do or have. Money, for example, is not a value, although the things you might do with money could be considered values: fun, creativity, peace of mind, service to others. Travel is not a value. Gardening is not a value. But both are examples of cherished activities that honor certain values, such as adventure, learning, nature, spirituality. And yet, though values are intangible, they are not invisible to others. You can walk into a room of strangers and get a sense of what people value by what they wear, how they stand in the room, how they interact with others, and with whom they interact. You know something about their values just by their presence in the room. You can sense the values in the room: power, friendship, intimacy, connection, independence, fun, and more.

As coach you will be able to help clients clarify their values as you hear about their lives, their action, the things they choose, the things they don't choose. You will see them when they honor their values and when they don't, and you'll both learn something either way. It's one of the reasons why the values clarification process is something you return to from time to time.

The Value of Values Clarification

The most effective way to clarify values is to extract them from the client's life experience. Ask clients to describe the values they see in their own life, perhaps clustered together, using their own words. This way the values rise naturally out of the life context. Values are extracted from the client's life, rather than selected off a checklist. When clients are presented with a list, it's often tempting to go shopping for values: "This would be nice to have . . . this would be well admired." Because people have a tendency to judge their values, they tend to list values they think they should have, like spirituality or integrity, and exclude values that society says are not so admirable, like personal power and recognition.

Working one-on-one with the client, either in the intake session or in a regular coaching session, the two of you will uncover a number of values once values have been identified. There is plenty of opportunity to coach values by asking questions such as, "Where do they show up? What values do you sell out on first? Which are the most immutable? Which ones are sometimes neglected?" Another fruitful exercise asks the client to prioritize the values, ranking the top ten from the most important value on down. The main result in this exercise is not the finished priority list. The client is free to change the order on that list any time. The real importance is that it forces clients to see the value itself beyond the word. By choosing the order, clients must consider one over the other. Some coaches will set the stage by making it a kind of game: if you can only take ten values with you into a strange and possibly dangerous territory, which are the values you absolutely must have? So it's not about which value is most important. It's about what clients learn about their values by having to give up something they care about.

The next step is to ask clients how they are honoring these values on a scale of 1 to 10: 1 means the value is not being honored in their lives; 10 means it is honored completely all of the time. There are almost certain to be values that are ranked at 4, 5, 6 in some important aspect of the client's life—most likely a place where there is upset or a pattern of anger or resentment because the important value is getting squashed. It's a great opportunity for coaching: "What's that about? What would it take to honor that value in those circumstances? What is the price you pay for not honoring that value? What's stopping you?"

In coaching, the values help determine the "rightness" of choices. They also illuminate unfortunate choices. Clients can look back over decisions they've made and see where their values were honored or ignored. Knowing the client's values makes a tremendous difference in the coaching too. You can quickly see how certain courses of action for the client will be blessed with a sense of flow and ease because the activities are congruent with their values. By knowing when the client's values are *not* being honored, you can also see the potential iceberg in front of the *Titanic*.

Values can be used at the client's decision point. As the client chooses various action steps, their values become the litmus test for action: "Will this action move you closer to honoring your values or farther away? If you make this decision, what value will you have honored?" When the client is considering an important life decision, ask how this course of action will honor the top ten values and to what extent. Making decisions based on the client's top values will always, repeat always, lead to a more fulfilling decision. It may not be the easiest, or the most enjoyable, or the most fun. It may require sacrifice and even have painful consequences. But on balance, over time, it will be the most fulfilling because it represents who the client is. Again and again we have seen clients make decisions based on their bank balance, or their fear of creating discomfort, or their worry about others' displeasure. They make decisions based on what is easiest at the moment or decisions that minimize the size of the waves. Such decisions never work out for their fulfillment because they have sold out on themselves and their values. (See the Coach's Toolkit for more on values clarification.)

Fulfillment and the Gremlin

When you are honoring your values regularly and consistently, you might say you have a formula for living happily ever after. In that case, why don't we honor our values all the time? The answer often is that the Gremlin has imposed a different set of ground rules for action. The Gremlin says, "You can't take that job (even if it honors your values of adventure and independence); you need to make more money," or, "You can't let your family down," or, "You don't have the discipline a job like that would require." The Gremlin says, "That's too risky," or "It wouldn't make any difference even if you did," or "You'll never change." Above all, the Gremlin wants the status quo because it's more comfortable than the unknown world you are creating by changing. Change is the Gremlin's enemy. In order to make the choices necessary to live a truly fulfilling life, clients need to change, and that is an automatic wake-up call to the Gremlin. Be aware that the Gremlin will appear, and be prepared to notice it in your coaching.

Fulfillment and a Compelling Way

Clarifying values is one way to help clients make choices that lead to more fulfilling ways of living. Finding the "compelling way" is a different approach with a similar result: it pulls the client into fulfilling action. The rationale for a compelling way gets back to the very definition of fulfillment: It is not about having; it is about being fulfilled. Consequently, fulfillment is possible every day, even in the present circumstances. The key is to look for the compelling way.

Let's say your client is feeling out of shape, tired, overweight, with a goal of losing thirty pounds, trimming up, and restoring a sense of fitness and energy. Naturally there will be a tremendous sense of accomplishment when she meets her goals. But she doesn't have to wait until she's lost the thirty pounds to find fulfillment. Through coaching she can design a plan of action that will put her on the path to the goal. In fact, what she designs is the compelling way that draws her to the goal. She can feel a sense of fulfillment every day she is on that path. Knowing that there's a compelling way is sustaining for clients on days when it's easy to become discouraged. The time to talk to clients about finding a compelling way is when they talk as if their lives will be available to them some time in the future—that they need to attain some state or accomplish some action before they can come alive. The question to ask is, "How can you have that fulfilling life today? What is the compelling way for you today?"

Fulfillment and Future Self

Standing at the foot of the mountain with your whole life in front of you can be daunting. But if you could get a glimpse of the future—get a sense of where you would be, say, twenty years from now—it might give you some confidence about the future and even some information about how to get there. Short of providing a time machine, the only way to make that possible is to have clients create an image of their future self. The creative power in discovering one's future self is hard to imagine until you've had the experience.

The future self is the one who no longer cares about the opinions or judgments of others. The future self is the one who totally knows his own strengths, the potholes in the road ahead, the heart of the decision. Even when clients think they don't have the answers, almost inevitably their future self does. The future self can look back with detachment and compassion and let the client know what the right decision is. The future self represents a powerful image of a life of fulfillment, a life of accomplishment. Although it's composed of what the client knows today, it is created without today's restraints. Since it is created out of imaginary space, it is not limited to what is "realistic" in the client's version of the world. It gives clients a chance to imagine a fulfilled life outside of their usual box.

There are a variety of ways for clients to access their future self. In the Coach's Toolkit you'll find a visualization exercise that has proved to be effective. The future self can be invoked by the coach whenever the coaching focuses on questions of fulfillment—especially when the client is unsure about the path ahead or feels locked into a path that is unfulfilling. One way to experiment with possibilities is to have the client imagine how the future self might solve this problem or work through this situation.

Fulfillment and Life Purpose

A life purpose statement is another way to capture the essence of what it means to be fully alive. To be living life intentionally, to be making choices that increase the value of life to self and others, is a description of being fulfilled today and every day. There are many ways to elicit the client's life purpose, and there is more than one way to describe this motivating definition of what our lives are about. Some call it a mission statement or a vision statement. It is a description that gets to the heart of what a person's true life legacy will be—the difference his or her life will make on the planet. It is the answer to the questions: What will I leave behind? What difference will I make in the lives of those I touch? The life purpose is a path. It is like East. Clients will never get to the place called East, but they may be on the path their whole lives going in that direction. There will be plenty of voices, internal and external, telling them to go in different directions. And sometimes they will listen, especially when they are unsure of their purpose. Finding and claiming a life purpose gives clients a powerful direction for their lives. The truth of the life purpose statement can make them virtually unstoppable.

Defining one's life purpose is a process that usually takes time. It can involve personal reflection, reading, keeping a journal, or interviewing others. Finding the one statement that rings true requires peeling back the layers until that one statement addresses the central questions of life for this client: Where is the hunger I am here to feed? Where is the pain I can comfort? Where is the teaching I am called to do? Where is the building I have the tools to accomplish? Life purpose is about clients using the talents they have been given as well as the unique learning of their lives, their expereince, and their wisdom. A fulfilled life is a life in which they are able to live life on purpose—intentionally, not by accident. They are able to live life with a purpose in mind. You'll find a number of exercises in the Coach's Toolkit designed to help clients clarify a life purpose statement.

The value of the life purpose statement in coaching is the focus on a fully alive, fully expressed, fulfilling life. It's like the uranium cube that powers the reactor. Working and living in a way that fulfills one's life purpose is another way of describing a life of fulfillment. The coaching that goes into creating the life purpose statement is rich with self-discovery, value clarification, and vision. It is territory for challenging clients to use all the talents they have been given. It is also a fruitful place for acknowledgment when clients make the sometimes difficult decision to follow their purpose rather than take the easy way. Living a life of purpose, a life based on one's values, is rare indeed.

Fulfillment and the Coach's Role

Here's the irony. Clients come to coaching for fulfillment. And then most of them, right away, begin to cheat on themselves by asking for less, lowering their standards, holding back. The path to fulfillment can be difficult, unfamiliar, and scary. Choosing to live our lives based on our values is not what society taught us. It is not the easy, well-trodden way. Most of us settle for what we can have. We make choices based on what others want, what would be easiest, what would cause the least discomfort. We give up. It's no easy task to get on the track for fulfillment. In fact, we say choosing a fulfilling life is a radical act.

The coach's role is to challenge clients to pursue their own fulfillment. It is not an easy journey. Even when clients don't want to go there, your job is to be out front, encouraging, pointing the way. Remember, the way was designed by the client. When you base the approach to fulfillment on values, it is never about the results. It's always about the process and the learning. In this approach the mutual goal is to empower and enlighten the client.

Client Balance

In a chaotic, high-speed world of schedules, commitments, stress, demands on time and energy, there is a yearning for something called balance. But balance is not a state we can get to or arrive at because it is always in motion. Balance is dynamic; it only exists in the midst of action. We are moving toward balance, away from balance, or through it. We may want to slow the tempo of the whirling in our lives, but there is no way to make it stop. The day it stops they will shove a lily in our neatly folded hands and close the lid on our now perfectly balanced life. In the meantime, balance is a fleeting experience not unlike the slalom skier racing downhill or the ballerina on point. Balance requires consistent, conscious, and controlled motion.

You can experience this for yourself by standing for a minute or two on one foot. Go ahead and try it now. And if you really want to simulate your life, rush around the room for about five minutes first, as fast as you can, starting and stopping, then spin in place twelve times to simulate waiting for people to return phone calls, waiting for the teller, waiting in the checkout line. *Now* try balancing on one foot. Those who are still standing will notice the fine adjustments being made in the foot and body in order to maintain equilibrium. Note, too, that balance is a skill that can be developed. It's as true of life balance as it is physical balance. With intention and practice—and the help of a coach—we can learn to get down the mountain with more grace instead of mowing down the slalom gates time after time.

When Enough Is Enough

Life is full today. The pace is fast and it seems to be accelerating. Clients are caught up in the spinning eddies. Look at your own life. How many meals do you eat in the car on the way to the next appointment or the next errand? How does that compare to five years ago? Who remembers the phone messages on pink slips of paper? A Smithsonian attraction today, it was only a few years ago that a handful of these pink notes represented a surge of busyness. How many voice-mail messages do you listen to in an average day? And then they invented e-mail. Pagers, cell phones, audiotapes in the car—all accessories of the well-dressed communicator today. Look at your calendar or planner. Could you possibly cram any more in there? These days even kids have their own day planners. In the 1980s we got the message: "You can have it all." Today, more and more people are saying: "You can have it!"

We're experiencing the indigestion brought on by the abundant buffet of the 1980s. It's like Thanksgiving dinner. You may sit down at the holiday table with intentions to eat in moderation. Then appetite, desire, and ritual take over. The result is lethargy, a stuffed feeling, and in the end your hungry eye lands on another piece of pie. Many clients are coming to coaching because they can no longer handle it all. They need help pushing themselves away from the buffet of life.

Life-Giving Choice

Instead of automatically reaching for another snack, coaching provides an environment in which the whole ritual comes to a halt, at least for thirty minutes a week. It's a place to ask what is really important, what needs to be different. There is no absolute right or wrong in this. One person's life-giving choice is another person's compulsion. For some, balance can only happen by slowing down, lightening the load, taking time out. There is a growing movement in this country toward voluntary simplicity. Coaching can provide the accountability and support for those who want to pursue a simpler, slower, intentional lifestyle. Others want to find balance in the fast lane; they revel at the speed and fullness. These are the slalom skiers of life careening down the mountain. They live by the credo of George Bernard Shaw: "I want to be thoroughly used up when I die, for the harder I work the more I live. I rejoice in life for its own sake. Life is no 'brief candle' to me. It is a sort of splendid torch which I have got hold of for the moment, and I want to make it burn as brightly as possible before handing it on to future generations." In the midst of that burning desire to live life fully, there is plenty of occasion for coaching to help these clients burn brightly without burning out. Coaching can help them attain a gyroscopic sense of balance that allows them to sustain their health, their relationships, their well-being, as they expend energy.

Who's Driving This Bus?

"Out of balance" is the condition of being driven by circumstances—when clients act as though they don't have the power of choice. You can hear it in their syntax: "I can't . . . I have to . . . I need to . . . it doesn't work that way." Or they assign the power of choice to someone else who then controls the conditions: "I can't because she would never . . ." Often it is the Gremlin that has climbed into the driver's seat and won't relinquish the wheel. Fear constricts the hand of choice, sometimes paralyzes it. When choice is gone, balance is gone—and with it the possibility for fulfillment. When you see that walls are closing in on the options and the client is starting to abdicate the power to choose, it's time to open the shutters to new perspectives.

A Balance Formula

There is a seven-step approach designed to lead clients from powerlessness to possibility and finally into action to create a more balanced life.

Step 1: Help clients see they are fixated on one way of looking at the issue. When clients are being driven by their lives they will say things like: "That's just the way it is." Not only aren't they considering alternatives, but they are blind to those other options: "Men my age can't find senior management positions" or "With my schedule I just can't make the time to exercise." When they are stuck in their perspective, you must start by helping them see the trap they are in. Help them see that they are anchored to this point of view. Make the chain that holds them in place visible. Point out the signals that indicate their balance is out of whack: they report feeling overwhelmed, stuck, paralyzed. When they are fixated by one perspective or when their explanation is "that's the way it is, that's just a fact of life," they are gripped by a single point of view. Balance is the issue. Balance coaching begins by recognizing the trapped perspective and then increasing the range of choices. A coaching example: "When you say 'that's just the way it is' or 'it's out of my control,' it sounds like you're sort of helpless and there's no escape. Is that true?"

Step 2: Identify additional perspectives. Perspective is one of the gifts that the coach brings to the coaching relationship—not the "right" perspective, mind you, simply other points of view. Creating perspective expands the aperture though which clients look at their life circumstances. Part of coaching is inviting clients to see their life or certain issues from different angles. When they see things from only one perspective, the old way of looking, they are less resourceful and victimized by the circumstances. When they are able to reexamine their viewpoint, they are able to see possibility and change.

What's driving the choice? Is it habit, self-limiting self-talk, routine? The ability to find new perspectives is one reason that clients are drawn to coaching. Coaching offers an effective setting in which to question their current position and become creative about looking at new alternatives. It can be as simple as asking the client to imagine eight different ways of solving the problem—without becoming attached to any one of them. In fact it's best if one or two solutions on the list are totally unreasonable. The more fanciful possibilities create a sense of playfulness that breaks through the walls of "can't" and stretches the boundary of possibilities to include ideas that were once outside the wall. For example, the client who can't find time to exercise could:

- Hire a live-in personal trainer
- Turn the family room into a gym
- Quit her job
- Say no to being on the Civic Committee
- Find a workout partner
- Get up thirty minutes earlier; go to bed thirty minutes earlier
- Teach the kids to do the laundry so she can work out instead
- Get a job working at a spa for six months

A coaching example: "Let's make a list of other possible perspectives. What's the first thing that comes to mind? It doesn't have to be reasonable. You don't even have to choose it—we're just building a list of possibilities. What's another one?"

Step Three: Get inside the different perspectives. The key to having more choices is to actually look at the world through the lens of that choice. "What would the world be like if you made that choice?" By challenging clients to get inside each point of view, you help them to expand their sense of possibility and learn quite a bit about how they could live differently. Maybe having a live-in personal trainer isn't realistic, but joining an aerobics class at work is possible. Maybe turning the family room into a gym isn't the answer, but borrowing her sister's stationary bike for a few months is possible. At this point the choices themselves are not so important as what the client learns in the process of considering different choices. A coaching example: "Just live the perspective for a moment. Try it on, take a look around. What would it be like to operate from this perspective?"

Step Four: Choose the perspective. Now it's time to choose one perspective as a pathway to action. It does not eliminate the possibility of going back and choosing any of the others. It simply means let's try one for now. By choosing one of these perspectives, clients take the first steps out of the Land of Stuck into a different perspective. They may not decide to live there long, but they've moved toward balance. And that's a big step worth acknowledging. A coaching example: "That's great. When you choose that, you honor your values and move closer to your purpose."

Step Five: Create a plan that addresses the situation. Choosing a new perspective is a huge step for clients. By doing so they reclaim a piece of their power. Now it's time to take the next step by creating a plan of action. It was just a barren piece of new territory before. With the planning step, we can see the foundation being built and the first 2×4s going up. The plan creates shape and form and now the new perspective starts to live in the world. The plan forces clients out of their dead end and connects them with their world. They have to start considering the resources available to make this happen. What will it cost in time and money? How will important relationships be affected? This is a creative process in which the coach can participate with brainstorming if that seems appropriate. This is also a great opportunity for the coach to offer encouragement, support, championing, and acknowledgment as clients bravely plan to change their lives. A coaching example: "What's your plan?"

Step Six: Commit to the plan—seriously. Planning can be just another cerebral activity. There's a lot of thinking about different ways of making things happen, allocating resources, pencil scratching, and calculating. The plan is external, however. As a coach you want the plan to live inside, in the client's muscle and bone, not in the brain where a mild distraction could easily displace it. So before you invite clients to take action, make sure they've really made a commitment to this plan. People gain a mysterious strength and resolve when they make a commitment. For commitment goes beyond making a choice: we make a choice between lasagna and linguini; we make a commitment to others, to life, to a course of action that implies no turning back. This is the point where you draw a line and ask the client to cross into new territory: "Will you commit to that plan and take action? Will you do that?" Up until this point clients may have been just playing along with your game. Chances are a shift will happen for them once they realize they are committing to a different way of operating in their world. It's their last chance to say they were just playing along to make you feel better, or because they thought they should, or were afraid to stop the game, or whatever reason their Gremlin might have for not showing up. This is not about exercising any more, or paying bills on time, or making sales calls, or whatever else precipitated this looking for alternative perspectives and a different course of action. This is about taking control of their lives. And so you must ask: "Will you commit to this plan?" In fact this act of commitment is so powerful that coaches sometimes ask their clients to actually draw a line—real or imaginary—on the floor in front of them, take a deep breath, and cross the line. And it is just as powerful when it is done over the phone as when it is done in person. A coaching example: "We've come a long way in expanding the list of options, choosing an option, and creating a plan. Now—there's the line on the floor. Take a deep breath. When you're ready to commit to the plan, step across the line. But only when you're truly ready to commit."

Step Seven: Take action. By now, taking action should seem like a relief. The hard part was finding new ways of looking at the world. The strain was actually inhabiting those different perspectives and getting inside the possibilities. The challenge was choosing one and then making a commitment to it—really making a commitment with no turning back. Now the client is moving toward balance. There will be much to learn in the action that is taken. Will there be failure and backsliding? Of course. And there will be learning in *that* as well. A coaching example: "Congratulations. You're now in action, driving the bus, living up to your purpose. There may be times when you want to bail out or take the easier way. We'll work on that when we come to it."

Sample Dialogue

COACH: I get the sense that you're just going through the motions. Your energy is way down lately. I can hear it in your voice—it's like you're slumped in your chair.

Client: I am.

COACH: What's that about?

Client: Everything's going along about like it should. It's just boring, not very alive.

COACH: Kind of a Zombie Place?

Client: Right. Sort of plodding along.

COACH: So we'll draw a circle and put a label on this perspective, "The Zombie Place," right there on the top of the circle. You're stuck in the Zombie Place.

Client: Until things change at work, there isn't much I *can* do. I'm just punching the clock.

COACH: Now I'm going to ask you to move over 90 degrees. What's another perspective? Another way to look at your life right now? It doesn't have to be the right one—just another perspective.

Client: It could be a plateau. I went through a lot of changes last year. Maybe there's more up ahead and maybe this is the plateau.

COACH: Like a resting place between changes. Let's move another 90 degrees. What's another perspective?

Client: It could be the transition period.

COACH: Good. What's another perspective?

Client: This could be the place where the learning occurs.

COACH: Like a special place with a special message for you. I could offer another perspective. Is that okay?

Client: Sure . . . like what?

COACH: This could be a successful place. Could you look at life like it was successful right now?

Client: Actually, I can. Things are going according to plan—it's just so different from all the excitement and activity of last year.

COACH: So the Zombie Place is just one way of looking at it?

Client: Right.

COACH: What's the perspective that's the most powerful for you? Which perspective would you rather choose?

Client: That this is the Learning Place for me—the time to catch my breath and catch up on the learning from all that activity and change.

COACH: Let's look at that for a moment. Now that you're standing in that perspective, what do you notice? What are you saying yes to?

Client: I notice that I'm being reflective, not just biding my time. I'm thinking about what I've been learning. I'm saying yes to meditating. And to keeping a journal about my learning. Maybe starting to look at what's on the horizon, too.

COACH: Great. And in order to say yes to that, you probably have to say no to some other things. What would they be?

Client: I'd have to say no to going to work so early.

COACH: So you'd have to say no to going to work early. What else?

Client: Say no to late night TV so that I get a full night's rest.

COACH: This is good. You've come from the Zombie Place to this place of learning and investigating—a more rested place, too, it sounds like.

Here the coach might invite the client to get inside other perspectives: What does it look like there? What will you be saying yes to? What will you be saying no to?

COACH: Which is the perspective you'll choose?

Client: I want the perspective of the Learning Place.

COACH: So let's talk about your plan of action. You mentioned meditating and keeping a journal. What will you do? When will you do it?

Client: Morning is best for me. I'm too tired when I get home at night and I don't think I could get the peace or privacy to do the meditating or journal writing at work.

COACH: Then what are the specifics of the plan?

Client: Meditate from 7 a.m. until 7:15, then do about fifteen minutes or so of journal writing.

COACH: Looks like a plan to me. Is this five days a week? Six? Seven?

Client: Not Saturday. I've got commitments with the kids I need to take care of early in the day.

COACH: Anything else about the plan?

Client: No, that's it. Six days a week.

COACH: Okay. Just a couple more steps and then we'll be complete. One of the weaknesses in planning is that plans live in the brain, where they can be easily misplaced or disregarded. So I'd like to get your commitment to this plan. And I'd really like you to get the commitment inside, in your body, attached to your emotion and spirit. So imagine there's a line across the floor a few feet in front of you—and you are going to step across this line to demonstrate your commitment to the plan.

Client: I'm ready.

COACH: So when you step across the line, you are stepping into action. Whenever it feels right, go for it.

Client: I'm stepping across. That's one small step for a man . . .

COACH: One giant step into a new perspective on your life. Congratulations!

Client: That's a powerful experience.

Balance Is Personal

As you can see, balance is a personal issue. In fact, every client will have a unique model of what balance looks like. Clients see that graphically in the Wheel of Life exercise. (See the Coach's Toolkit at the back of the book.) This is an important coaching opportunity. Ask clients to score their level of satisfaction in various areas of their lives. As they go around the wheel, draw the line in each segment that corresponds to that level. If they say their satisfaction level is 10, great—it's all the way out on the rim. If their satisfaction level is 2, it's near the hub. When they have drawn an arc in each segment corresponding to their level of satisfaction, take a look at the shape of the resulting wheel. For most people it will create a bumpy ride indeed because some segments are so far out of balance. Most clients have not thought about what balance means to them or what it is they truly want. Too often it means continuing to have everything they have today—but with less stress, less tension, pressure, and pain. Clients may desire more balance in their lives as if it were a thing that can be acquired like furniture—as in "I'd like more balance in my life." Coaching balance is about helping clients see the circumstances of their lives, clarify what is important, and move from perspective to choice. In the process, the coach helps them find their own unique vision of balance.

Assessing Balance over the Long Run

Because it is dynamic, in motion, balance is a process, not a place, and is therefore assessed over time. How much time? It depends. If the time frame you choose to evaluate balance is Wednesday from 9 a.m. to 5 p.m., for example, life might look pretty out of balance: all work and no play. The point is that balance must be seen over a time frame that encompasses the ebb and flow of life. On any given week, then, the coaching call might take a snapshot of the client's movement toward balance or away.

Keep in mind that there will be periods of time that look significantly out of balance to the outside observer. Ask any entrepreneur or small business owner what life was like during the early stages. During that period, their time, energy, thoughts, and feelings were probably focused more on the business than any other area of their lives, awake or sleeping. And yet it's one thing to say, "For a period of time, I need to focus all my attention on one significant aspect of my life." So long as it doesn't become a permanent condition, the concentration can be part of a long-term balance strategy. It's when the out-of-whack period becomes an out-of-whack way of life that the issue of balance must be raised.

The bumpy ride is certainly an indication that the wheel of life is out of balance—that the significant areas of life around which we rotate are in need of serious alignment. Just recognizing the rocky ride becomes a way of beginning the process of change. The awareness immediately raises the question: What would it take to experience life with more fluidity? In essence, what are the choices that must be made to start heading toward balance instead of away from it? Ultimately balance is about decisions.

The Perspective Game

One exercise that increases the range of perspectives for clients is called the Perspective Game. (There are empty wheels for this in the Coach's Toolkit. See Figure 6 for an example of a filled-in wheel.) This diagram looks a lot like the wheel of life, except the eight areas are empty. Each of

Question: Where do I go next in my life?

Figure 6   The Perspective Game

the wedges is dedicated to a different perspective on the same question, each representing a different way to assess the question. Let's say your client is single and lives in the city where she grew up so she is close to family and friends. Although she's frustrated with a job and career choice that feel like a dead end, it has some prestige and she's living comfortably. Even so, she feels handcuffed to the job, to the city, to the way of life. A lot of her conversation starts with: "I can't because . . ." The inquiry question for her homework assignment might be: "Where do I go next in my life?"

As the client comes up with options the wheel wedges are gradually filled in:

- Get married
- Join the Peace Corps
- Go back to graduate school
- Move to the French Riviera
- Adopt a child
- Move to a trailer home in the woods and write
- Take a six-month sabbatical
- Get a new job

Ask your client to view the inquiry question from the perspective of each segment of the circle. Emphasize the experience so she really gets a sense in her bones of what the world looks like from each perspective. After discussing each of the areas, ask her what she learned by viewing the question from each of the perspectives: Which response felt the strongest? Which one felt the weakest? Which perspective was hard to adopt? What did you learn about yourself?

This exercise gives clients a deeper understanding of the positions available, opens up the range of possibilities, and conveys a sense of the right choice. The perspectives created through the segments of the wheel create the basis for confidence in making life choices.

Saying No

One of the side effects of increased perspectives is an accompanying increase in the number of choices. With so many enticing choices before us, we are now faced with an unusual phenomenon: a super-abundance of choices. We not only have an abundance of things we feel we must do and things people expect us to do, we also have the abundance of all the things that simply look too good to pass up. The consequence, as so many have noted, is that people are spending their lives— expending themselves—as if it were all unlimited, and it's not. So one of the most empowering skills to learn is the simple, unheralded ability to say no. The ability to say no to the boss, the spouse, the friends, the TV, the overtime, the recreation and social engagements—not necessarily all of these things, perhaps, but some combination that creates balance. Learning to say no—and it is a learnable skill—is one of the most difficult skills the client can learn. It is also one of the most valuable, because learning to say no becomes a way to honor the client's values. To say no involves a choice. It actually means saying yes to something and no to something else. It's about choosing: choosing to say yes to things that make us more alive and saying no to things that suck the life from us. It's as simple as asking clients: "What do you want more of in your life? What do you want less of?"

Working with a client to say no can be a major part of a coach's job during the initial months. This is where we run into the client's habitual response: to say no is rude; to say no means you're not a team player; to say no means you're selfish; and so on and so on. Yet for every yes you say in life, you are saying no to something else. If I say yes to working late hours every day, I am saying no to family and rest; I am saying yes to fear about losing my job and yes to powerlessness; I am saying no to serenity. If I say no to getting up and exercising in the morning, I may be saying yes to being warm and cozy, or yes to an extra ten pounds or getting more sleep, or simply saying yes to the Gremlin.

This is an important issue for client and coach to examine. To discover where the client responds with an automatic yes or no opens up new options. For the client to consider what the no is in every yes sheds light on blind spots or habits. Here's an assignment for clients that can be both confrontational and expansive: request that they say no five times a day for a week. For the really stuck or overwhelmed client the learning is huge. One learning that usually surfaces when examining yes and no is where the client is addicted and without choice.

Commitment to . . .

Coming face to face with issues of balance puts clients in a position of making choices and declaring what they are committed to. When they reach this point it's time to stop talking. This is the step of commitment that will lead to action. This is more than endorsing a plan. It's an affirmation, a statement of intent and direction. Commitment allows clients to announce how they will devote their time, attention, talent, and resources. And because the coaching relationship is an alliance between coach and client, this commitment is a covenant between them, a shared promise that the coach must hold as securely as the client.

These commitments are the foundation of the client's agenda. If clients falter, or waver, or even forget what they committed to—usually with the help of the Gremlin—the coach will stand fast rather than participate in the retreat. Unfortunately this is a time when some coaches default on the relationship. If the client forgets, coaches do not forget. They don't beat the client over the head; they don't shame the client. But they do not stand by and watch clients betray themselves. The coach has to bring the commitment back into the foreground.

One of the reasons why coaching is expanding so rapidly as a profession is that people are well intentioned. They know what they need to do, know what they want, at least in general terms. They say they'll do this or do that with genuine goodwill, but then life gets in the way. Let's say your client made a commitment to spend more time with his family. Then unexpectedly the company has a new and exciting project for him—maybe even a promotion, more money. "Hey, the family could use the money, right? If it's good for the career, it's good for all of us, right?" And yet the new project may mean overtime hours, pressure, and distractions as well as excitement and the potential for job satisfaction and even career advancement. This is a great opportunity to examine what your client would be saying no to if he says yes to the new project.

This is the time when the coach needs to remind the client of the commitment: "This is what you said was important; this is what you said you were committed to. How will this new project honor your commitment to your family?" It's a question the client may not want to hear, but it's what you must be ready to ask. In fact, the client may decide that the project is even more important and the coach must simply adjust to the client's revised agenda. But before that happens, the coach needs to examine the perspectives and test the change of direction: Is this an example where you need to say no? How will this honor your values? Going out five years from now and looking back, what is the decision you would have wanted to make today?

The coach continues to hold the commitment and advocate the client's initial vision until there's no doubt the client is making the choice in harmony with his sense of fulfillment—not because of a sense of obligation or a desire not to miss out on the opportunity. Life is out there, ready to distract clients from their commitments, ready to sabotage the movement toward balance. Both coach and client must be vigilant. Both must be ready to check for the truth and sustainability of the commitments the client makes.

And yet, standing at the threshold of action is sometimes where clients get stuck. There are lots of reasons. Sometimes the Gremlin will not permit change of any kind. Sometimes it's because they are unwilling to act until they are *sure* they have chosen the right course of action. They want to have it figured out first. They want some assurance that they'll succeed with the action that is planned. They want it to be perfect. That would be nice. Sometimes it may even be possible. But more often than not, the creative process, which is what change is all about, is messy. Look at the painter, the sculptor, the gardener. The first step seems to be to create a mess or step into one. Coaching for change is often a process of encouraging clients to get into action and learn from the action. There is no such thing as pinpoint accuracy. Sometimes we can "ready, aim, fire." Sometimes we simply need to "fire . . . aim . . . fire . . . aim." And learn from the results each time.

A Balanced Point of View

As a coach, your job is to maintain a constant background awareness of your client's sense of balance. Even when the client is ready to commit to a course of action that will lead to a desired outcome, part of your job is to see the impact of that action on other parts of the client's life. As their coach you are still focused on the big picture of the client's overall fulfillment, balance, and process. This doesn't mean you discourage the client from acting. It is never the coach's role to hold the client back. In fact, based on your designed alliance your job may be to challenge clients to take bigger steps and push to the edge of their abilities—all the while watching their course and checking for balance.

Balance, as a principle, means addressing all aspects of life. As always, it depends on the client and the client's agenda. The coach's role is to grasp the big picture of the client's life: to see the whole and the relationships within the whole. Part of the coach's job is to speak up when the client is swerving out of balance—before he hits anything hard.

Balance, in fact, is always part of the coaching backdrop whether it shows up in every coaching call or not. Whenever you encourage the client to expand the range of possible choices, whenever you invite additional perspectives, whenever you help the client move beyond "that's just the way it is," there is some aspect of balance in the coaching. Balance itself is rarely the focal point of the work you do with the client. Instead, the work focuses on the area that is out of balance and needs attention, learning, and action. Even though balance may not be the point, it is often the warp and weave of the fabric that holds the whole of the client's life together.

Client Process

It makes one pause to realize we are human "beings" and not human "doings." Maybe it's just an accident of the language but it's instructive. There is an important distinction here between the doing of life and the being of it that is especially relevant to coaching. Clients usually come to coaching to do things differently or to do different things. They want to set goals, get a plan, get into action, and use the accountability of coaching to stay on track along the way. A great deal of the coach's focus is on the path that leads to fulfillment or balance in life. Balance coaching in particular emphasizes a structure for advancing from perspective to planning to commitment to action. Process coaching is about where your clients stand today in the process of their lives.

There is an intriguing dualism of doing and being; two pieces that form a whole. Doing is focused, directed, intentional; being immerses the client in the flow of life. Doing is about generating, creating, and being responsible; being is about allowing it to happen, letting go, accepting what is there. Doing is often a fierce determination to make something happen; being is blending with the motion of life. For a full approach to coaching and a full approach to life, we need to attend to both doing and being. In our lives and in our work as coaches, we need to hold both simultaneously like holding water and fire in our hands.

The Look of Process

Being can look lots of different ways. We can be frantic, stuck, happy, melancholy, up-tempo or glacier-slow. The being state is there whether we notice it or not. In fact most of the time we *don't* notice it. Our attention is on what we are doing, not on who we are being.

This concept of just "being" can sound odd or even contrived to some people—especially people who are so active, or so wired for doing, they may have forgotten what it is like simply to *be*. To be a teenager, to be in love, to be a mother, is to live a tremendous range of experience. It's not a one-dimensional state. Take, for example, being a parent. Once you become one, you can generally expect to be a parent for the rest of your life. Whatever you do with the parenting experience, you are now in a process of being a parent that will continue every day whether your attention is on it or not. Notice that "being" a parent doesn't remove the need for action. No doubt you've noticed that parents are active. Obviously, to be a parent isn't about contemplating quietly. You are being a parent and doing parenting things simultaneously.

In co-active coaching, the focus of process coaching is on where clients are now and how they want to be. Process can be compared to the river of life. Life has a constant flow but it changes form. In one part it is steady, then it hits rapids, then a waterfall. There are eddies and whirlpools, backwater and swampy parts. It narrows and suddenly speeds up. Process is about being wherever you are on the river and not trying to dam the river, walk upstream, or stop the river. When you're in the rapids, the only thing to do is be in the rapids. You can wish it weren't so, but it is the place in the river you are inhabiting at this moment, so there you are. You have this life you are living. Sorry, there is no exchange window. You can't turn it in and get another one. While you are busy making plans for the future you are also in the present. You are in the process of your life.

The Coach and Process

Part of the coach's job is to be with the client in the process—to be in the flow with the client. One of the simplest examples of this is mirroring clients when they show up for the coaching session. Try matching their speed, intensity, breathing, and language. Ask yourself: "What is the energy level on the other end? Where is the client in the river of life today?" Reading the Level III energy helps you connect even more strongly with your client. If your client is feeling the blues and you show up as the High-Voltage Coach, you two could be off to a bumpy ride. It isn't a *rule* that you match the client's energy—sometimes it's better not to—but it's a way of noting the client's state and joining him there.

Be aware that clients almost never come to coaching for the process. They mostly come for setting goals and getting into action to achieve those goals. And in their minds that's all about doing: action steps, to-do lists, and accountability. Yet there are times when it is indeed the process that needs coaching. Often it is a blocked process that is keeping clients from the balance and fulfillment they want in their lives. About the time they're thinking about giving up, or deciding that the coaching isn't working, the shift to process coaching leads them to examine their process, to learn how they operate, and quite often keeps them in the coaching relationship.

Where to Look

It's easy to be distracted by the activity on the surface. Imagine the river on a bright afternoon: the sun reflecting off the water in glittering sparkles can be practically blinding. The action of life can be dazzling. But when you look at the river through a polarizing filter, you can tune out all the distracting sparkles and see the flow of the water. That's the coach's job—to notice the turbulence and watch for the dangerous places. Remember that the river, powerful as it is, always finds the path of least resistance. So when process is the coaching focus, it's almost always because there is resistance somewhere. Look for the turbulence and the struggle. Your client may be trying to dig a channel to get the river to go in a different direction.

A word or two is in order about the expression "be with," which we used often with process coaching. Think of it in the same way you would think of visiting a friend in the hospital. Your goal is to *be with* your friend. There is really nothing for you to do, except be there. And it is more than just showing up. To be with is to be present and fully engaged, attentive, open, receptive, involved, even interacting, but with no other goal than simply being together with someone in the experience. To be with is a powerful Level III connection between you and the other person. They know you are with them at a deep level. When you are with clients at this deep level they are free to share more than their thoughts and analysis; they can be open to sharing the honest emotion of their experience as well.

Can't Go There

Process coaching often shows up when the river takes a turn into territory the client doesn't want to enter. As a coach, your curiosity is piqued. Where is it the client doesn't want to go? What is it the client doesn't want to deal with? The possibilities are numerous: "I don't want any more letdown" . . . "I don't want the worry about money" . . . "I can't be with the failure I created in my last job" . . . "I can't be with the embarrassment" . . . "I can't be with the confusion in my life" . . . "I can't be with the happiness this person brings to my life" . . . "I can't be with the demons." So clients are stuck and uncomfortable, sometimes downright miserable, because the river won't hold back. The river takes them there anyway. And *you* can't talk them out of it with your words any more than they could talk themselves out of it. They are in the river.

Such clients are looking for some way to stop the river of life from going in a certain direction. They don't realize what it costs them to cut out those parts of their life they don't want to be with. So draw a large circle (Figure 7). This is the client's whole life. Now start excluding the pieces they don't want to be with. Color them in. Here is the anger they can't be with . . . and the disappointment . . . and the risk taking . . . and with each piece that is colored in, there is less life left for the client. Now imagine trying to have a whole life and the effort it will

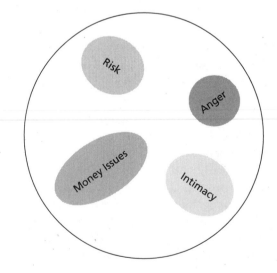

Figure 7   Redirecting the Flow

take—and the turbulence it will create—to rearrange the flow of the river around all those big obstacles in the path.

Gremlin Activity

When coaches see clients resisting and struggling, it is often a sign that there is a Gremlin at work keeping the client from making life changes. In this case, coaching strategies typically focus on noting the Gremlin's activity, invoking the client's life purpose, or reinforcing the client's values. All of these tactics tend to pin the Gremlin in a bright light and force him to disappear. If the usual tactics have no effect, however, chances are there is something in the client's life that has him profoundly stuck. It is the thing he can't be with.

Process coaching is not about having your clients eliminate the experience they find uncomfortable. Process coaching is about having them include the feelings—including the Gremlin's desire for escape. The Gremlin wants to avoid all the experiences that are uncomfortable. The coach's job is to help clients become fully engaged in their lives. Let's say the client is sad. Rather than try to find a quick fix and ignore this major component of the life process, the coach allows the client—even encourages the client—to be sad and thereby get over the sadness. When clients are able to accept life—including the parts that are hard to be with—it gives them more versatility and self-confidence.

Assessing the Currents

In balance coaching we talked about creating new perspectives, choosing, making a commitment, and stepping into it. Commitment in process is about looking at your life and really seeing what it is you're committed to. You say you're committed to bringing peace to the planet, for example, or you're committed to your marriage. That's one kind of commitment. Another kind shows up in your life through the choices you make regardless of what you say. Your client might say she's committed to finding a new job, but the action in her life says she's *really* committed to struggling about work. When you look into clients' lives to see what they're really committed to, you can see that a client is committed to, say, being angry or afraid, or playing it safe—because that's what's there. That's what the process of his life is showing you.

It's as though there's an undercurrent that has the power to pull the client down by the ankles. The question is: What is the current? As a coach you might point out to your client: "You say you're committed to losing weight and getting fit—but the evidence of your life says something else. What shows up in the process of your life is that you are committed to staying comfortable or resisting change, committed to the drama of struggling or the stimulation." Whatever their words, their life says they're committed to something else—to being a victim, to being a lone wolf, to being broke, to being right, to complaining. This subconscious undercurrent has the power to run people. When it shows up on the surface as resistance or turbulence, it becomes noticeable and available for coaching.

There are other kinds of currents as well. In fulfillment we talk about aligning with currents like the future self, the life purpose, and the compelling way. These are powerful positive currents that pull us into the future rather than pull us down. Even values alignment is a kind of finding the flow—becoming congruent.

Process Coaching

Process coaching is called for whenever clients need to go deeper into their experience. It is often called for when clients are stuck in a strong emotional state that is blocking them from moving on. This can involve a variety of emotions: sadness, anger, loss, or even overwhelming joy. This state of being stuck can happen during times of major life transition when there is a flood of emotion so strong that clients have difficulty getting into action. Process coaching allows clients to fully be in their experience rather than talk about their experience on a superficial level, or try to talk their way around it or talk themselves out of it.

Start by Noticing

Start by noticing the resistance and ask: "Where is the place you don't want to go?" Start probing, removing layers. Continue to ask: "What's that about? . . . What would happen if that happened?" Perhaps you say to your client: "I notice we keep making new plans and commitments each week and nothing's happening. What is the resistance there? Would you be willing to look at that? Take a deep breath, get settled, and tell me—what's going on in there?"

When the client responds by telling you she's afraid, reinforce that you've heard her response but keep probing: "You're afraid. What is it you're afraid of? Failing again. I know, that would feel awful." Notice the significant turning point here. You just acknowledged the feeling. You join the client in her conclusion that failing would be awful. A different path would take the coaching to the "failing is learning" theme or some other problem solving, but you're in the river's current here and the client can't hear that comforting message over the roar of the river of failing. Process coaching will not talk her out of feeling bad about failing. Feeling bad is what is true for her right now. You need to be with her in this feeling—while you still hold onto the big tree on the shore. Then go deeper.

Expand and Explore

Once you start on this path of going into the process, you are committed to it. You need to be willing to stay with it and expand and explore the process with the client. Continue to deepen the experience. Be imaginative in your probing to amplify it: "Where do you feel the failure in your body? What else do you see? What is your posture? What is your breathing like?" Remind the client you are still there: "Are you ready to go on? Let's turn up the volume to increase the intensity. Put your hand on the knob and turn it up a notch. Now what do you notice?"

In process coaching you'll find that the most effective coaching structure is often the use of metaphor. It gives clients a story and images to express their strong, often unarticulated feelings. You might suggest, for example, that you and the client dive into the problem and swim around in it. Or ask the client to explore the cave and use her flashlight to shine into all of the corners and crevices. Or roll up her sleeves and reach her hand into it right up to the elbows. Or be a scientist and investigate it and then record her findings.

After a short time, the client will reach a point where the experience of exploring this thing is complete. As coach you are asking questions like: "What else do you see? What more is there in here for you?" But you'll notice that the client has stopped going deeper. Your intuition and experience will let you know that the client is complete. Now you can move on: "What's the learning in this for you? What is the gift for you? What is the thing you will take from here? What do you want to leave behind? What might you do differently next time?"

Creating a Bigger Life

Together you and the client have created an experience of living successfully with this part of his life. Together you have created an experience of accepting the part he has been unwilling or unable to name and be with. Now he can begin to include it in his life.

That is the whole point about process coaching. It is about making space for one's whole life: not only the parts that are easy and pleasant but all of the mess, the embarrassment, the shameful pieces, the regrets, all of the things that are hard to be with, by having the client be in the experience rather than just talk about the experience. When clients can include *everything* that life has to offer, rather than hiding from it or resisting it, it's as though they can then take a much bigger breath, get it all in, and thereby create a much bigger life. It's a profound experience and gives them much more room to operate.

Feelings as Information, Not Symptoms

One aspect of process coaching is hard for many coaches: being with the emotion of it. This exploration touches very deep feelings in clients—feelings they often express emotionally as well as verbally. There may be long-restrained anger or bravely controlled tears. In the process of entering forbidden territory and opening that door, there may be quite a flood of feeling. Coaches are sometimes alarmed and confused by this. They think that because the client is reacting with feeling, the relationship has changed to therapy. But emotions and therapy are not the same thing. Emotions are just emotions. When someone is crying it doesn't mean they are ill. They are crying because they're crying—that's how people express strong feelings.

It's okay for coaches to allow emotion—crying, sadness, pain, anger—and actually to encourage it. Emotion is a legitimate form of expression like words and music and dance. Don't be a detective about it. Don't look at why they're crying—which is the typical response. The cause itself is not important; accepting the feeling is important. Nor is it up to the coach to try to heal it or fix it or stop it—another typical response. Just explore it and acknowledge it: "That is a powerful feeling. There's some pain in there, I can tell."

Emotions are part of the normal functioning of a human being, not symptoms of disease. The whole, healthy, resourceful client has full access to his or her emotions. It's the hiding, denying, submerging that gets clients in trouble. Feelings are ways we have of expressing ourselves; they are a way our body has of discharging and discovering whatever is inside. And if we don't get to discharge and discover, we don't grow. We can even get sick—physically and emotionally—by holding things in. It's also important to recognize the cleansing effect of tears or anger or joy. Process coaching is where tears and other emotions will show up because you're encouraging, even challenging, clients to visit the hard places and give in to the experience so they can include it in their lives. Unless you can explore those places, coaching lacks depth and breadth. Your client can still move forward, but process is where the deepest change really happens.

Even though process coaching can be powerful emotionally, there's still room for humor. The ability to explore forbidden territory with humor can give clients license to approach the dark areas on light feet or feel more curiosity about the depth of the murky water and less like they are about to drown.

Pitfalls of Process Coaching

There are also some pitfalls to watch out for in process coaching. Process coaching tends to be messier, in general, than fulfillment coaching, with its emphasis on values and Gremlin and vision, or balance coaching, with the solid structure of a seven-step approach to action. Process coaching is also inherently more emotionally charged. Because of the unique nature of process coaching, there are a number of pitfalls to watch out for.

Getting Beyond Technique

Coaches sometimes fall into the trap of thinking that process coaching is in the technique—especially the imaginative probing. Your intuition and your own style will guide you when it comes to looking for ways to ask clients to describe where they are. "Where do you feel it in your body?" is often a useful question because it gets clients out of their intellectualizing and into the experience.

But a pat series of questions that go into body exploration is not process coaching. The technique is just an entry point—a tunnel. If you're using it simply as a technique, it is likely to come across to the client as superficial—in which case you as the coach are modeling "superficial" and not "risk taking." So why would a client be willing to go deeper and take risks? As a coach you need to be with the client or process coaching will not take place. Clients will know if you're there with them at an unspoken level. They will sense your Level III presence. You need to be willing to be with them.

Getting Scared

Sometimes coaches get scared because emotions surface and because process coaching is inherently messy. Balance coaching has a tidy seven-step sequence. Fulfillment coaching has its values clarification. But process coaching involves slipping under the water, into the river, not knowing exactly what you will find. Not knowing, not being in control, afraid that this is therapy, a deep desire to fix and run—these are all common reactions of scared coaches when they discover they're in the midst of process coaching. And yet process coaching is the extraordinary experience of being with another person at a very deep level beyond thinking and understanding—being totally in the flow of their life with them. It is a profound experience for clients. They have rarely known anyone so willing to simply accompany them on a dangerous journey without giving advice, trying to talk them out of it, making them feel bad or weak, without telling them it will be all right, or any of the usual patronizing gestures—just authentically being there. It is an extremely safe and reassuring space for clients, a place where they can really be *themselves*.

Getting Addicted

Once they've experienced the power of process coaching and the new resourcefulness of their clients, some coaches start to see opportunities for process coaching everywhere. It's intoxicating and they become addicted to the experience—to the endorphins or adrenaline or emotion. But process coaching is not a magic potion. It should be used with care along with coaching for action. Remember that in co-active coaching, the coaching direction is part of the designed alliance. If you are continually forcing the agenda toward process coaching, you are not honoring the alliance. There needs to be a balance between being and doing.

There is one final pitfall of process coaching, and that is going halfway and stopping. Once you begin down this path, it is best to keep going, bravely as necessary, until the client is clear and resourceful again.

Sample Dialogue

Client: Looks like I'll have to dust off the old résumé again, after all.

COACH: You finally heard about the job overseas?

Client: I heard. And it wasn't the answer I wanted to hear. So I'm cranking up the search machinery again.

COACH: You had a lot riding on getting that job. I remember how excited you were after the last interview. Sounds like you're kind of shrugging it off now—as if it weren't that important. What's the truth there?

Client: Disappointment.

COACH: Yeah.

Client: I was really pumped for that interview. I don't see how it could have gone any better.

COACH: It's a huge letdown.

Client: I don't really want to dwell on it.

COACH: I understand. Still, it looks as though your life wants to dwell on it.

Client: Boy, that's the truth. I can't remember being this depressed before. Maybe I had too much riding on getting the hell out of the country.

COACH: What's it look like to you? I'm sensing sadness. What's your experience?

Client: It's actually like getting punched in the stomach. I feel like it took my breath away. It really hit me in the gut. Like I can't even stand up straight.

COACH: What's the painful part?

Client: The loss, the waiting, the wasted energy.

COACH: Would it be all right if we explored that right now? I think it's important to go through this, not step over it.

Client: Sure. I hate it, but it's not going away.

COACH: So what's it like there?

Client: It's dark . . . sharp and dark . . . hard to see, jagged edges.

COACH: What does your face feel like?

Client: I feel it in the back of my eyes, like this pressure. My forehead is tight, stressed, and there's a ringing in my ears, and, like, voices.

COACH: What are the voices saying?

Client: The usual Gremlin stuff. But this time more voices all at once: "You weren't really qualified. You stunk at the first interview. You were over your head all along. They saw through your fake act of competence." You know, that stuff.

COACH: Okay. What I want you to do now is turn up the volume on it, just a little at first. It's at 5 right now. Turn it up to 6.

Client: The voices?

COACH: The voices, the pain, the pressure, everything. Really explore that place—and explore it deeply. I'll be right here.

Client: Okay. I'm turning up the volume. There's 6.

COACH: What do you notice?

Client: Failure. Like a huge wave of failure, it's breaking over everything.

COACH: A wave of failure. Are you in a safe place?

Client: Yeah, it's running past me.

COACH: When you're ready, try turning it up another notch to 7.

Client: Now I really feel the loss. Like a dream died. Like my last chance to build something important just vanished.

COACH: You're really mourning the loss of the dream. How big is that?

Client: It's huge.

COACH: I can tell. What do you notice now?

Client: That I can turn down the volume.

COACH: Do you want to do that now?

Client: I do.

COACH: What happens to the sense of loss and failure that had such a hold on you?

Client: I didn't realize how tight a grip it had. It's a little looser now.

COACH: And you also discovered you have some control over it. You have the power to experience it—and to limit its impact on you.

Client: I'm not just a victim. I can still choose.

COACH: So here's my request for next week: I want you to stay for a while in this place of disappointment, loss, and failure. Will you do that?

Client: You're kidding.

COACH: Actually, I'm not. You know how to do whatever you need to do in the job search—write a résumé, do the interviews, whatever needs to be done. The hard thing for you is to live with the disappointment. That's the learning edge for you. If you could be with that, what would it give you?

Client: Freedom. It's just . . . I don't have to be happy about it, do I?

COACH: No. And you don't have to avoid doing any of the things you'd normally do. It's just that this isn't the last time you'll face this sense of loss and failure. If you can be with it now—and develop some muscles to handle it—you'll be in better shape the next time you feel the disappointment.

Client: Like an emotional fitness program.

COACH: The universe provided a great gymnasium for you. Let's take advantage of it and build some strengths for disappointment and failure in your life. I have an inquiry for you to journal on: "What am I learning from my disappointment?"

Client: I think there's a lot to learn.

Process and Accountability

There is a pondering, contemplative, go-with-the-flow quality with process. And yet, as we pointed out earlier, process includes action. Thus process can be coached for accountability just like fulfillment or balance. In this case the coach and client are looking for ways to forward the action and deepen the learning of swimming in the process of life. Let's say your client is stuck at telling the hard truth to boss, employees, spouse, and children—so stuck she can't move on. As her coach you might challenge your client to tell the hard truth fifteen times this next week and notice what happened so she can be with confrontation rather than avoid it or deny it. Now she is accountable for being with this difficult situation. Or the client might agree to write down three hard truths each day and note whether or not she spoke them out loud to the person involved. Or the client could write in her journal each day on the question: What are the hard truths I hide from myself?

You can also add the process perspective to traditional issues of accountability. If your client commits to writing thirty pages of his book next week and says he'll do it but it will be hard—there'll be blood all over the pages—you counter: "Then your challenge is to do thirty pages next week and make it be *easy.*" Or you can decide what clients are going to do and then ask them how they want to *be* in the process. How can they do what they want to do and make it be fun, or fast, or childlike, or triumphant, or tender? Do they want to be playful, intense, creative, focused, committed? How many ways can you make the experience "be"?

Where Do You Stop?

Before we leave the subject of exploring the hard places, it is worth asking a pointed question: Where do you stop in your coaching? What areas in your life are hard for *you* to deal with? The answer is important because these are the places you'll be reluctant to go with your clients. Let's say you have trouble dealing with money, or anger, or abandonment. These are places where you may stop in your coaching. They are places your clients may need to go—may even be willing to go. But if you are unconscious of your own process, you will not be able to coach in these places and you'll shortchange your clients, because as soon as they start to go there, you'll steer them away. Coaches, therefore, must do their own rigorous process of self-discovery—ideally with their own coach. Begin to work on these areas so they can be included in your own life and become accessible in your work with coaching clients, too.

Integrating Fulfillment, Balance, and Process

There are always a dozen different tunnels to go down with every client in every situation. For those who were looking for the coaching rule book or user's manual, there isn't one—at least there isn't a programmed way to lead you unerringly to the next coaching step or question. The tunnel you choose depends on your Level III awareness, your intuition, and your willingness to go looking without having it figured out first. The first tunnel you choose may not be productive. That's okay. Coaching is a long-term affair, not a one-time shot. You might have a number of starts and stops in various tunnels in a thirty-minute coaching session. You might try a little fulfillment coaching about values, balance coaching about new perspectives, and process coaching about how frustratingly slow the process is—all in a matter of minutes. You become very agile with the skills and in tune with Level II and III listening. It really does become a dance—dancing in the moment.

Most people, even coaches, find it easier to see the place of fulfillment coaching and balance coaching. These are the two tunnels that coaches and clients are likely to go down first. The activity and accountability are clear signs, visible and measurable, that give coaching muscle and bone. But if we are to coach the whole of the client's life—and ensure that the client has a full life, fully accessible, fully expressed—then we need to understand and be able to use process coaching too. It's the heart to go with the muscle and bone.

Tips and Traps

We've spent most of the book talking about principles, contexts, and skills of coaching. We've given examples and described applications. Now it's time to get down to some of the nuts and bolts of coaching. To explore all the issues about setting up, marketing, and managing a viable coaching practice would require an entire book of its own. But there are a few topics that should be addressed here because they directly affect the coach and client relationship.

The Time Frame

Coaching takes place over time. It's one of the cornerstones of coaching. The commitment to time is important for a number of reasons. Above all, it reflects the truth about deep and lasting personal change: it takes time. The blinding flash of insight or epiphany on the mountaintop are always possible, but for most clients change is a process that is more like agriculture than rocket science. It takes digging around in the dirt, planting, cultivating, harvesting. It also takes clients time to figure things out, to be clear, to divest themselves of the self-limiting reasons and the old ways of thinking that held them back. Most coaching relationships start with a commitment to a minimum of three months, but agreements for six months or longer are not uncommon.

This sense of the time frame also helps clients to make commitments rather than seeking a temporary fix. Coaching is not a patch job. It is a course change for life. That time frame encompasses the first big dip in the process and also the first plateau. Clients begin their coaching relationship filled with enthusiasm, energy, even euphoria about beginning anew. That glow starts to diminish after a few weeks when the process of change begins to get tough or uncomfortable. The Gremlin may be aroused, and clients frequently find that change is messy. Life under construction is like any remodeling project: chaos, inconvenience, decisions to make, people to negotiate with. It's easy to lose sight of the finished vision when the air is filled with a cloud of plaster dust. The time frame has room in it for the client to pause and examine the discouragement or the plateau.

Often clients will use the initial energy and momentum of their fired-up state of mind to make terrific progress at first. Then at some point they usually reach the limits of their comfort zone for change. They will pause at the threshold—usually with a Gremlin holding them back—not sure they can move on. That plateau happens in the first few months. So too does drifting off—clients bored with their own game. So too will the testing—clients experimenting to see how far they can wander off and ignore their commitments before you call them to task. It all takes time to build the relationship and establish the ground rules.

There is also the client's personal sense of timing to consider. What is an appropriate pace of change? If you push too hard too soon, even the clients who are willing and ready may take on too much and fail. Failure is not bad—it is a learning opportunity. But early in the relationship a little more learning, with a little less failing, may keep the client motivated to continue. When it is right to push and when to ignore, when to hold back and when to go full out, are sensitive issues. The point is to ensure that the client is making maximum progress. Like an athlete training for an event, the cycle that builds muscle fastest and provides lasting strength is a cycle of intense work followed by rest. Intentional muscle overuse and breakdown are followed by rebuilding that is stronger than before. The coach's sense of timing is therefore very important. It is a sense that combines experience, intuition, and listening at Level III.

Clients will sometimes want to take time off—maybe a week or a couple of weeks. They may want to change to an every-other-week schedule.

The danger is that they'll lose their momentum and commitment. The development that is happening for them when they are meeting weekly with you starts to wane if the short-term reinforcement isn't there. You may also need to question whether the need for time off is authentic or just a clever Gremlin game to sabotage the change. If clients come back after time away and have a hard time getting on track, if they seem to have lost ground or the fire in them has dimmed, it is a learning opportunity for you and your client. The dimmed fire might be exactly what the client needed too. As coach, you know that change happens over a period of months. This is a definite advantage as you help clients make choices. For example, clients will sometimes make a commitment to a course of action that you know from experience or intuition is almost certainly doomed to failure. You can intervene and rescue the client from a bad idea. Or you can allow the client his or her learning, knowing that time will provide the learning most needed.

This also releases the coach from the pressure of believing he or she must be a miracle worker on every call. The trap coaches must watch out for is the urge to force the coaching, to think that breakthroughs and major life-changing insights must occur on every coaching call. In fact, they are more likely to occur—when they occur at all—during the week between coaching calls. Coaches who get caught up in a mission to produce extraordinary effect in the coaching call are in danger of pushing their own agenda to be seen as a great coach instead of holding the client's agenda.

Eye to Eye

In the coaching relationship, coach and client are able to look each other in the eye as peers, collaborators, mutually committed to the best possible outcome the relationship can produce. (See Figure 8.) Clients enter the coaching process with goals. They are looking for assistance that will help them sort through the goals, point them to a more effective process, and accompany them to the finish line. As coach you are a full partner in that process. You are also creating the conditions of resourcefulness, self-reliance, and confidence so that you will not be needed in the future.

Part of the underlying purpose of coaching is to produce a stronger client who is capable of self-directed change. A portion of what you provide as coach is transferred to the client permanently. In co-active coaching, the way that happens is by regarding each other as peers: eye

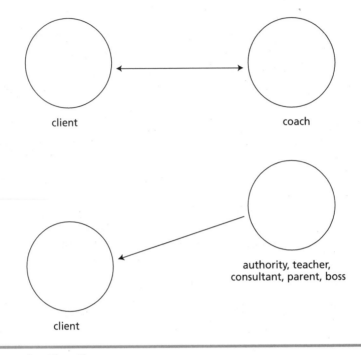

client   coach

authority, teacher,
consultant, parent, boss

client

Figure 8   Elevation

to eye. If you stand on a pedestal, you run the risk of always limiting the client's ability to fully reach his own strength. It's like being in the role of a parent: sometimes clients will want to earn your approval; sometimes they will want to rebel against your authority. So long as you are a parent instead of a peer, they can take the role of the inferior one or the victim. It gives them a convenient reason why things continue to turn out badly. When you are able to work with clients eye to eye, you empower them to be their own final authority. Gradually their reliance on you will fade and they'll take the strength of the relationship with them.

The Flow of Coaching

There is no universal law that governs the flow of coaching, yet there seems to be a natural pattern with many variations. It is definitely *not* a linear sequence. Coaching is about creating human change over time, and anything so human is inherently unpredictable. Still, our experience shows that there are trends that tend to repeat as people begin coaching, experience the effect of coaching, and see themselves in action and learning.

Emphasis on Action: What Do I Do?

Clients come to the alliance with "things" to do: things that need to be dealt with, a backlog of to-dos, or habits to develop. They are motivated by the accountability of doing what has to be done. Goals and action plans are important: making choices, finding focus, saying yes and saying no. This is a very active period and a time when clients are learning about the process, the structure, even the language of the coaching relationship. They learn about inquiry, confront their Gremlin, meet their future self, discover volumes about what they value, what they believe, what they want from life. They go through a creative, sometimes fumbling process figuring out what structures work for them: maybe it's their journal, regular meditation, taking karate lessons. They move from reaction in their lives to self-direction. They see change around them in new ways of acting, new skills learned, new experiences tried, even new clothes, new hairstyles, new books to read. Creative turmoil is part of this early stage. It's an excursion into the client's life in a way he's probably never experienced before, focused mostly on taking action. At this early stage, the learning is mostly a by-product.

Ways of Being: Who Am I?

It takes a while for the learning to catch up and sink in. As time progresses, clients settle into the doing of their lives and begin to view their own life from a higher perspective. Like an athlete who has been training for months, they can see the muscles and the endurance they have gained. The early pain of getting into action has subsided. Now they begin to take a longer view. They begin to look more at ways of being—to explore attitudes and take even deeper excursions into methods that impact their lives. Although the agenda they bring to the coaching call still contains issues for the week, there is a growing inclination to look inside at personal operating principles and the big picture of their lives. Often the field of vision expands from "What is happening in my life?" to "What is happening in my relationships and in my community?" The client asks: "Where can I make a contribution? Where can I make a difference?"

Self-Creation: What's Next?

Eventually clients reach a stage at which much of coaching is about self-creation, innovation, and design with new personal standards and operating styles. They have strengths they didn't realize and a desire to use them. At some point clients reach a point of satisfaction—a point when they are ready to move on from the coaching. It is a point at which the questions no longer arise from the coaching relationship. The client has found a voice for searching and asking, a voice for real self-expression. For some clients this whole process from the initial discovery session to completion might take three months. For others, the process might take many years because the coaching relationship keeps being reinvented as clients move through the stages and phases of their lives. Certainly a thirty-year-old person's questions about doing and values and choices will change by the time he is forty. Coaching is valuable at each passage.

When clients reach the point of continuous self-reflection, self-directed action, and self-expression, they may be ready to leave the coaching relationship. At this point it's helpful to suggest a continuing relationship on a much less frequent basis, perhaps once a month or every two months, or to suggest quarterly check-ins for a longer time period, an hour or more, perhaps with prework to help clients clarify where they stand. Still it is likely to be a heartfelt parting when clients complete their coaching work. You may know in your head that it's nothing personal: simply the client's normal evolution to full-fledged self-reliance and responsibility. Yet the two of you have shared many experiences and adventures, often intimately. As much as you cheer the client's accomplishment and new sense of power, there is likely to be sadness at the parting.

Closing the Book

A definitive finish is an important way of putting the cap on the relationship. It's important for coach and client alike—whether this has been a long, fruitful, intimate relationship or one that for whatever reason didn't work out. The process of conscientious completion is a way of closing the book. Perhaps you and this client will resume a coaching relationship in the future. In any case just walking away is not appropriate. It violates all the tenets of the coaching relationship. In the relationship there is truth telling, acknowledgment, risk taking, discovery, and learning—and the completion is an opportunity to exercise all of these. The simplest way to complete the process is for the client to prepare a list before the final session of all the pluses and minuses: What worked and what didn't work? This can be a time for reviewing clients' accomplishments: What are they proudest of? When were they the most afraid? When did they feel most empowered? When were they most surprised by themselves? What did they notice about the changes in themselves and their relationships with others? This debriefing allows clients to see the full range of their experience and the progression of the work they have done. It is a final opportunity for the coach to acknowledge who the client had to be in order to do the things the client has done. It is also a final opportunity to coach clients on the design of their future.

This sense of wrapping up and moving on is a natural part of the end of each year, as well. Many coaches use an end-of-year completion ritual as a way of claiming the learning from the past year, discarding the junk, and entering the new year with a clean slate. This can be a literal exercise: you can have the client prepare a list of all the pluses and minuses of the old year, read them out loud to you on the last coaching of the year, and then rip, burn, or in some way destroy the old list. The completion ritual might also include establishing goals or resolutions for the new year.

Ruts and Recharging

Let's be honest. There are times when coaches go blank in their coaching. They get into the routine and the rut of working with the same people on the same issues, using the same questions and same technique, and soon they are putting themselves to sleep. The coach has done a great job of making the client responsible for the agenda and the action, but now the coach himself is withering.

Recharging your coaching battery can take a wide variety of forms. The coach can show up with his or her own agenda one week. There's a radical act. After all we've said about clients designing their own agenda, turning the tables might be just the thing to get coach and client thinking in fresh ways. In fact clients often appreciate this intervention: they get tired of always having to come up with the agenda and it gives them a break.

There are lots of ways to break out of the mold:

- Start the client on a relevant book you have read. Have her discuss how she plans to apply what she's learning.
- Pick a subject for daily journal work that is different from the current client issue but supports it. A big inquiry almost always fits: something like "Where am I kidding myself?"
- Recommend that the client conduct informational interviews with friends or co-workers on such issues as "What are you saying no to in your life these days?" or "What is my reputation?"
- Ask the client to prepare a written vision statement, or write a song about his vision, or create a collage out of pictures cut from magazines.

The goal is to find creative ways to express the central themes of the client's life.

About every three or four months it's also a worthwhile strategy to simply ask the client: "What would need to happen to quadruple the value of the coaching for you?" Some coaches repeat the intake session every four to six months—usually somewhat scaled back but perhaps focused on one aspect. For example: spend a whole hour exclusively on values clarification or the future self or life purpose. Or try creating a customized personal performance profile that describes three or four habits the client would like to acquire in the significant areas of his life. The coach can then refer to this profile during ongoing coaching calls.

Some coaches create themes for the month or themes for the week that they share with their clients. A series of these themes can create a cascading effect of learning. One week you ask: "What expectations do you have in life?" The next week you ask: "How do your expectations serve you?" Then: "What do your expectations cost you?" Then, "How can you let go of your attachment to your expectations?" Then: "What are you so attached to you can't let go?" And so on, following the thread.

Getting out of a coaching rut can also be done by changing the coaching environment. If you normally sit when you take coaching calls, try standing up for a week. Or move your phone to a different room. Or go to a resort in the mountains and coach from your room looking out over a panorama of snow-capped magnificence—all for the sake of getting out of your coaching rut, of course.

All Seriousness Aside

It's time to say a word or two about the use of humor as a coaching tool. As a coach you set the tone for how clients interact on the call—and indeed in their lives—by the direction you provide. Coaching is serious business. We are talking about people's lives here, their happiness, their sense of purpose and achievement. Still, a skillful dose of irreverence can cure an abundance of taking life too seriously. It takes sensitivity, of course, but a light touch at the right moment can turn near catastrophe into amusement. Humor sheds light. It brings people out of the hole. It gives them perspective.

Humor is good for the soul and it makes the coaching work better. Clients are more willing to play with options, to take risks, to enter dangerous territory. Look at your own coaching or listen to a tape of one of your coaching calls. What is the tonal environment you are creating? Is it getting ponderous and losing its energy? Humor sparks things up.

There is liveliness and energy when there is laughter. Humor is another tool in the coaching kit to keep you sharp and effective. Don't lose it.

The Other Skills: Telling and Demanding

Telling and demanding are two skills that do not appear in the usual discussion of coaching skills because they are for advanced-level coaches. Training really competent coaches requires a long period of curing people of the urge to tell and demand. In co-active coaching we insist on respecting the client's agenda and not giving advice. We place a high value on the art of asking questions—not telling—so that the learning and action come from the client, not the coach. Our strongest interventions—requesting and challenging—have the built-in caveat that clients can always refuse or make a counteroffer.

Yet there are times when the correct coaching tactic is to tell and demand. This is the big wake-up call. When the client is absolutely trapped in confusion, when the resistance is intransigent, when the game is destructive and repetitive, when it's time to stop the self-destructive sabotage, it is time for the coach to call a halt. This is not the time to go halfway. It is the time to tell and demand: "This is destructive. Stop it now!" This is not a request or a gentle prod, it is not telling or giving advice, it is not offering solutions. It is the big intrusion. And it is so rare coming from the coach that it will have triple the usual impact on the client.

It takes an experienced coach to handle such a powerful tool. It is used only because of the coach's absolute commitment to the client's full life. It may be the only way to stop a Gremlin that has the client by the throat or the only way to shake the client out of habitual self-limiting belief. It involves phrases like: "I will not tolerate you selling out on yourself like that. You know you're strong enough. I know you're strong enough. Just do it." Imagine the acknowledgment that is built into this explosive intrusion. It has the power of dynamite.

Schedules and Structures

Coaches come to the profession with their own work habits, their own comfortable ways of doing things, as well as their own personal style and temperament. For some, the pace of a thirty-minute phone conversation is ideal. for others, it is too short; they need an hour to get into an in-depth conversation with a client. The schedule and structure of coaching depend on the individual preferences of the coach and are affected by the nature of the clients the coach draws to his or her practice. In short, the co-active coaching model can be applied in a wide variety of coaching forms.

Weekly Sessions

There are a number of good reasons for creating a coaching practice based on weekly coaching sessions by phone for thirty minutes. It's comfortable and convenient for the coach—and usually for the client too. The weekly calls are frequent enough to sustain momentum. The thirty-minute time frame is efficient. It forces a rigorous sense of getting down to business; there is little wasted time. It's an easy, low-overhead way for most coaches to establish their practice because they can easily coach from a home office and work with clients literally around the world.

But it's not the only way to structure a coaching practice. Many coaches are comfortable and familiar with a face-to-face coaching session. They may already have an office arrangement in place. A biweekly one-hour session might be more suitable for some coaches and for some clients. Some coaches work three weeks by phone and one week in person. In the end there is no rule about what your practice should look like. It's whatever works for you and for your client.

Daily and Weekly Schedules

Many coaches prefer to schedule several clients back to back on the half hour. The coaches get in an energy groove and the coaching seems energized. Just remember to schedule breaks after about four calls or you are likely to find yourself wishing you had a catheter. For weekly scheduling, some coaches have all their calls on two or three days and use the other days for marketing, public speaking, writing, or personal time. A note for the self-employed: Schedule your breaks months in advance—and that includes daily breaks, days off, weekend getaways, and vacations—or it will be too easy to book that time for others. Then make sure you actually take the time off. You will need the rest. And besides, what kind of example would you be setting if you couldn't arrange some balance in your own life?

Group Coaching

Throughout the book we have talked about one-on-one coaching. But group coaching is another viable form of coaching and uses many of the same skills and the same basic format. Some coaches work with couples in a coaching relationship. Coaches also work with small groups: perhaps members of a work team in an organization, an executive or management team, or people with a common coaching goal such as a real estate sales group, or a group of financial planners, or parish ministers, or home care nurses. The initial intake session focuses on the common goals of the group and the outcomes they desire from the coaching work. The design of the alliance is part of the initial session too, often with specific goals or outcomes for each member. The group meets with the coach on a periodic basis determined by the group.

Group coaching is often done by phone teleconferencing. Sessions might last one hour and take place once a week. Calls might last thirty minutes and take place at the same time every morning five days a week. There is enormous focus and action in group telecoaching—especially when the group meets daily. The agenda for the group call is typically preset with time for each person to report on accountability, report successes and failures, invite group brainstorming or discussion, look for individual learning, create assignments for the next call, and so forth. Coaching the group call requires a certain agility and a facility in group dynamics to ensure that everyone participates and the needs of the group are met. Group calls will surely test your Level III listening skills.

Another variation on group coaching is a short-time-frame group process. Often three weeks long, this twenty-one-day supercharged format uses daily team coaching to keep the team and its members on track and making progress, uncovering obstacles, dispelling resistance, and motivating each other to accomplish a difficult short-term goal.

Different Coaches, Different Styles

One of the purposes behind this chapter has been to expand your image of coaching and how it is practiced. Although the half-hour weekly phone call is common, there are many adaptations and variations among professional coaches with successful practices. Good coaching that *works* is the bottom line.

Here we want to emphasize once more that there are no cookie-cutter coaches. The principles, contexts, and skills of coaching are valuable for understanding what to do, but there is no magic coat of coaching that you can put on and be assured of success. Clients are human beings and come with quirks and strengths and traits that are sometimes hard to love. Coaches too come in a variety of forms with different inherent strengths, different life experiences, and different ways of getting from here to there. The fact is, there is no infallible recipe to make you a perfect coach. So instead, bless all the differences. They make life interesting and create more ways for more people to enjoy the power of a coaching relationship.

A Vision for the Future

The vision was never about coaching. It was always about people living lives of radical fulfillment, balance, and aliveness. Coaching emerged as a means. We assembled pieces to create a coaching method. We talked and we read and we experimented. Coaching was given form and structure and skills. We played with what worked and discarded what didn't. We came up with a vocabulary and designed a model that we're proud of because it explains what co-active coaching is about. Over the years we have become even more excited about being coaches, training coaches, and above all spreading the word about the power of coaching to change lives. But the vision was never about coaching. It was always about people living fully, passionately, enjoying their work and giving their best.

Today the profession of coaching is still in its infancy, still finding its voice, still learning to walk. But clearly it has the size and the impact of a profession with active professional and personal coaches not only in North and South America but in Europe and the Pacific Rim. That the profession continues to grow at an impressive rate is a tribute to the human desire for excellence and the spirit of being fully alive. It is the clients of coaching who make this a profession of substance and growth.

The Making of a Profession

Ralph L. Sanderson's "Essay on Professional Ethics" lists five criteria that traditionally distinguish professionals:

- Members of a profession possess specialized knowledge or skills.
- They hold themselves to a higher ethical standard than other members of society.
- They are self-governing in the sense that they regulate entrance into the profession, monitor the performance of members, and expel those who violate their responsibilities.
- They provide important benefits to society.
- They are accorded certain rights and privileges ordinarily denied to other occupational groups.

Like a photographic print in the developing tray, the details of coaching as a profession are still emerging. Even so, it is very clear that the profession meets the founding criteria. Compare coaching today, for example, with the profession of financial planning. Back in the late 1970s there were people in various businesses who offered financial planning services to clients. But there was no official organization—no sense of financial planning as a profession the way we might think of certified public accountants. There was a need, however, for professional financial planning. Gradually, a profession of like-minded people formed with a desire to serve their clients' needs and an equal desire to protect the integrity of the profession. The movement to establish a professional identity seems to coincide with an equally powerful desire to set the *professionals* apart from other practitioners by means of ethical standards and certification.

Ethics and Standards

Holding oneself accountable for certain standards is part of being a professional. Those standards are typically developed and endorsed through a professional association. The International Coach Federation (ICF) has developed the following ethical guidelines for its members:

Preamble: A Coach believes in the dignity and integrity of every human being and is committed to eliciting the inherent capability and resourcefulness of every individual. A Coach pursues, through an interactive process, the development of client-designed strategies and solutions which move the client toward the rapid attainment of his or her goals. A Coach is respectful and protective of the vulnerability of each client, while constructively holding the client to a high standard of self-responsibility and accountability. The Coach maintains an objectivity and competence where he or she claims it and practices in the best interests of the client, the community, and society.

1. Coaching Relationship and Contract

At the beginning of any coaching relationship, ICF Coaches will articulate the terms of the Coach/Client relationship in a clear, written communication or agreement. (Such an agreement may be recordable by Web site, brochure, e-mail, or a signed paper agreement.) Terms of the Coach/Client agreement will include the qualifications of the Coach; the nature of the services available; limitations, boundaries, and perspectives of the Coach or the services offered; a Statement of Client's Rights; and terms of the contract, i.e., times, frequency, and methods of communication, and fees for the Coaching service.

2. Client Protection

The Client's well-being is the central focus of a Coaching relationship and thereby obligates the Coach to maintain a high level of integrity and trustworthiness throughout the contract. Therefore, Coaches are respectful of Clients' needs and requests; constructive in their feedback; attentive to the boundaries and limitations of each party; mindful of confidentiality issues and conflicts of interest; forthright and authentic in addressing any such issues as they emerge. The Coach will under no circumstances take advantage of a Client personally, socially, sexually, or financially. The Coach will disclose any and all personal gain accrued by the Coach/Client relationship, including, but not limited to, useful knowledge, personal growth, and fees received for referrals or recommendations made to and/or pursued by the Client. The Coach not only will communicate but will continuously demonstrate that the intended outcome of an exchange of information, discussion, referral, or recommendation is the Client's growth and well-being, not the promotion of the Coach's self-interest.

3. Confidentiality

The Coach will make every effort to honor the Client's confidence, although the Coach cannot provide an "a priori" guarantee. The Coach will advise the Client of circumstances which might influence the Coach's objectivity or judgment, and any decision, or factors relating to a decision, to reveal the client's confidential information to a higher authority. Clients will be apprised that their confidence is not privileged under law and can be subpoenaed via the Coach. To the extent that a Coach is uncomfortable holding a Client's confidence, the Coach is advised to consult a mentor coach in an effort to jointly determine how best to handle the situation. In rare cases,

if the confidential information is of an "outrageous," "illegal," or "dangerous to the client or others" nature, the Coach is obligated to consult a mentor coach, and/or an attorney, in order to determine whether to notify
authorities, with or without the Client's consent. The Client is apprised and
agrees that any materials provided by the Coach may not be resold, published, or used outside the coaching relationship without the explicit permission of the Coach.

4. Conflicts of Interest

Any conflict of interest is to be discussed and resolved with the Client's best
interest in mind. Whenever a conflict becomes apparent, the Coach is ethically obligated to identify it and attempt to resolve it. If, during the coaching relationship, the Coach cannot serve the Client objectively, respectfully,
or without internal or external conflict, the Coach is ethically obligated to
terminate the coaching agreement/contract. Such a termination provides
reasonable advance notice and a reasonable explanation of the conflict at
the center of the termination decision.

5. Referrals and Terminations

Whenever internal or external conditions arise which seem "uncoachable"
or unworkable, the Coach is ethically committed to reveal his or her observations and opinion to the Client. The Coach will suggest a viable solution(s) to
the problem, making every effort to avoid injury to the dignity of the Client.
If the solution includes a referral to another Coach, the referring Coach is ethically committed to refer to three (3) more suitable Coaches, one (1) of which
may be the ICF Referral Service. If the Coach's suggested solution includes
termination without referral, or postponement of the coaching contract until
a more suitable time, the Coach is ethically committed to provide a clear
explanation of the rationale underlying the recommendation.

6. Ethical Violations

If a Coach knowingly, consistently, or outrageously breaches the Ethical
Guidelines of the ICF, the Coach will be asked to work with a mentor Coach,
and/or be expelled from the ICF association. A Coach who receives a reprimand by the ICF is encouraged to train with a mentor Coach for a period of
months (length of time to be determined by ICF Board) or until the essence
of the complaint is corrected. Expulsion from ICF will mean that the Coach
will no longer be authorized to claim or use membership in the ICF, nor represent previous membership in the ICF, as a competency claim. A reprimand
leading to expulsion of a Coach from the ICF constitutes a forfeiture of any
prepaid dues to the organization by the Coach being expelled.

The Coaches Training Institute recommends additional rules of professional conduct:

1. We hold the content of the relationship with our clients as confidential. Even the names of our clients are confidential unless they permit us to mention or use their name.
2. We do not break the law for our clients. We do not act as accomplices to our clients' acts of violence.
3. We do not enter into financial agreements with our clients based on results—for example, the client will give you a 10 percent bonus based on the sales bonus they receive from their corporation.
4. When we enter into agreements with corporations, we regard its employees as our clients and respect their right to confidentiality.
5. We do not work with clients we cannot champion and speak of in a positive manner.
6. We manage our own Gremlins in such a way that they do not retard the client's progress.
7. We treat our colleagues, competitors, and the coaching profession with honor and respect.
8. We agree to promote the client's agenda, to point the client toward fulfillment, balance, and process, and to forward their action and deepen their learning.

These codes of professional ethics and standards give us a clearer understanding of the profession's stand in certain areas. But they are more than minimum standards of legal behavior. They are the clearest way to express the integrity that is at the very core of coaching. Even without a widely accepted code, ethical coaching would stand on its own. This is a profession that, by its nature, embraces high ethical standards. The commitment to a whole, healthy, and resourceful client ought to be reason enough for ethical behavior. Coaches should have a clear sense of values in the decisions they make and be able to conduct themselves ethically and professionally. Beyond the code of conduct agreed to by the profession, that's the deeper commitment—to integrity of self.

Referrals

The question of ethical behavior often comes up with respect to coaching boundaries. What are the limits of coaching? When is it therapy the client needs, not coaching? There is no scientifically dependable test for this decision, of course. The choice is always up to the coach.

Because there's a potential for overlap between coaching and therapy, coaches must be cautious in aspects of their practice that might invite confusion in the mind of the client. Both therapy and coaching, for example, might deal with the same difficult life circumstance such as betrayal in a relationship or failure of a business. Both therapist and coach might approach the situation similarly: looking for learning and looking for action that will lead the client to a more resourceful state. Even much of the conversation might sound similar, and in both cases the client might express deep feelings including anger, pain, tears. In this case it's up to the coach to see the big picture, to see the potential risk of offering coaching when therapy is called for, and to talk about it openly with the client. Many coaches keep a referral list for such situations when perhaps the best resource for the client is a therapist, career counselor, or other consultant.

Or perhaps this is indeed a coaching relationship, but for some reason—perhaps the client, perhaps the situation—you are not comfortable coaching. The client may be a colleague or a friend of your spouse. The client's personality may not be compatible no matter how hard you try to be professionally detached. Or you may simply decide that this client is uncoachable, at least by you. There are many reasons for deciding that the relationship won't work on the client's behalf. In this case the thing to do is face the truth with integrity and make it easy for the client to leave.

Imagine a World . . .

Those of us who have trained coaches and coached clients know the extraordinary impact coaching can have on people's lives. We've felt it in our own lives. At times it is awe inspiring. Now extrapolate from that handful of people in one person's sphere of coaching experience to a whole world where coaching is part of everyday life. In this world there are restaurants and health clubs, occupational therapists, and, yes, professional coaches. Their value and function are well understood. Today, by contrast, most coaches spend a significant amount of time simply explaining what coaching is. This widespread understanding of the essence and value of coaching would eliminate one huge step in the process of bringing people to coaching relationships. Imagine a world where the fundamental skills and approach of coaching were widely used—not just by coaches, but by everyone. What if the culture co-opted the principles of fulfillment, balance, and process and made them a basic expectation for everyone? What if the axioms we take for granted in coaching relationships found their way into everyday life? Imagine what that would be like.

In this world where fundamental coaching principles abound, people are committed to a fulfilling life and work. They are more likely to stop tolerating a second-rate life and decide they won't settle for anything less than a full way of living that uses their talents and skills completely. Kids learn that fulfillment is not something that will happen for some people some day when they are rich or famous—it's available in this moment, and the next one, and the next one for those who are on a path of fulfillment.

Imagine a world where everyone has a compelling vision of their work: a sense of choice and purpose. Imagine a world of passionate, committed people determined to make a difference in the lives of others as they live life fully themselves. This would be a world that got everybody's best, everybody's stretch, everybody's gift—instead of merely their compliance, their bodies sitting at a desk, working at a machine, or standing behind a counter with 10 percent of their brains plugged in. With coaching, the same people might be in the same jobs a year later but with an entirely different frame of reference. The whole value of work would change because it would no longer be about what job you have but about what difference you make—what values you honor in the work you do.

Imagine a world where the axioms of coaching operated everywhere: in interpersonal relationships, in work dynamics, in international relations. Imagine the difference it would make if people designed the alliance before embarking on a business project, or a relationship. What would it be like if people routinely told the truth to each other—even the hard truth—and stood up for no less than that? Imagine how our political system would change. Imagine a world where people are willing to truly listen not only to the words but to everything behind the words. Imagine a world in which you could hear and receive the hard truth and find the learning in the truth instead of diving for your defenses. What if we held out for each other and our children the biggest picture possible of what they could be instead of pointing out their limitations? What if we expected their greatness instead of expecting them to fail or fall short? What if we were fully committed to having our friends, partners, and children succeed beyond their dreams—but still left room for them to fail without making them bad, just human, and we continued to treat failure as a form of fast learning?

What if we simply acknowledged people's strengths instead of picking at their flaws?

This would be a world of curiosity and wonder and listening in extraordinary new ways. It would be a world in which we give our intuition a place to work. It would be a world where we hold each other to account for who we are and what we say we will do. In this world we are as committed to the truth about ourselves as we are to the truth we tell to others.

This would be a world that values learning and growth over comfort and looking good. Imagine a world of compelling visions let loose to create and prosper, totally supported, totally encouraged, totally celebrated. Imagine.

The Coach's Toolkit

Intake Forms and Checklists

For Use with Individual Clients

Individual Client Intake Checklist
Coaching Agreement
Personal Information Fact Sheet
Wheel of Life Exercise
Primary Focus
Individual Client Inverview
Strategic Planning Checklist
Completion Log
Coaching Preparation Form

For Use with Corporate Clients

Corporate Client Intake Checklist
First Meeting Checklist
Corporate Client Profile
Performance Awareness Appraisal
Job Performance Wheel
Management/Leadership Wheel

Additional Coaching Forms

Coaching Definition
Wheel of Life Exercise
Priorities Wheel
Management Competencies Wheel
Blank Wheel
Planning Wheel
Merry-Go-Round
Goals and Commitments
Daily Habits
Daily Habits Tracking Log
Action and Planning Log
Gremlin Clarification
Saying Yes—Saying No

Coaching Exercises

Future Self
Life Purpose
Values Clarification

Coaching Resources

Powerful Questions
Inquiries
Structures
Sample Co-Active Coaching Skills List

Intake Forms and Checklists
for Use with Individual Clients

These sample forms represent a possible approach when working with individual clients, especially during the coaching intake session. Please do not think that these are the "right" forms to be used. They are supplied here to give you a sense of direction and to support you in creating your own forms that reflect your style and approach to coaching.

Individual Client Intake Checklist

(Items to go over with the client)

1. Welcome the client.
2. Explain how the session will go today.
3. Explain about coaching.
4. Outline your background.
5. Discuss confidentiality and security.
6. Ask the client, "May I mention that you are a client?"
7. Design the alliance: "How do you want to be coached?"
8. Grant the coaching relationship power.
9. Explain balance and score the Wheel of Life.
10. Discuss values clarification and explain the Gremlin.
11. Fill out the Primary Focus form.
12. Review any other forms: Strategic Planning Checklist, Calendar, etc.
13. Fill out on the Completion Log any actions to be taken.
14. Set up the next three appointments in calendars.
15. Discuss how the calls will go, explain about the inquiry, and remind the client about the "ups and downs" of the process.
16. Fill out Coaching Agreement and Client Information forms, noting the impact of vacations, late or missed calls, and other arrangements.
17. Receive money for the intake session and the first month. Explain about the monthly billing process (written invoice or phone invoice).
18. Talk about the issue of commitment, about being human, and about learning and change taking time.
19. Other:
20. Thank the client and express your eagerness to begin work.

Coaching Agreement

Client Name: _____

This agreement, between coach _____ and the above-named client will begin on _____ and will continue for a minimum of three months. The fee for the initial meeting is $_____ and the fee for the initial three months is $_____ per month, payable in advance each month.

The services to be provided by the coach to the client are coaching or tele-coaching, as designed jointly with the client. Coaching, which is not advice, therapy, or counseling, may address specific personal projects, business successes, or general conditions in the client's life or profession. Other coaching services include value clarification, brainstorming, identifying plans of action, examining modes of operating in life, asking clarifying questions, and making empowering requests.

Upon completion of the three months, coaching will convert to a month-to-month basis. The client and coach agree to provide one another with a fourteen-day notice in the event it is desired to cancel further services. It should be noted that an average of four weeks per month is used in calculating the monthly fee.

The coach promises the client that all information provided to the coach will be kept strictly confidential.

Throughout the working relationship the coach will engage in direct and personal conversations. The client can count on the coach to be honest and straightforward in asking questions and making requests. The client understands that the power of the coaching relationship can only be granted by the client—and the client agrees to do just that: have the coaching relationship be powerful. If the client believes the coaching is not working as desired, the client will communicate and take action to return the power to the coaching relationship.

Our signatures on this agreement indicate full understanding of and agreement with the information outlined above.

_____ _____ _____ _____
Client   Date   Coach   Date

Personal Information Fact Sheet

All personal information is confidential and treated appropriately.

Client Information

Full name _____

Name you like to be called _____

Address _____

_____

Telephone Numbers

Home telephone _____ Work telephone _____

Message and/or car telephone _____

Pager and/or other telephone _____

Fax number _____ E-mail address _____

Employment Information

Occupation (what you do to earn a living) _____

Employer name _____

Personal Information

Date of birth _____

Marital status_____ Number of children _____

Significant other's (S O's) name _____

S O's date of birth _____

Wedding/special anniversary date _____

Name(s) and age(s) of child(ren) _____

_____

Wheel of Life Exercise

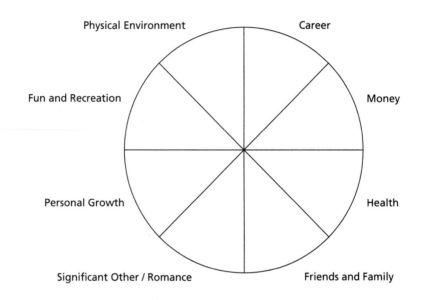

Directions: The eight sections in the Wheel of Life represent balance. Regarding the center of the wheel as 0 and the outer edge as 10, rank your level of satisfaction with each life area by drawing a straight or curved line to create a new outer edge (see example). The new perimeter of the circle represent the Wheel of Life. How bumpy would the ride be if this were a real wheel?

Example

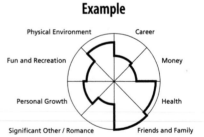

Primary Focus

Identify five areas that you want held as your main focus during this coaching relationship. For each focus area provide a simple heading and a description of a measurable result. For example:

BE MORE PRODUCTIVE.
I have a system to follow up on calls and letters, I'm on time, I get all tasks accomplished, I have realistic goals for new projects.

1. _____

   _____

   _____

2. _____

   _____

   _____

3. _____

   _____

   _____

4. _____

   _____

   _____

5. _____

   _____

   _____

Individual Client Interview

As a coach, it's important for me to understand how you view the world in general and yourself in particular. Each person has a unique way of thinking and a unique way of interacting with those around him or her.

Answer each of these questions as clearly and thoughtfully as possible, expressing the best of who you are. These are "pondering" questions designed to stimulate your thinking in a particular way that will make our work together even more productive. I suggest that you take several days to compose your responses to these questions. Thank you.

1. What accomplishments must, in your opinion, occur during your lifetime so that you will consider your life to have been satisfying and well lived—a life of few or no regrets?

   _____

   _____

   _____

2. If there were a secret passion in your life, what would it be?

   _____

   _____

   _____

3. What do you consider your role to be in your local community? In the United States? In the world?

   _____

   _____

   _____

4. If you could devote your life to serving others—and still have the money and lifestyle you need—would you do it? How would it look?

_____

_____

_____

5. If you trusted your coach enough to tell him or her how to manage you most effectively, what tips would you give?

_____

_____

_____

6. If you had a five-year goal and you had the continuing services of a coach to help you make it happen (and money were not an issue), what would that goal be? What difference would working with a coach make?

_____

_____

_____

7. What's missing in your life? What would make your life more fulfilling?

_____

_____

_____

8. Do you believe in God or in the concept of a higher power? If so, describe the most useful and empowering aspects of your relationship with God. If not, what reference point do you use?

_____

_____

_____

Strategic Planning Checklist

(Items to be evaluated for action and calendaring on a weekly basis)

1. What is important for me to do this week?

2. What career or business issues needs to be planned for or acted on?

3. What can I do to increase my Values or Wheel of Life scores?

4. What family member/friend/colleague/employee shall I connect with this week?

5. What birthday or special occasion do I need to plan for?

6. _____

7. _____

8. _____

9. _____

10. _____

11. _____

12. _____

13. _____

14. _____

15. _____

Completion Log
(To be used by coach and/or client)

Item to Complete	Do By	Done
1.		
2.		
3.		
4.		
5.		
6.		
7.		
8.		
9.		
10.		
11.		
12.		
13.		
14.		
15.		
16.		
17.		

Coaching Preparation Form

(Note: Some clients fax or e-mail this information prior to the coaching session.)

Preparing for the coaching session will allow you to optimize your results and our time together. Prior to the session, you may wish to answer the following questions:

1. How am I, today, right now? How has my week been?

   _____

   _____

2. What do I want to get out of the call today?

   _____

   _____

3. What action did I take since our last session? What were my wins/challenges?

   _____

   _____

4. What do I have to report? What do I want to be held accountable for?

   _____

   _____

5. What issues do I want to deepen on our call today? What are the challenges, concerns, achievements, or areas of learning to be addressed?

   _____

   _____

6. Debrief of last week's inquiry:

   _____

   _____

7. What else?

   _____

   _____

Intake Forms and Checklists
for Use with Corporate Clients

These forms are geared toward corporate clients. Only a few samples are provided here because there are many vehicles currently available, such as 360-degree feedback and regular performance appraisals. Again, identify what would best serve you, drawing from this and the previous section.

Corporate Client Intake Checklist

1. Before the initial session have a conversation with the client. Let the client know what to expect, what to bring (such as calendar or performance reviews), how much time it will take, and anything else that would allow the client to get prepared and look forward to the session.
2. Be sure the environment and room setup for the first meeting are safe, quiet, and not distracting. No phones, beepers, or other machines are allowed to intrude.
3. Welcome the client and set the tone. Let the client know of your eagerness to work with him or her.
4. Explain how the session will proceed: the amount of time, whether you will be taking notes, whether he or she might want to take notes, a sense of what will be covered (balance, values, goals, action plans, other), information on what will result from this session, and anything else that will inform and put the client at ease.
5. Discuss coaching and explain how it has developed as a profession. Cite examples of people (with their permission) who have used coaching and how it has benefited them. Tell the client about the kind of tools you might be using, about the options for how often you will meet, whether by phone or in person, and so on. Give an overview of coaching, not the details. Indicate here that the coaching relationship is one of design and alliance.
6. Discuss your background. Now ask for permission to coach the client.
7. Describe confidentiality and define exactly what it will mean. (If complete confidentiality is not possible, design the ground rules together—for example, the coach will report only when the client is present or the client will report and inform the coach. Assure the client you understand the impact of confidentiality on the effectiveness of coaching and will always be conscious and sensitive to that. This is the time to begin building trust—the keystone of the designed alliance.
8. Explain in detail how clients design the alliance to get them where they want to go. Then design the alliance, giving the client examples of how you might work with him or her. Include accountability, brainstorming, the amount of attention to the client's personal life, skill development, 360-degree feedback, and the like.

9. Explore values clarification and the Gremlin, and do some form of vision work.

10. Fill out the Primary Focus form with the client. It is useful to include some personal area of focus from his or her personal life or personal development. In this way the client learns that the coaching is personal, not just about his or her job. This is where the client discusses what's really important. Plan to spend a good bit of time on this step.

11. Review other forms and tools you may find useful, such as planning calendars, information tracking forms, and personal inventory forms.

12. Design clear goals with due dates, and ensure that these items get posted in the client's calendar. Define accountability and illustrate how it works. Assure the client that he or she is the designer of action plans, and that the coach is not a disciplinarian.

13. Discuss the anticipated high and the corresponding low (the loss of enthusiasm that often occurs four to eight weeks into the coaching). Explain that it is the client who grants the coaching relationship power, ask that he or she do so, and ask if you may remind him or her of this from time to time. Point to the expected emergence of the Gremlin.

14. Discuss how future coaching sessions will go. Set up future session times and establish ground rules for tardiness, missed sessions, vacations, and other interruptions.

15. Set up the nature of assignments and inquiries.

16. Close the session with optimism and a potent sense of the client's future.

First Meeting Checklist

Coach: _____

Phone: _____

E-mail: _____

Meeting time and location: _____

Bring the following items to the first meeting:

- Completed Client Profile
- Personal planner/calendar and notepaper

Corporate Client Profile

Please take time to answer the questions on the following pages. Some of the questions capture information about where you are today. Others will get you thinking about what you want from coaching, from your job, and from life in general. This information will set a good foundation and allow us to move forward.

Bring Your Copy to the First Meeting.

Client Information

General
Name _____

Mailing address _____

Mail stop _____

Building number _____

Department _____

Home telephone _____

Work telephone _____

Fax number _____

E-mail address _____

Work Information
Job title _____

Years with company _____

Coaching

1. What do you want to make sure you get from the coaching relationship?

_____

_____

_____

2. How do you want me to be as your coach?

_____

_____

_____

3. Other:

_____

_____

_____

Job

1. What do you want from your job?

_____

_____

2. What projects are you leading?

_____

_____

_____

3. What are your key job goals?

_____

_____

_____

4. What skills or knowledge are you developing?

_____

_____

_____

5. How do your job goals support your personal goals?

_____

_____

_____

6. What else can you do to advance the company's objectives?

_____

_____

_____

Personal

1. What do you have to contribute that is unique?

_____

_____

_____

2. What special knowledge do you have?

_____

_____

_____

the coach's toolkit

3. What do you believe in?

_____

_____

_____

4. What do you do when you're really up against it?

_____

_____

_____

5. What activities have meaning and heart for you?

_____

_____

_____

6. What needs in the world are you moved to meet?

_____

_____

_____

7. What two steps could you take immediately that would make the greatest difference in your current situation(s)?

_____

_____

_____

8. What can I say to you when you are most "stuck" that will return you to action?

_____

_____

_____

Performance Awareness Appraisal

Note the performance skills asked of you in the performance of your job. Mark where you are today with an X. Mark where you want to be with an O.

Skill or Quality	Scale 0–10 Importance	
	To Me	To Company
1.		
2.		
3.		
4.		
5.		
6.		
7.		
8.		
9.		
10.		

Low   High
0   2   4   6   8   10

Job Performance Wheel

Directions: Score your sense of satisfaction with the above labeled aspects of your job performance. If one does not apply, replace it with a more appropriate label. Use the scale of 0 to 10 to assess your performance. Identify areas you wish to improve. Determine what actions you will take to improve your scores.

Management/Leadership Wheel

Organizing and Staffing

Planning and Budgeting

Controlling and
Problem Solving

Promoting
Stability and
Order

Promoting
Change

Motivating and
Inspiring

Establishing Direction

Aligning People

Directions: Score (0 to 10) your satisfaction with your ability to:

▓ **Planning and Budgeting:** establishing detailed steps and timetables for achieving results and then allocating the resources necessary to make it happen

▓ **Establishing Direction:** developing a vision of the future, often the distant future, and strategies for producing the changes needed to achieve that vision

▓ **Organizing and Staffing:** establishing a structure for accomplishing plan requirements, staffing that structure with people, delegating authority for carrying out the plan, providing policies and procedures to guide people, and creating methods or systems to monitor implementation

▓ **Aligning People:** communicating the direction by words and deeds to all those whose cooperation may be needed so as to create a team that understands the vision and strategies and accepts their validity

- **Controlling and Problem Solving:** monitoring results in detail, identifying deviation from the plan, and then organizing to solve these problems

- **Motivating and Inspiring:** energizing people to overcome major political, bureaucratic, and resource barriers to change by satisfying basic, but often unfulfilled, human needs

- **Promoting Stability and Order:** creating the potential of consistently producing key results

- **Promoting Change:** creating the potential of producing useful change (such as desired new products)

Additional Coaching Forms

(To be used during future coaching sessions)

Coaching

A powerful alliance designed to forward and enhance the lifelong process of human learning, effectiveness, and fulfillment.

Wheel of Life Exercise

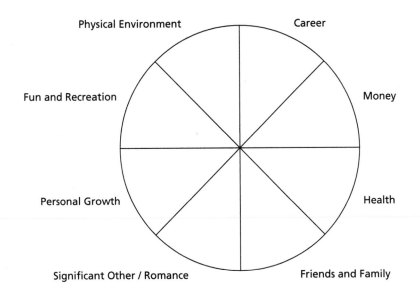

Directions: The eight sections in the Wheel of Life represent balance. Regarding the center of the wheel as 0 and the outer edge as 10, rank your level of satisfaction with each life area by drawing a straight or curved line to create a new outer edge (see example). The new perimeter of the circle represent the Wheel of Life. How bumpy would the ride be if this were a real wheel?

Example

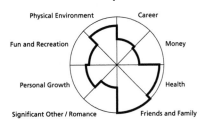

Priorities Wheel

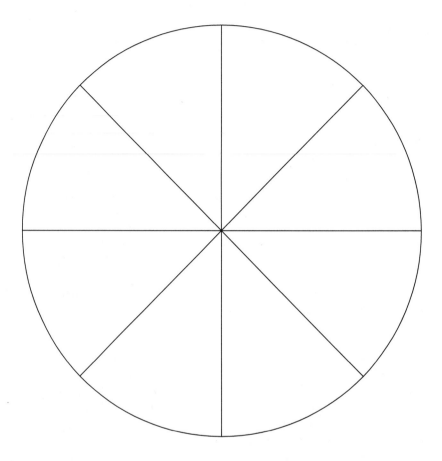

Directions: Using the "Wheel of Life" model, label this wheel with eight priorities in your job or your life. Upon completion of the labeling, score your sense of satisfaction with your priorities on a scale from 0 to 10. Identify one or two scores that you want to impact immediately. What actions will you take? When will you take these actions? What support do you require to ensure that the actions occur?

Management Competencies Wheel

Directions: The eight sections in the Wheel of Life represent balance. Regarding the center of the wheel as 0 and the outer edge as 10, rank your level of satisfaction with each competency area by drawing a straight or curved line to create a new outer edge (see example). The new perimeter of the circle represents the Wheel of Life. How bumpy would the ride be if this were a real wheel?

Example

Blank Wheel

(To be labeled by coach or client)

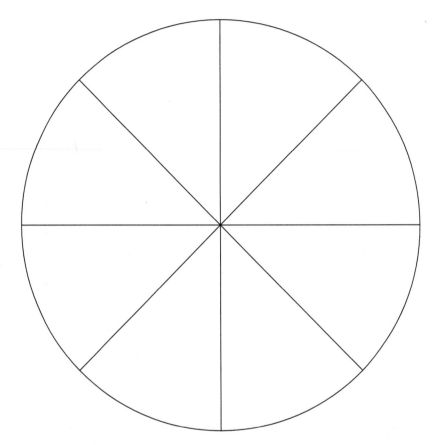

Planning Wheels

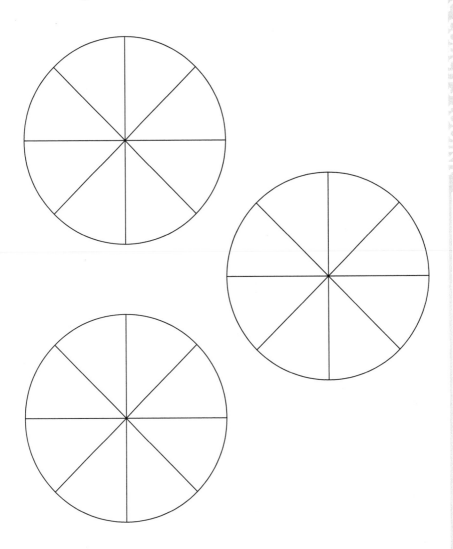

Directions: Label each wheel with the name of a wedge from a previous wheel (for example, the Wheel of Life) or with a desired outcome. Label the wedges with results or actions pertinent to the wheel title, and use the resultant wheel for creating a game plan.

Merry-Go-Round

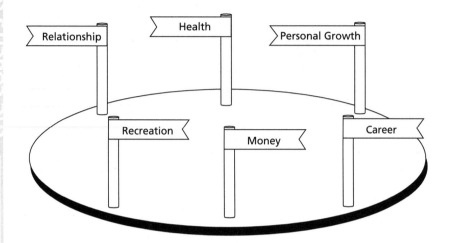

Goals and Commitments

When you have a goal, there is a specific point in time by which you either have accomplished it or not. It is measurable and specific. You have either increased your income by 30 percent by July 31st or not. Commitments are ongoing quality-of-life shifts. A commitment is not measurable. It may have to do with the state or quality of *being* you want to create in your life. "I am committed to having joy, self-expression, and community in my work" and "I am committed to loving and celebrating my body" are both examples of commitments. Using the Wheel of Life as your guide, identify your goals (with specific due dates) and your commitments.

		Goals	**Commitments**
Career	1.	_____	_____
	2.	_____	_____
Money	1.	_____	_____
	2.	_____	_____
Health	1.	_____	_____
	2.	_____	_____
Friends and Family	1.	_____	_____
	2.	_____	_____
Significant Other	1.	_____	_____
	2.	_____	_____
Personal Growth	1.	_____	_____
	2.	_____	_____
Fun and Recreation	1.	_____	_____
	2.	_____	_____
Physical Environment	1.	_____	_____
	2.	_____	_____

Daily Habits

Small constructive actions done on a daily or routine basis can quickly give you a sense of accomplishment and forward momentum. These daily habits (or success practices) form the foundation on which major change takes place. Take a look at your "Wheel of Life" score to get ideas for habits that would support you in moving forward. What action, if taken on a regular basis, would make a difference for you in one of the areas of the wheel? These habits can be related to either your professional or your personal life (i.e., process all incoming mail daily, exercise four times per week). Remember those things that will nourish you and provide you with satisfaction, such as spending twenty minutes a day with your children or thirty minutes on spontaneous self-indulgence, soaking in a hot tub and/or getting a massage twice a week, taking a walk in the woods three times a week, calling one close friend a day, etc.

1. _____

2. _____

3. _____

4. _____

5. _____

6. _____

7. _____

8. _____

9. _____

10. _____

Daily Habits Tracking Log

New Daily Habits for the Month of _____

Habit	1	2	3	4	5	6	7	8	9	10	11	12	13	14	15	16	17	18	19	20	21	22	23	24	25	26	27	28	29	30	31
1.																															
2.																															
3.																															
4.																															
5.																															
6.																															
7.																															
8.																															
9.																															
10.																															

Directions: Write your new daily habits in the space provided. Each day, color in the box for that day and that habit to track your progress. The objective is to fill in all the boxes during the month. You may take weekends off.

Action and Planning Log

(Use this form to write down specific To Do's and Long-Term Goals)

To Do's

Action Item   **Date Action
                                                   to Be Taken**

_____   _____

_____   _____

_____   _____

_____   _____

_____   _____

_____   _____

_____   _____

Long-Term Goals

_____

_____

_____

_____

_____

Gremlin Clarification

My Gremlin's name is:

_____

My Gremlin is fond of saying or often says:

_____

_____

_____

_____

_____

Inside my organization/community/family, Gremlin comments we use are:

_____

_____

_____

Saying Yes—Saying No

By saying YES to   **I am saying NO to:**

1. _____ _____

          _____

2. _____ _____

          _____

3. _____ _____

          _____

4. _____ _____

          _____

By saying NO to   **I am saying YES to:**

1. _____ _____

          _____

2. _____ _____

          _____

3. _____ _____

          _____

4. _____ _____

          _____

Coaching Exercises

The exercises that follow have been referenced throughout the book. Greater detail is provided here to enable the coach to better deliver such potent exercises to the client during the intake or in a future coaching session.

Future Self Exercise

The following visualizations are based on a future self exercise used in The Coaches Training Institute workshop. Feel free to use these exact words. We recommend that you have the client get comfortable, perhaps lower the light level, make sure there will be no distractions, and play quiet, meditative music. When the client is grounded and ready, begin the visualization. Pause at appropriate times throughout the visualization to give the client sufficient time to be with the location or answer the questions. Allow a little time at the end for debriefing, but make the continued exploration of the visualization the homework for the upcoming week. The week after debriefing the visualization in detail, do the second visualization exercise to reveal the gift the future self will be giving the client.

Visualization 1

Get into a comfortable position. Now allow your eyes to close and begin by focusing your awareness on your breath. Breathing in and breathing out. Breathing in easily and effortlessly. Then breathing out. Each breath allows you to become more relaxed and comfortable. Outside sounds only allow you to go deeper inside: a reminder of how good it is to leave the noise and stress of the outside world and journey into the quiet and peace of your own inner world.

(Include the next paragraph only when you want the client to go to an even deeper meditative space.)

> As you allow yourself to go deeper into a state of relaxation, perhaps you can remember a time when you stood before a pond or a lake and it was quiet and peaceful. You may have tossed a pebble into the center and noticed the ripples spreading out. One ripple after another, flowing outward, farther and farther. The ripples slowing down, becoming farther apart, until the water was once again calm and peaceful. I'm going to invite you now to imagine that your body is like that body of water. And as you drop a pebble into the center of your body, you can feel ripples of relaxation rippling out.

Waves of relaxation flowing through your body. Up through your torso into your chest and your back. Up through the vertebrae and spreading out into each and every muscle of your back. Through your shoulders and arms, up through your neck, your jaw, face, scalp. Feeling those ripples relax you as your muscles let go and become soft and loose. Feeling the ripples of relaxation flowing down the bottom of your torso. Flowing through your abdomen and your pelvis. Down through your thighs, calves, ankles, and toes. Know that each time you drop a pebble into the center of your body you can become more relaxed.

As you become more relaxed, you find yourself becoming more quiet and peaceful. Now bring your attention to the spot between your eyes: the third eye. Imagine a light there. What color is the light between your eyes?

Now imagine that light becoming a beam that extends out into space. Follow that beam as it leaves this building, as it travels above the city, as it continues out, so that you can make out the entire area. Keep going further and further out into outer space and notice the curvature of the earth. As you keep going further and further out, you find yourself enveloped by the softness and quiet of space. Notice the big blue-green ball below you with the white clouds wisping around it. Allow yourself to enjoy this perspective for a moment.

Now notice another beam of light very near to you, a different color from the one you followed into outer space. Begin to follow that beam back down to earth. The beam is taking you back to earth twenty years from now, twenty years into the future. Keep following this beam down, noticing the curvature of the earth and the geography stretched out below you. As you come closer to the end of the beam, keep noticing where you are. This is where your future self lives, you, twenty years from now. Come into contact with earth and notice where you are. Notice what dwelling or nature surrounds you. Now move to the dwelling of your future self. What does it look like? What kind of landscape does it have? Are there trees? Flowers? What kind? Get a sense of this place.

Now get someone to come to the door. On the other side of the door is your future self waiting to greet you: yourself twenty years from now. As the door opens, what do you notice? Greet your future self and notice the way your future self returns your greeting, welcoming you into this time and place twenty years in the future. Take in this person—your future self. What does this person look like? Notice how this person stands, what this person is wearing. Get a sense of this person's essence. Notice the inside of this dwelling. What kind of person lives here? What are the colors of this place?

Now move with your future self to a comfortable place for a conversation. Perhaps your future self offers you something to drink. Settle in and make yourself comfortable for a talk with your future self. There are questions that you might want to ask your future self. Begin by asking: "What is it, future self, that you most remember about the last twenty years?" Take a moment now to hear the answer. (*Pause.*) Now ask your future self the following question: "What do I need to know to get me from where I am now to where you are? What would be most helpful?" Listen to what your future self has to tell you. (*Pause.*) Good.

Now take a moment and ask your future self your own questions. What other questions would you like to ask your future self? (*Pause.*) And now ask your future self one final question before you go: "What name, other than your first name, are you called by? A special name. It could be a metaphor or a symbol of your essence. What is this name?" (*Pause.*) Good. Bringing this visit with your future self to a close, thank this person for being here with you today and sharing so much wisdom.

Now find your way back to the beam of light and journey back up the beam, watching this world twenty years in the future grow ever smaller as you move out into space. Again you see the ball of blue and green below you, clouds swirling around it. Notice that your beam of light has intersected with a different beam of light that will take you back to this year and this location. Follow this beam of light back to the present time on earth. As you travel down this beam, notice the earth growing bigger and bigger. Moving further down the beam, notice the geography of the area, the skyline and landscape of the area, and, finally, come back into the room here. Good. In a few moments I'm going to count from three to one. At the count of one, you will be refreshed and alert, as if you've had the perfect amount of rest, knowing you can remember everything you wish of this inner journey.

When you open your eyes, please remain silent and jot down things you want to remember about your journey. *Three.* Coming back to present time, becoming more alert and refreshed. *Two.* Stretching your body, feeling the ground beneath you. And *one.* Eyes open, refreshed and alert.

Visualization 2

Just make yourself comfortable and allow your eyes to close and begin by taking long, slow, deep breaths. Breathing in through your nose and holding it . . . and breathing out through your mouth. Just allow yourself to be aware of your breathing. Easily, naturally, and freely.

I'm going to invite you to take a mental inventory of your body now. Beginning at the top of your head, become aware of any tension or tightness you might find. And just give that tension or tightness a color and let it drain out the tips of your toes and the tips of your fingers. Just allow that tension or tightness to drain away. And moving down your body bring your attention to your neck and arms. Again, if you find any tension or tightness, just let it drain away. Take your awareness now down along your back, down into your abdomen and pelvic area. Again, notice any tightness you might find there and just eliminate it. Imagine it just melting away, draining out through the tips of your toes. Noticing if there is any tension or tightness in your legs or your ankles and feet and just allow it to drain out your toes. Now imagine you're like a strong and sturdy tree, putting roots down into the ground, allowing those roots to go deeper and deeper, spreading out, connecting you solidly to the earth.

Now bring your attention to the spot between your eyes: the third eye. Imagine a light there. What color is the light between your eyes? Now imagine that light becoming a beam that extends out into space. Follow that beam as it leaves this building, as it travels above the city, as it continues out, so that you can make out the entire area. Keep on going further and further out into outer space and notice the curvature of the earth. As you keep going further and further out, you find yourself enveloped by the softness and quiet of space. Notice the big blue-green ball below you with the white clouds wisping around it. Allow yourself to enjoy this perspective for a moment.

Now notice another beam of light very near to you, a different color from the one you followed into outer space. Begin to follow that beam back down to earth. The beam is taking you back to earth twenty years from now, twenty years into the future. Keep following this beam down, noticing the curvature of the earth and the geography stretched out below you. As you come closer to the end of the beam, keep noticing where you are. This is where your future self lives, you, twenty years from now. Come into contact with earth and notice where you are.

Now move to the dwelling of your future self. You know the way. You've been here before. Your future self is waiting for you. Waiting to talk with you. As your future self greets you, notice what it is like being with this person again. Look around you. Drink up the environment. Notice the colors here.

Now is your opportunity to ask whatever questions you'd like of your future self. You might want to know your next step. Who you need to be right now in order to move forward. Or ask your future self anything that feels right to you. (*Pause.*) Now take a moment to listen to your future self's response. (*Long pause.*)

I am going to invite you now to take a deep breath and allow yourself to step into the being of your future self. Allow yourself to merge into this person's body. Experience what it feels like to be this future self. Be aware of how you feel. Of how good it feels in your future self's body. What does the world look like through your future self's eyes? Walk around, feeling yourself move as your future self. Notice if there's one particular place in your body where you can feel your future self's power most strongly. This is the power of being your future self. Allow that feeling to expand, filling your whole body, into your very cells. You may want to touch that place on your body now to anchor that feeling. And know that whenever you wish to connect with your future self, you can touch that place on your body and bring forth these positive, powerful feelings. When you touch that place, these feelings and this experience will flood your body, easily and effortlessly.

Now, looking out through your future self's eyes, look at your present-day self. What do you notice about your present-day self? Looking out through your future self's eyes, what is it that you want to tell your present-day self? (*Pause.*)

Now take a deep breath and shift your awareness, leaving the body of your future self and becoming your present-day self once again. Allow yourself to be fully present in the body of your present-day self.

As you look back at your future self, notice that this person has a gift for you: a special gift to remind you of who you are becoming and what you are moving toward. As your future self offers you the gift, ask if there's any meaning to it. Is there anything you need to know about it? (*Pause.*)

It's time to leave now. Thank your future self for the wisdom. From now on your future self will be an inner resource you can use whenever you need to. Whenever you seek guidance, whenever you need to know what your next step should be, you can contact your future self, a powerful ally and resource for you. Say goodbye now, knowing that you will remember everything you need to from this visit.

Now find your way back to the beam of light and journey back up the beam, watching this world twenty years in the future grow ever smaller as you move out into space. Again you see the ball of blue and green below you, clouds swirling around it. Notice that your beam of light has intersected with the first beam of light that will take you back to this year and this location. Follow this beam of light back to present-time earth. As you travel down this beam, notice the earth growing bigger and bigger. Moving further down the beam, notice the geography of the area, the skyline and landscape, and, finally, come back into the room here. Good. In a few moments I will count from three to one. At the count of one, you will be refreshed and alert as if you've had the perfect amount of rest, knowing you can remember everything you wish of this inner journey.

Three. Coming back now, coming back to present time, becoming more alert and refreshed. *Two.* Stretching your body, feeling the ground beneath you. And *one.* Eyes open, refreshed and alert.

Life Purpose Exercise

We say that people are born with a life purpose. Some people never look for their purpose and so it remains unspoken their whole lives. But it is there. The life purpose is the reason we are on this planet. It is the thing we are meant to accomplish, the gift we are meant to bring. Life purpose is not about a job or even an avocation. It is the round-the-clock, twenty-four-hour, every-day-of-your-life expression of who you are when you are reaching your full potential.

When clients are "on purpose" they are fulfilled. They are contributing and making a difference. When they are not on purpose, they feel discontented and unfulfilled. Even if clients don't have a life purpose statement, they still have a life purpose. Even if they can't articulate a life purpose statement to their satisfaction, they can tell the difference between when they are on purpose and when they are not on purpose. It is very challenging for them to *not* do this purpose. It feels terrible, dead, disconnected.

The coach's job is to work with clients to design a life purpose statement they can use as they clarify their purpose in the world. Such a statement allows them to connect with their life purpose easily and quickly. The life purpose statement is like a big neon sign that will help them find their way out of the swamp when they get stuck. Because it is a personal statement for the client's own use, it can be as grand and sweeping or as transformational as the client can stand. It is not open to the ridicule or judgment of others.

The process we use for finding and articulating a life purpose statement follows a series of steps.

1. The coach presents a visualization or exercise that generates impressions and allows clients to gather insight about their life purpose. (Four visualizations are included in this section.)
2. Coach and client debrief the visualization(s), looking for the impact the client wants to create. Client and coach brainstorm and collaborate. Here the coach's job is to listen and keep encouraging all the words that come out of the visualizations. The coach listens for any repeated words or common themes. The coach also uses his or her intuition to sense the impact words or phrases. Life purpose coaching is extraordinarily intuitive. The client and coach keep listening for the words that have the strongest "hit."

The coach compiles the big hit words and replays them for the client so the client can hear them and see which ones resonate most. This forms the beginning of an impact statement.

This initial impact statement is likely to be general: "I want people to be happy." "I want people to be in better relationships." The problem with a general impact statement like this is that it is too vague to motivate the client to action. So the coaching then focuses on taking the client deeper into the impact so it is more specific and the client has something to grab on to. The impact statement needs to be clear enough and strong enough so that the client can access it when he or she is off course. It describes the impact (naturally) the client wants to have, such as to have people embrace life, act authentically, see their true selves, find their personal power, discover their creativity, experience their magnificence, or restore them to life.

3. Once the impact statement is found, the next step is to find a metaphor that captures the essential quality of the life purpose. For example, "I am the magician . . ." "I am the lighthouse . . ." "I am the dynamite . . ." "I am the rock in the shoe . . ." "I am the alarm clock . . ."

   The metaphor can also be an action: "I wake people up . . ." "I explode the lies . . ." "I uncover the inner truth . . ." "I call people home . . ."

   Note that finding a metaphor is generally not easy for clients. It is often hard for them to see themselves in the form of a metaphor or image. Also note that finding a life purpose statement takes time. It is a process of peeling back the layers to get at the essence of a person's purpose. In this initial coaching session on life purpose the client will likely find one version that is rough but workable. It may take months or years to refine the statement. The metaphor also may change over time. The goal is to find a version that rings true for the client, knowing there is more work to be done.

The metaphor and impact statement should be concise and should create maximum impact for the client—in general, not more than fifteen words maximum. The life purpose statement should follow this general format:

I am the _____(metaphor) so that
people _____ (impact statement).

The following are examples of life purpose statements:

I am the lighthouse that guides people to their dreams.

I am the dynamite that transforms people's lives.

I am the rock in the shoe that causes people to remember to be alive.

I am the alarm clock that awakens people to their magnificence.

Note that life purpose statements can be corny, grandiose, and flowery. All of that is okay. These are not for publication. They are for you and your clients to use in order for the clients to fully feel the power of the life purpose in them. The coach needs to champion and encourage clients to create a truly *big* life purpose statement. The life purpose is not something they will necessarily accomplish in this lifetime, but it should have tremendous, compelling power to motivate clients to be in action in their lives and to be on purpose. The visualizations are just the beginning—a place to start to collect the raw material. There are lots of additional ways to have clients envision their life purpose. They can draw pictures of their life purpose, or find a piece of music to use as their theme song. Encourage clients to be creative and look for whatever inspiration they can find to help them articulate their life purpose. The coach's role is to encourage, to continue ongoing coaching in order to clarify the statement, and, of course, to use life purpose in the coaching as clients look at what will be fulfilling for them in their lives.

Visualization 1

Imagine that you're in a large group of people milling about in front of a stage. Up on the stage is your future self. Your future self begins to speak to this large group of people. Suddenly you become aware of a shift that has come over you and the entire audience. Your future self has in some way had a profound impact on you and on the rest of the people in the audience. You are all altered or changed in some fundamental way. Aware of this impact on yourself and others, you leave the room altered for the rest of your life.

Questions:

What was the impact your future self had on you and the others?

How were you and the others transformed?

Who was your future self being to have such an impact?

Visualization 2

Turn the clock back and look at a time in your life when you felt your full power—a time when your spine, arms, and fingertips were tingling with excitement, a time when you simply didn't care what anyone thought of you. You were absolutely alive! (Pause)

Questions:

Where were you?

What were you doing?

Who was around you?

What was occurring in them at that time?

What was your impact on them?

Visualization 3

Return to the auditorium once more. The stage is there and a large group of people are milling about. There is a buzz in the room. Everything is the same as before except this time it is you on stage. Look out over the crowd. Feel the feelings you have as you are about to address the gathering. Just as you step up to the microphone, time freezes for an instant and you hear a voice in your ear that says your name and then says, "In the next thirty seconds you will have a chance to have any impact you want on this entire group. It will be only one chance, one impact, but all of these people will be changed in some way; they will have a different life because of the impact you have had on them. Thirty seconds. 15 . . . 10-9-8-7-6-5-4-3-2-1."

Question:

What impact did you have? What happened to the people?

Visualization 4

You are getting into a rocket ship. The rocket ship takes off. You are on your way to an undeveloped planet in the universe. It's a fine planet in every way, but it's uninhabited. You can create this planet however you want it to be created. You have the power to have it be any way you want. When you land, what is it that you're going to make happen—what's the impact you want to have, that's going to create the planet the way you want it to be? (Pause)

The ship is landing on the planet. The door opens. You touch the planet and say, "It's going to be this way." What is "this way?"

Values Clarification Exercise

Values are who we *are*. Not who we would like to be. Not who we think we should be. Who I *am* in my life, who we *are* in our lives, right now. Another way to put it is that values represent our unique and individual essence, our ultimate and most fulfilling form of expressing and relating. Our values serve as a compass pointing out what it means to be true to oneself. When we honor our values on a regular and consistent basis life is good, life is fulfilling.

As coaches we know how beneficial it can be for clients when they are clear about their own values. Important life decisions are easier to make and more fulfilling when the decisions are viewed through a matrix of well-understood personal values. However, the process of clarifying values is often difficult for clients. Frequently the process makes people intellectualize and fantasize, whereas you want them to look into their lives and uncover the values that are already there, in their day-to-day actions and interactions. That's one of the reasons selecting values from a list seldom works: the list becomes an opportunity to vote on the most desirable or socially acceptable values, rather than serving as a mechanism to identify who we are. Selecting values from a list reinforces the intellectual urge to figure it out and get the words *right*. Clients' values are observable, they live in the world; thus clients won't benefit from picking their values from a list. The coach's job is to assist the client in viewing his or her life in such a way that existing values are revealed.

Sometimes clients can't seem to get a perspective on their values. Coaching works well in such cases because the coach can ask questions and provide scenarios that take clients into their *lives* rather than into their *heads*. Values clarification coaching allows clients to examine and articulate their values in a safe yet courageous environment. The exact wording will matter to the client in the long run, but in the short run what is most important is that the approximate label for the value resonates with the client. As a practical matter for coaches, values clarification is enormously helpful in learning to know the client, and in helping the client know him- or herself. Coaches and clients use values to help facilitate fulfilling choices, to strategize appropriate actions, and to recognize situations in which values are an issue.

Many clients nevertheless struggle with finding the right words. They are constrained because they feel they have to find the perfect word and the value has much more emotional meaning than the definition of a single word allows. In fact, each individual has his or her own unique meaning for each value. We may have different meanings even though we may use the exact same word. Earlier we mentioned techniques that can minimize vocabulary anxiety. The first tip is to use a pencil, with an eraser. Clients often experience a sense of reluctance when values have to be written in ink. The coach can emphasize the advantages of the eraser so the client realizes that getting it *right* the first time is not an important factor. The second tip when doing values clarification is to use several words together to form a string describing the value. Separating the words with slash marks helps make the string easier to read. For example:

Integrity/honesty/walk-the-talk
Integrity/whole/congruent
Leadership/empower/collaborative
Leadership/decisive/powerful

When creating the values string, ask the client to place the most significant term at the beginning, such as Integrity or Leadership in the examples above. Point out that it may take several months to come up with a fairly complete list of values. Since values show up over time in our lives, it is unlikely that we will be able to capture them accurately and completely in one sitting. When values are fully defined and elaborated upon they become a powerful tool in pointing a client toward fulfilling choices as he or she approaches a major crossroad or gets off track.

The process of identifying values is facilitated by the coach when various scenarios are proposed to the client. The following scenarios will give you a place to start. Experiment with these and continue to explore other methods for allowing the client to see their values.

A Peak Moment in Time

Ask the client to identify special, peak moments when life was especially rewarding or poignant. It's important that the time frame be quite limited—as in "a moment"—or there will be too much in the experience to allow the client to pinpoint specific values. When the client has a specific moment in mind, start probing: "What was happening?" "Who was present and what was going on?" "What were the values that were being honored in that moment?" Acknowledge what you are hearing and keep probing, periodically testing words to see what values the client responds to. "That sounds like a huge win. Is that a value around accomplishment or achievement?" or "What a special day. It sounds like you were honoring a value around nature and a value of connection. Does that sound right?" There will be an energy hit when the words ring true. Ask the client to expand on the first word. "What does accomplishment mean to you?" "What words elaborate on your value of connection?" Keep looking at peak moments, seeking experiences the client found particularly rich and fulfilling.

Suppressed Values

Another way to isolate values is to go to the opposite extreme, looking at times when a client was angry, frustrated, or upset. This will often lead to identification of a value that was being suppressed. First have the client name the feelings and circumstances around the upset; then flip it over and look for the opposite of those feelings. For example, the client might say, "I felt trapped, backed into a corner. I had no choices." The coach might then say, "Trapped, cornered, without choice. If we flip that over it sounds like there might be a value around freedom or options or choice. Is that in the ballpark?" Being nonattached, the coach does not care whether the words feel right to the client, as long as they spark in the client meaningful language that resonates with his or her sense of self. To further illustrate, the coach might say, "So you felt quite frustrated when they kept spinning their wheels, doing the same thing over and over again? Is the other side of that a value around creativity or innovation?"

Many of us have situated our lives in such a way that we automatically and easily honor many of our values without even being aware that we are doing so. Therefore we may not recognize them as *values* until something gets in the way of our honoring them. The key here is to point out to the client that every upset or moment of distress is likely to signal that a value is being suppressed.

Must Haves

Another way for clients to identify their values is to look at what they *must have* in their life. Try it yourself. Beyond the physical requirements of food, shelter, and community, what *must* you have in your life in order to be fulfilled? Must you have a form of creative self-expression? Must you have adventure and excitement in your life? Must you have partnership and collaboration? Must you be moving toward a sense of accomplishment or success or surround yourself with natural beauty? An underlying question for the process is: "What are the values you absolutely must honor—or part of you dies?"

Obsessive Expression

We are all capable of obsessive behavior—insisting on honoring our value, inflating it into a demand rather than a form of self-expression. You've probably had an experience like this in your own life—such as when your roommate's value of orderliness became an obsessive demand for perfection. When we insist on something, when it is a case of "my way or the highway," then it is likely that a Gremlin is in the neighborhood. Our friends and family often do us a service by pointing out the obsessive expression of our values. "You are so controlling!" "All you think about is your students." "You hog all the attention." These statements might point toward a value of personal power/leadership, and learning/growth, and recognition/acknowledgment. Have your clients examine when they take certain values to the extreme. "What is it that people say about you? What do you say about yourself? What is it that people tease you about or that drives them nuts?" There are important values here that have mutated for some reason. Look for the value, and don't focus on the mutation.

The Values-Based Decision Matrix

One of the most potent tools for making fulfilling life choices is the Values-Based Decision Matrix. This matrix is launched during the initial values clarification process. (Please note that the listing of values may take several months prior to its completed form.) After you and the client have brainstormed a list of values, ask the client to rank the top ten values in priority order. Then ask the client to score his or her sense of satisfaction—the degree to which he or she is honoring each value—using a scale of 0 to 10. Most clients find this exercise very revealing, and they are often shocked at what they learn about themselves. Generally, the coach pays particular attention when a client indicates that a score is below 7. This is a likely place for coaching, since low scores mean the client may be selling out, putting up with an intolerable situation. It also means that there is a "play it safe" Gremlin to examine, and the client may have been unaware of that. The coach may want to revisit this process from time to time to keep the client grounded in his or her sense of self.

Over the years we have noted that typically when things are going particularly well in a client's life, the scores are high. When the client is struggling or is experiencing a low ebb, the values matrix can help determine where corrective action is needed. When a client is looking at making a major decision, such as whether to make a job change, or to start a new business, or even to have a child, the Values-Based Decision Matrix can be particularly revealing. Ask the client to score his or her values today. Next, ask the client to project out two months, a year, or to sometime in the future. "Imagine that you did make the change; anticipate and write down what your scores would be if you did. Next, imagine that you did not make the change and record those scores." This exercise will provide the client with useful insight around making a fulfilling choice. Be alert because this exercise will also provoke the Gremlin and you may hear such statements as: "But I'll make more money" or "I think I should take the risk" or "But he wants a son." The question to pose to the client might be "How does taking this action allow you to honor your values—to be true to yourself?"

The following sample Values-Based Decision Matrix represents the responses of a client determining whether or not to take on the leadership role in her company. As you can see, Leadership is not among the top ten values. Review the numbers as if these were your values and your decision. Note how provocative and revealing such an examination can be. What is not on this list of values are tangible measures, such as money and status—factors that are usually the basis for decision making, yet rarely lead to fulfilling choices.

Sample Values-Based Decision Matrix

Prioritize and List Values	Date: 7/98 Score Value	Date: 1999 YES Score Value	Date: 1999 NO Score Value	Date: Score Value	Date: Score Value	Date: Score Value
1. Learning/Growth	9	9	6			
2. Self-Expression	7	9	8			
3. Freedom/Independence	5	7	8			
4. Innovate/Create	6	8	7			
5. Partnership/Collaborate	8	9	8			
6. Organized/Order	7	8	7			
7. Integrity/Honesty	9	9	7			
8. Fun/Humor/Play	7	6	8			
9. Connection/Intimacy	8	6	8			
10. Adventure/Risk Taking	5	8	7			

Additional Forms

Three additional forms that can be used when working with values are included in this section. They are the Values Worksheet (p. 232), to assist the client in identifying values; the Standards and Obstacles Worksheet (p. 233), to help with establishing standards and obstacles for honoring values; and the Values Action Log (p. 234), to assist in creating values-based action plans. The sample list of values (p. 235) is to be held by the coach and not provided to the client. When we are on the spot we often forget values; using the list enables the coach to prompt clients around their values—especially when the coach senses a client may be negating or overlooking some obvious value, such as spirituality or humor.

Values Worksheet

Rank in Priority Order	Value/Description	Score Level of Satisfaction Scale of 1 to 10 (10 = Highest)

Standards and Obstacles Worksheet

Value	Honoring Score	Standard (How is value honored?)	Obstacle to Honoring Value	Strength of Obstacle Score
1.				
2.				
3.				
4.				
5.				
6.				
7.				
8.				

the coach's toolkit

Values Action Log

Value	Action to Be Taken to Increase Score	By When?
1.		
2.		
3.		
4.		
5.		
6.		
7.		
8.		

Sample Values List

The following list is representative of words or phrases that illustrate values. Remember as you work with this exercise that you may combine two or three values as long as critical distinctions are not lost. For example, whereas the combination "Honesty/Integrity/Truthfulness" maintains a single distinction, "Honesty/Integrity/Freedom" combines concepts and thereby loses clarity.

Humor	Participation
Directness	Performance
Partnership	Collaboration
Productivity	Community
Service	Personal Power
Contribution	Freedom to Choose
Excellence	Connectedness
Free Spirit	Acknowledgment
Focus	Comradeship
Romance	Lightness
Recognition	Spirituality
Harmony	Empowerment
Accomplishment	Full Self-Expression
Orderliness	Integrity
Forward the Action	Creativity
Honesty	Independence
Success	Nurturing
Accuracy	Joy
Adventure	Beauty
Lack of Pretense	Authenticity
Zest	Risk Taking
Tradition	Peace
To Be Known	Elegance
Growth	Vitality
Aesthetics	Trust

Keep Looking

Because values are such an important part of the way clients order their lives and make choices, it is essential to continue to look at this area. Values could conceivably be looked at in every coaching call—either to help make a choice or to clarify and reinforce a course of action. "What is the value that would be honored if you did that?" When your clients honor their values, three things happen: one, they add additional fuel to the motivation fire and help build steam for action; two, they under-mine the work of the Gremlin because action based on values is more powerful than the Gremlin's reasons for not taking action or for taking some other course of action; and three, they have a fulfilling life.

Coaching Resources

The following resources expand on coaching skills and contexts mentioned throughout this book. These resources should be considered a work-in-progress. The active professional coach will add to these lists over the life of his or her career.

Powerful Questions

Powerful questions are provocative queries that put a halt to evasion and confusion. By asking the powerful question, the coach invites the client to clarity, action, and discovery at a whole new level. As you can see from the following examples, these are generally open-ended questions that create greater possibility for expanded learning and fresh perspective.

Anticipation

What might happen?
What if it doesn't work out the way you wish?
What if that doesn't work?
And if that fails, what will you do?
What is your backup plan?

Assessment

What do you make of it?
What do you think is best?
How does it look to you?
How do you feel about it?
What if it doesn't work?

Clarification

What do you mean?
What does it feel like?
What seems to confuse you?
Can you say more?
What do you want?

Evaluation

In what way?
Is this good, bad, or in between? In what way?
How does this fit with your plans/way of life/values?

What do you think that means?
What is your assessment?

Exploration

May we explore that some more?
Would you like to brainstorm this idea?
What other angles can you think of?
What is just one more possibility?
What are your other options?

Example

Will you give an example?
For instance?
Like what?
Such as?
What would it look like?

Elaboration

Will you elaborate?
Will you tell me more about it?
What else?
Is there more?
What other ideas do you have about it?

Fun as Perspective

What was fun about . . . ?
What was humorous about the situation?
How can you have it be fun?
How do you want it to be?
If you were to teach people how to have fun, what would you say?

For Instance

If you could do it over again, what would you do differently?
If it were you, what would you have done?
How else could a person handle this?
If you could do anything you wanted, what would you do?
For instance?

History

What caused it?
What led up to . . . ?
What have you tried so far?
Can you remember how it happened?
What do you make of it all?

Implementation

What is the action plan?
What will you have to do to get the job done?
What support do you need to accomplish . . . ?
What will you do?
When will you do it?

Integration

What will you take away from this?
How do you explain this to yourself?
What was the lesson?
How can you lock in the learning?
How would you pull all this together?

Learning

If your life depended on taking action, what would you do?
If you had free choice in the matter, what would you do?
If the same thing came up again, what would you do?
If we could wipe the slate clean, what would you do?
If you had it to do over again, what would you do?

Options

What are the possibilities?
If you had your choice, what would you do?
What are possible solutions?
What if you do and what if you don't?
What options can you create?

Outcomes

What do you want?
What is your desired outcome?
If you got it, what would you have?
How will you know you have reached it?
What would it look like?

Perspective

When you are ninety-five years old, what will you want to say about your life?
What would you think about this five years from now?
How does this relate to your life purpose?
In the bigger scheme of things how important is this?
So what?

Planning

What do you plan to do about it?
What is your game plan?
What kind of plan do you need to create?
How do you suppose you could improve the situation?
Now what?

Predictions

How do you suppose it will all work out?
What will that get you?
Where will this lead?
What are the chances of success?
What is your prediction?

Resources

What resources do you need to help you decide?
What do you know about it now?
How do you suppose you can find out more about it?
What kind of picture do you have right now?
What resources are available to you?

Starting the Session

What's occurred since we last spoke?
What would you like to talk about?
What's new/the latest/the update?
How was your week?
How's life?

Substance

What seems to be the trouble?
What seems to be the main obstacle?
What is stopping you?
What concerns you the most about . . . ?
What do you want?

Summary

What is your conclusion?
How is this working?
How would you describe this?
What do you think this all amounts to?
How would you summarize the effort so far?

Taking Action

What action will you take? And after that?
What will you do? When?
Is this a time for action? What action?
Where do you go from here? When will you do that?
What are your next steps? By when?

Inquiries

An inquiry is a kind of powerful question that is typically used as a homework assignment between coaching calls. You are asking the client to consider and ponder these inquiries for the week. Instead of looking for the one right answer, the client is in a mode of self-reflection, discovery, and learning. This list of inquiries is not comprehensive: active coaches will be adding inquiries throughout their career.

Beginning Inquiries

What do I want?
What is it to have a full, rich life?
What am I tolerating?
Where am I not being realistic?
What is integrity?
How do I operate?
What is it to live in alignment with my values?
What is it to be powerful?
What is it to be present?
What is my prevalent mood? Is that a habit?
What is choice? What is it to choose?
When do I allow myself to not be my word?
What is the difference between a wish and a goal?
Am I being *nice* or am I being **real**?
What do I do to avoid feelings? (Alcohol, food, work?)
Where is my attention? (On self, others, work, daydreams, my vision, values, complaints?)

What Works?

What keeps me going?
What is working?
What frees me up?
What is it to be prosperous?
Where am I too hard on myself?
What is present when I'm at my best?

What is my structure to win?
Where am I the solution?

Motivational

When am I unable to laugh at myself?
What do I need in order to reach my goals?
What is the distinction between feeling good and fulfillment?
Great goals are compelling; vague goals are forgotten: which type are my goals?
What am I building? (A cathedral or a block of stone?)
Who am I becoming?
What motivates me?
What is it to be undauntable?
How do I choose to be this week?
What does it mean to allow or include?
What is it to be creative?
What powerful questions can I ask myself each morning?
What is it to be tenacious?
What is it to be passionate?
What flag am I bearing?
What is it to be powerful/resilient/ resourceful/empowering/determined?
What pain do I notice in people around me?
What is it to speak/act from my heart?
How have I withheld myself from life?
Is what I am doing, right now, life affirming or life numbing?
What is it to be intuitive?
What is it to be focused?
What is it to be a leader?

Stopped/Blocked Client

What is the lie?
What am I resisting?
If I were at my best, what would I do right now?
Where do I give my power away? To whom? When?
What are my false assumptions?
What do I pretend? (To know or not to know?)
What do I need to leave alone?
What's out?

What is needed in this situation?
What is it to be exceptional?
What will I gather evidence for this week?
What is it to generate or cause?
What are my wants versus my musts?
Where am I an automatic no or yes?
Where do I limit myself?
What are other possibilities?
Where am I too comfortable?
What is it to move toward the fear?
What does it mean to "lean into it"?
Where am I selling out on myself?
What else can I do to honor my values?
What requests can be made to get me going?
What is the powerful interpretation?
Where am I uncompromising? Where am I too flexible?
What does _____ cost me?
Where do I hold back?
What am I withholding?
What am I unwilling to risk?
What is it to surrender?
Where am I suffering?
What will free me up?
What are my assumptions?
What are my expectations?

Pleasure

How can I pamper myself today?
What is it to be grateful?
Who can I make smile this morning?
What will recharge my batteries?
What is fun?
How can I contribute to my reserves of fun/leisure/balance/resourcefulness/
    patience?
How can I have this be easy?
Who can I get to play with me on this project?
What is it to be tickled?
What is grace/serenity?

What makes me laugh?

Do I choose heavy or do I choose light?

Since I am going to do this anyway, do I choose to have it be neutral, hard, or fun?

What can I do to my physical environment to have it nurture me/relax me/empower me?

What is fulfilling, what feels good, and so what?

What is pleasure?

What acknowledgment can I give myself today?

What is kindness?

What is it to go softly into life?

What is abundance?

How can I have this be playful and light?

How can I double my vitality?

What should I give myself permission to do today?

When will I take a break today?

What thrills me?

What is it to be awed?

What is it to be generous with myself?

What is it to be considerate?

What is it to be gentle with myself?

What is it to gawk/savor?

What am I grateful for today?

Provocative

What do I regret/resent?

What am I unwilling to change?

Where might I be in denial?

What am I overlooking?

Where am I taking my foot off the gas?

What is the decision I have been avoiding?

Where do I stop short?

What is a big enough game?

What have I wanted to do and haven't?

What keeps me from winning?

Where have I denied myself/others?

Why bother?

What am I being right about?

What complaint/fear/bad habit/discomfort can I do something about
   today?
Where am I asleep at the wheel?
What am I settling for?
What will this goal get me?
What am I overlooking?
How do I sabotage myself?
What is it to transcend my sense of failure/sense of resignation/feelings
   of "I can't"?
Where am I selling out on myself?
What am I willing/unwilling to change?
What am I stepping over?
What is my reputation?
What do I expect of myself?
What is grace/enthusiasm/prosperity/abundance?
What is it to be proactive?
What is it to be centered/optimistic/supportable/nonattached?
What is it to be fluid/flexible?
What is it to be compassionate?
What is completion? Where am I incomplete?
If my whole attention is focused on producing the result, what will I have
to give up?
Why am I taking this action?

Assignments

Forgive yourself once a day.
Count the number of times a day you notice the Gremlin.
Laugh/smile twenty-five times a day.
Cite twenty-five things that make you smile/laugh.
Be present for fifteen minutes at a time three times a day.
List your five most prevalent Gremlin conversations.
What is the most insidious side of your Gremlin?
List your justifications.
List your expectations.
Play a bigger game this week.
Eliminate . . . words from your vocabulary this week.
Add . . . words to your vocabulary this week
Do the hard thing first each morning and after lunch.

Say no _____ times a day.

Make _____ mistakes a day.

Take_____ risks this week.

Ask_____ people out for coffee each day this week.

Say "so what" . . . times a day.

Answer the question "Why bother?" with every new action.

Count the times you speak powerfully.

Only speak powerfully this week (not positively but *powerfully*).

Catch yourself growing (making mistakes).

Acquire evidence of some new ability. (Using the "bushel basket" metaphor, gather evidence of accomplishments, compassion, being proactive, going for it, and so forth.)

Choose what you have in every moment.

Enjoy two big belly laughs each day.

Completion

What is it to be complete?

What's next?

What territory have you taken?

How far have you come?

What gold nuggets are you taking away?

Who have you become?

What have you built?

What is the new elevation from which you regard your life?

What did it take to get here?

What have you learned about yourself?

What does it take to maintain?

What is momentum?

What will keep you on track?

What is it to be filled with loving-kindness?

What is it to live life fully?

What is it to love deeply?

What values require your constant attention?

What will you be giving away?

What is your contribution to the world going to be?

Who did you have to be to reach this place?

How will you know to ask for support?

What acknowledgment would you like to give yourself?

Structures

Structures are those devices that help create focus and discipline for the client. Putting a note in the client's calendar is a simple structure to jog the memory and get people to take a desired action. A structure is a method for helping people to remember and take action on what is designated as important. But a structure only works if people notice it. Whether or not they do what the structure indicates, the structure will lead to learning. There's an unlimited number of structures to get people into action. Here we cover some of the basic categories.

Basic Structures

Here are some suggestions of structures that have worked:

- Call your coach's voice mail or your own voice mail every day when a certain task is done.
- Wear a rubber band on your wrist when you want to remember to do something, such as breathe deeply, speak powerfully, sit up straight, turn complaints into requests, or tell someone something positive.
- Throw a dinner party once a month. This can be a structure for cleaning house or keeping up relationships with friends.
- Find an exercise partner.
- Devise an intentionally fabricated deadline on the day you start the project—such as scheduling a time to show a colleague or friend your completed project in two weeks.
- Schedule appointments with one friend a week for two months.
- Put a chair in front of the door when you come in at night to remind yourself to bring important documents tomorrow.
- Send yourself an e-mail or voice mail to request that a certain task be done.
- Ask a friend to send you a predesigned postcard once a month to encourage you to . . .

Counting is a structure. When you want to pay attention to certain behavior—when your Gremlin shows up for example, or when you acknowledge others—simply count how many times you do it any given day. This is a structure that focuses your attention on noticing.

You can also count: number of cigarettes smoked, number of calories, number of cold calls, number of times you apologize, and the like. Counting does not require that you do anything other than notice. But by noting every time you do something, it heightens your awareness.

A talisman can be a structure. A toy lion by the phone can remind the client to be ferocious in pursuit of a goal.

A coach is one of the best structures. Coaching is a relationship of accountability and a place where clients stop everything while they look at their life, at how they are doing, and whether they are headed in the direction they want.

Time Management

This category includes any kind of calendar, day timer, or to-do list. It can be paper, computer, store-bought or hand-made, rigorously designed down to the quarter hour, or just an overview. The key to its effectiveness is how well it fits the client. There is a mistaken belief that there is just one right way. For all the evolution in format and technology from crayon to palm-top computer, the appropriate system is what works for your client.

Money Management

For most people, the register in their checkbook is about the only structure they have for managing this significant area of their lives. Other structures might include computer programs, a monthly budget, regularly scheduled money management discussions with their spouse, or the services of a financial planner or home budget consultant. This is by no means an exhaustive list; it merely gives you a sense of the variety of options available.

Using the Senses

For clients who are highly visual, any structure that appears in their daily field of vision is likely to work—posting sticky-notes to their computer or the cabinet above the desk, or the refrigerator door, for example. Postcards or pictures cut from magazines are another good structure. Repainting a room to change the visual space might be an important new structure for a client. Simply changing their chair position so clients are forced to look at their world from a different perspective—any structural device that engages them visually is likely to be powerful and effective. Think about how you could use the other senses as well: auditory structures like playing music or creating an audiotape of affirmations. A particular fragrance can be a very powerful structure—religious ceremonies and rituals have used the structure of smell for thousands of years because it's a structure that works. How could you use the structure of smell creatively in your clients' lives?

Some of the best structures come from your intuition and may not seem to make sense at first. Place watermelon seeds on the kitchen window sill . . . carry a flashlight in your briefcase . . . wear two different colored shoes today. One reason why structures work is because they interrupt the ordinary mind-flow and grab your attention. The more outrageous they are, the more likely they'll be to interrupt the semiconscious way we often glide through the days of our lives.

You may have a whole catalog of structures you have used with clients. That's handy and a great source of ideas. But it's also very effective to let clients create their own structures. In that case the structure is even better suited to the client.

Sample Co-Active Coaching Skills List

Accountability

Acknowledgment

Articulating What Is Going On

Asking Permission

Bottom Lining

Brainstorming

Challenging

Championing

Clarifying

Clearing

Confidentiality

Creating Trust

Dancing in the Moment

Forwarding the Action

Goal Setting and Planning

Holding the Client's Agenda

Holding the Focus

Inquiry

Intruding/Taking Charge

Intuiting

Listening

Metaphor

Meta-view

Powerful Questions

Reframing

Requesting

Self-Management

Structures

Visioning

Glossary

Accountability. Accountability is having your clients account for what they said they were going to do. It is determined by three questions: *(1) What are you going to do? (2) By when will you do this? (3) How will I know?* Accountability does not include blame or judgment. Rather, the coach holds the client accountable to the client's vision or commitment and asks the client to account for the results of the intended action. If need be, holding the client accountable includes defining new actions to be taken.

Acknowledgment. Acknowledgment addresses the Self and who the client had to be in order to accomplish whatever action he or she took or awareness he or she achieved. It is the articulation of your deep knowing of the other.

"I want to acknowledge the courage it took for you to show up on this call, knowing that you had some difficult things to share with me today."

Articulating what is going on. This skill involves telling clients what you see them doing; repeating or mirroring back to them what they have just said to you.

"You are really working hard at this project and it is frustrating for you that your partners are not working as hard as you are."

Asking permission. This skill enables the client to grant the coaching relationship access to unusually intimate or sometimes impolite areas of focus.
"Can I tell you a hard truth?" "Is it all right to coach you on this issue?"
"Can I tell you what I see?"

Bottom-Lining. This is the skill of brevity and succinctness on the part of both coach and client. Bottom-lining is also about having the client get to the essence of his or her communication rather than engaging in long descriptive stories.
"I went to work this morning and was distraught when I found a pink slip in my box."

Brainstorming. In this skill the coach and client together generate ideas, alternatives, and possible solutions. Some of the proposed ideas may be outrageous and impractical. This is merely a creative exercise to expand the possibilities available to the client. There is no attachment on the part of either coach or client to any of the ideas suggested.

Celebrating. Celebrating fully honors wherever the client currently experiences him- or herself in life. The coach uses this skill to deepen the client's appreciation of his or her own successes and failures, disappointments and wins. Celebrating is not necessarily about cheering. It is about bringing attention and acknowledgment to the client's process.
"You failed to make ten cold calls this week. I celebrate your failure."
"Hooray! I celebrate your success of getting a new client."

Challenging. Challenging involves requesting that a client stretch way beyond his or her self-imposed limits. Frequently, in the face of a challenge, clients will respond with a counteroffer that is greater than they initially would have allowed themselves to make otherwise.
A client needs to make cold calls to increase his business. He thinks he can make only one call a day. You challenge him.
"I challenge you to make ten calls a day!" The client counteroffers with, "I'll make seven."

Championing. When you champion clients, you stand up for them when they doubt or question their abilities. Despite the client's self-doubt, the coach knows clearly who the client is and that he or she is capable of much more than the client thinks. When the client is in the valley, the coach is on the next hill, waving a flag and saying,
"Come on. You can make it!"

Clarifying. When a client is unable to articulate clearly what he or she wants or where he or she is going, the coach clarifies the client's experience. Clarification may be used in response to the client's vague sense of what it is that he or she wants, confusion, or uncertainty. This skill represents a synergistic application of questioning, reframing, and articulating what is going on. It is particularly useful during the intake process.

Clearing. Clearing is a skill that is of benefit to both the client and the coach. When a client is preoccupied with a situation or a mental state that interferes with his or her ability to be present or take action, the coach assists the client by being an active listener while he or she vents or complains. This active listening allows the client to temporarily clear the situation out of the way and focus on taking the next step.

When a coach gets hooked by a client interaction or is preoccupied with issues that do not pertain to the client, the coach can clear. The coach clears by sharing his or her experience or preoccupation with a colleague or a friend in order to show up and be fully present with the client.

Client's agenda. The client's agenda consists of the client's life purpose, vision, values, and goals, and the principles of fulfillment, balance, and process. In short, it is everything that the client is and wants to be and do.

Confidentiality. *All* information that a client shares with a coach is held as confidential. This means that all information that a client confides in the coach is *not shared with anyone else* without the client's express permission. Confidentiality, the hallmark of the coaching profession, creates safety and trust and is the basis of the powerful designed alliance between client and coach.

Creating trust. The coaching relationship rests on a foundation of safety and trust. To create trust you might discuss safety, maintain confidentiality, tell the truth, offer clients an opportunity to ask for what they want, actively listen to what they are telling you.

Dancing in the moment. Dancing in the moment means being completely present with your client, holding your client's agenda, accessing your intuition, letting your client lead you. When you dance in the moment you are open to whatever steps your client takes and are willing to go in the client's direction and flow.

Designing the alliance. When the client grants power to the alliance, it then becomes necessary for the client to take responsibility for his or her part in the alliance. Out of their ownership of the alliance, clients design the alliance that will be most beneficial to and supportive of forwarding their actions toward their goals and vision. This is done through making requests of the coach, setting up the logistics of the coaching relationship, and discussing the best ways to facilitate client learning and action.

Failure. Failure is the lack of achievement of a goal or activity to which one committed oneself. Failure is often confused with being wrong, morally shameful, or bad. To fail merely means that you did not succeed at what you set out to do. It is an opportunity for reflection and correction which can then forward the action toward success.

Forwarding the action. This skill utilizes all other coaching skills, with an added emphasis on moving the client forward. It may be through use of a request or a powerful question. It may be through bottom-lining so that something gets done during the session. Forwarding the action may occur through bringing the client back to the focus of his or her goal, or through reframing something in such a way that the client is free to take action. Acknowledging a client can also forward action. The most powerful forwarding the action occurs when a coach has the client DO IT NOW during the coaching session. This provides immediate support and immediate celebration once the action is taken.

Goals. A goal is an outcome that the client would like to achieve. Goals are most helpful when they are measurable, specific, are owned by the client, have a date by which they will be accomplished, are made public (in order to achieve support and accountability), and constitute a reasonable stretch for the client.

Gremlin. The Gremlin is a concept developed by Richard Carson that embodies a group of thought processes and feelings that maintain the status quo in our lives. Often operating as a structure that would seem to protect us, it in fact keeps us from moving forward and getting what we truly want in life. Like our mind, the Gremlin will always be with us. It is neither good nor bad; it just is. The Gremlin loses its power over us when we can identify it for what it is, notice our options in the situation and then consciously choose what it is we do really want at that time.

Holding the client's agenda. Holding the client's agenda is both a philosophical stance and a skill employed by coaches. When a coach holds the client's agenda, the coach becomes invisible. That is to say, the coach lets go of his or her own opinions, judgments, and answers in support of facilitating the client's fulfillment, balance, and process. The coach follows the client's lead without knowing the RIGHT answer, without giving solutions or telling the client what to do. Holding the client's agenda requires the coach to put his or her whole attention on the client and the client's agenda, not on the coach's agenda for the client.

Holding the focus. Once the client has determined a direction or course of action, the coach's job is to keep the client on track and true to that course. Frequently, clients become distracted by events in their lives, strong feelings elicited by the Gremlin, or the wealth of other possibilities available. The coach consistently reminds the client of his or her focus and helps redirect his or her energy back to the client's desired outcomes and life choices.

Homework inquiry. This term refers to a powerful question given at the end of the session that is intended to deepen the client's learning and provoke further reflection. The intention is for the client to consider the inquiry between sessions and to see what occurs for him or her. The inquiry is usually based on a particular situation the client is currently addressing. *"What are you tolerating?" "What is it to be undauntable?" "What is challenge?"*

Intruding/Taking charge. On occasion, the coach may need to intrude, to interrupt or wake up a client who is going on and on, or who is kidding him- or herself. Sometimes the intrusion is a hard truth such as *"You are kidding yourself."* Sometimes the intrusion is simply stating what is going on, such as *"You are skirting the issue."* Intrusion is considered rude in American society. Co-active coaching views intrusion as being direct with the client, allowing him or her to honestly assess and immediately deal with situations.

Intuiting. Intuiting is the process of accessing and trusting one's inner knowing. Intuition is direct knowing, unencumbered by one's thinking mind. The process of intuiting is nonlinear and nonrational. Sometimes, the information received through intuiting does not make sense to the coach. However, this information is usually quite valuable to the client. Intuiting involves taking risks and trusting your gut.

"I have a hunch that . . ." "I wonder if . . ."

Life balance. Life balance is dynamic and is always in motion. The client is either moving toward balance in his or her life or away from balance. The job of the coach is to facilitate moving toward life balance as much as possible. The areas to be balanced in life generally include career, money, relationships with family and friends, romance, personal growth, fun and recreation, health, and physical surroundings. If one or more areas are receiving attention at the expense of the others, life will feel unbalanced and bumpy.

Life purpose. Life purpose is about why you are here on the planet. Who is it that you are moved to be and what is it that you are moved to create? It is an essence statement that serves as a reminder of who you are and the impact you naturally create in the world. When you are living your purpose, life is experienced as fulfilling, effortless, and satisfying. When you are disregarding your life purpose, life often feels empty, anguished, and unfulfilling.

Listening. The coach listens for clients' vision, values commitment, and purpose in their words and demeanor. To *listen for* is to listen in search of something. The coach listens with a consciousness, with a purpose and focus that come from the alliance that was designed with the client. The coach is listening for the client's agenda, not the coach's agenda for the client. Co-active coaching calls listening to your own thoughts, judgments, and opinions about the client's story Level I, while *listening for* is Level II and *conscious listening* is Level III.

Metaphor. Metaphors are used to illustrate a point and paint a verbal picture for the client.

Your mind is like a ping-pong ball bouncing between one choice and another. You're almost at the finish line. Go for it! You can win the race!

Meta-View. Meta-view is the big picture or perspective. The coach pulls back from the client's immediate issues and from the clarity of that expanded perspective reflects back to the client what he or she sees.

Planning and goal setting. The coach helps the client articulate the direction in which he or she wishes to go and actively monitors the client's progress. Clients can frequently benefit from support in planning and time management as coaches help them develop their skills in these areas.

Powerful questions. A powerful question evokes clarity, action, discovery, insight, or commitment. It creates greater possibility, new learning, or clearer vision. Powerful questions are open-ended questions that do not elicit a yes or no response. They are derived from holding the client's agenda and either forward the client's action or deepen his or her learning.

What do you want? What does that cost you?

Reframing. Reframing involves providing a client with another perspective. When a coach reframes a situation, he or she takes the original data and interprets them in a different way.

A client has just been informed that she was selected as second choice for a high-powered position in a very competitive market. She is disappointed and is questioning her professional competence. A reframe of the situation is: To be selected as second choice in such a competitive market indicates the high quality of your expertise and experience.

Requesting. One of the most potent coaching skills is that of making a request of the client. The request, based on the client's agenda, is designed to forward the client's action. The request includes a specific action, conditions of satisfaction, and a date or time by which it will be done. There are three possible responses to a request: yes, no, or a counteroffer.

Will you pay your telephone bill by Friday?

Self-Management. This skill refers to the coach's ability to become invisible in the service of holding the client's agenda. This means the coach must put aside all opinions, preferences, judgments, and beliefs in order to reflect and support the client's agenda. Another facet of self-management includes managing the client's Gremlin. The coach can aid the client in identifying the Gremlin and then providing tools that the client can use in managing the Gremlin. Clearing is also a tool for coach or client self-management.

Structures. Structures are devices that remind clients of their vision, goals, purpose, or actions that they need to take immediately. Some examples of structures are collages, calendars, messages on voice mail, alarm clocks, and so on.

Values. Values represent who you are right now. They are principles that you hold to be of worth in your life. People often confuse values with morals. Values are not chosen. They are intrinsic to you.

Vision. This is a multifaceted mental image and set of goals that personally define and inspire the client to take action to create that picture in his or her actual life. A powerful vision is sensuous, exciting, and magnetic, constantly attracting the client's desire to bring the image to fruition. Vision provides the client with a direction and can provide meaning in his or her life.

About the Authors

Laura Whitworth has worked with hundreds of entrepreneurs and professionals as a personal and executive coach and in 1997 was named one of the ten most influential coaches by *Professional Coach Journal*. As cofounder of The Coaches Training Institute and a founding member of the Personal and Professional Coaches Association, she has contributed to the formalization of the principles and ethics of the coaching profession.

Henry Kimsey-House has been a coach and workshop leader since 1981. Widely recognized as an innovator in experiential learning and creative course design, he is cofounder and curriculum director of The Coaches Training Institute and The Co-Active Leadership Program.

Phil Sandahl came to coaching after fifteen years as a freelance writer. Cofounder of the Minnesota Coaches Association, he is currently a coach and workshop leader who works primarily with the self-employed, especially those in creative fields.

Index

access to intuition, 32, 37–38, 54–56
accountability, xviii; as feedback, 74, 81, 128; in homework assignments, 74, 82–84; as measure of action/learning, 11, 80–81; motivation by, 84, 143, 161; and process, 143, 155–156; in relationship, 11, 82, 83, 85; requesting, 88–89; rewards and consequences for, 84–85; as structure, 91–92, 93; tracking for, 82–84
acknowledging, 74; decisions, 125, 131, 163; feelings, 148–149, 150; who the client is, 44–45, 47
action: being vs. doing, 143–144, 152. *See also* action/learning
action/learning, 74, 79–80; accountability for measuring, 11, 80–82; between coaching sessions, 82–84; coaching skills for, 85–91; in model of co-active coaching, 5–6, 11; rewards and consequences in, 83, 84–85; using structures for, 91–93. *See also* learning

active listening, 32, 33, 40. *See also* listening
agenda. *See* client's agenda
agreement, coach-client, 171. *See also* relationship
alliance, designed. *See under* relationship
articulating, 40–41
asking permission. *See* permission
attention, in listening, 32–39
awareness, 32–39, 66

balance: choice in, 7–8, 128–129; coaching for, 143, 144, 147, 166; commitments in, 139–140; as dynamic process, 127–128, 136; formula for, 129–135; integration with fulfillment and process, 145, 156; in model of co-active coaching, 6, 7–8; as personal, 135–136; and the Perspective Game, 136–138; and saying no, 138–139
being fulfilled, 115–117, 123
being heard, and listening, 31–32, 45
being vs. doing, 143–144, 152

being with, in process coaching, 145, 147, 151
blurting, 55, 59, 67
body language, 32, 35
bottom lining, 104
brainstorming, 17, 86, 131

Carson, Richard, *Taming Your Gremlin*, 9n
challenging, 90–91, 92, 165
championing, 105, 112
change, x, 67; client's need for, xviii–xix, 1; through cycle of action and learning, 5–6, 11, 79–80; environment as influence on, 15–18; Gremlin as enemy of, xx, 25–26, 122, 140
choices: in balanced life, 4, 7–8, 127–141; saying no as, 138–139; values and "rightness" of, 121–122. *See also* client's agenda
clarifying: action steps, 82–83, 87; in definition of fulfillment, 117–119; and listening, 41–42. *See also* values clarification
clearing, as self-management, 98–101, 106–107, 112
client's agenda, 97; commitments in, 139–140; guiding, 66, 88; and intuition, 59–60; in model of co-active coaching, 3–5, 6–8. *See also* choices
closed questions, 64, 69
coach: consultant vs., 5, 65; in flow of coaching, 160–163; in group coaching, 166–167; as mirror of client, 36, 144–145; as professional, 139–140, 156, 169–175; and purpose of coaching, 11, 12, 21, 125, 159–160; sense of timing by, 157–159; styles of coaching by, 167–168; therapist vs., x, 150, 152, 174; and value of coaching, 174–176. *See also* co-active coaching; tools of coaching
Coaches Training Institute (CTI), xii–xiii; rules of conduct, 173
Coaching for Performance (Whitmore), x
co-active coaching: for action/learning, 79–93; for balance, 127–141; Coach's Toolkit for, 177–252; curiosity in, 63–77; definition and background of, ix–x, xi, 3; for fulfillment, 115–125; in future, 169–175; intuition in, 49–61; listening in, 31–47; model of, 3–12; for process, 143–156; as profession, xi–xiii, 169–173; relationship in, 3, 13–28; self-management in, 95–112; tips and traps in, 157–168

commitments: for balanced life, 131–132, 139–140; discovery of, 19, 22–23; levels of, 79–80, 84–85; in process coaching, 147–148; requesting, 88–89; to time, 157–159
communication, 11, 81, 128; intuition as, 54–56. *See also* senses; tools of coaching
compelling way, 21, 22, 122–125
completion of coaching, 162–163
confidentiality, 16, 171–172
conflicts of interest, 172
confrontation and articulation, 40
Confucius, x
consequences. *See* rewards and consequences
consultant vs. coach, 5, 65
contexts: in model of co-active coaching, 6, 9–12. *See also names of specific contexts*
courageous coaching environment, 15–18
CTI. *See* Coaches Training Institute (CTI)
curiosity, 76, 151; and information gathering, 63–65, 67–69; and inquiry questions, 73–75, 77; in model of co-active coaching, 6, 10–11; and powerful questions, 69–73, 77; value and development of, 65–67

dancing in the moment, 12, 156
demanding and telling, 165
designed alliance. *See under* relationship
disconnections with clients: forbidden territory, 101–102; fresh air strategies, 100–101
discovery: from curious questions, 63–77; at intake session, 19–21; self-discovery, 4, 125, 156

emotions, 14; fear of, 151–152; feeling good vs. being fulfilled, 116–117; as information, 150–151. *See also* process coaching
empowerment: through change and learning, 14, 23; from relationship, 13–15, 16, 27, 160
environment, coaching, 28, 164; confidentiality in, 16; as courageous, 15–18; spaciousness in, 17–18; trust in, 16; veracity in, 16–17
environmental listening. *See* Level III listening (global)
ethics and standards, of professional coaching, 170–173

expectations, client's, 24–25

failure: facing, 24, 152–155; as learning, 24, 102–103, 110–111, 148–149, 158
feelings. *See* emotions
fieldwork. *See* homework assignments
fixations and balance, 129–130
focused listening. *See* Level II listening (focused)
forbidden territory, self-management of, 101–102
fresh air strategies, for self-management, 100–101
fulfillment: and balance, 129, 156; and compelling way, 122–125; hunger for, 115–117, 123; in model of co-active coaching, 6, 7; personal definition of, 117–119, 120; process coaching for, 145, 148, 156; and value, 119–122. *See also* value
future: client's design of, 19, 21–23, 123–124, 216–221; co-active coaching for, 148, 169–176

Gallwey, Timothy, *The Inner Game of Tennis,* ix–x
global range of listening. *See* Level III listening (global)
goals: discovery of, 19, 21, 22; setting, 87
Gremlin, 4, 9, 9n; and balance, search for, 129, 132, 139, 140; client's self-management of, 12, 85; coach's self-management of, 99, 102–103, 111–112, 172; as enemy of change, 25–26, 122, 140; tips for control of, 70, 147, 158, 159, 165
group coaching, 166–167

habits, 19, 22–23
harmony. *See* fulfillment
homework assignments, 24, 73, 82–84
humor, 151, 164–165

ICF (International Coach Federation), 170–172
information gathering vs. curious questions, 63–65, 70
Inner Game of Tennis, The (Gallwey), ix–x
inquiry, 73–75, 77, 243–248
intake session, 164; as discovery session, 13, 67, 104, 117, 167; elements of, 18–25; forms and checklists for corporate clients, 189–200; forms and checklists for individual clients, 178–188; outcomes of, 26–28
integrity. *See* ethics and standards

intelligence, intuition as, 53
internal listening. *See* Level I listening (internal)
International Coach Federation (ICF), 170–172
interpretations: of intuition, 51–54; separating, 109–110
interrogation vs. curiosity, 66
introspection, 73
intruding, 24, 72, 165; and intuition, 57–59, 61
intuition, 49–50, 67; access points for, 32, 37–38, 54–56; of clients, 59–60; coaching skills for, 57–61, 151, 158; as intelligence, 53; interpretation of, 51–52, 53–54; known vs. unknown, 50–51; in model of co-active coaching, 6, 10

judgment vs. interpretation, 53–54

leading questions, 64–65
learning, 117; from curiosity, 65, 73; from failure, 24, 102–103, 110–111, 148–149, 158; saying no as, 138–139; and time frames, 159, 166, 167. *See also* action/learning
Level I listening (internal): explanation of, 9–10, 34–35, 72; practice of, 45–46; reactions from, 98–100. *See also* listening
Level II listening (focused): explanation of, 9–10, 35–37; practice of, 45–46. *See also* listening
Level III listening (global), 158; explanation of, 9–10, 37–39, 46; in process coaching, 144–145. *See also* listening
life purpose and fulfillment, 124–125, 222–225
listening, xviii, 158; attention and impact of, 32–39; and being heard, 31–32, 45; coaching skills for, 40–45; levels of, 9–10, 31–32, 34–39, 45–46, 67; in model of co-active coaching, 6, 9–10; practice of, 45–47
logistics, 19, 23

mentoring programs, xi, xii
metaphor, 43, 47, 149
meta-view, 42–43, 46–47
mission statement, 124–125
model of co-active coaching: background of, xii, xvii–xix; client's agenda in, 4–5, 6–8; contexts of, 9–12; cornerstones of, 3–5

motivation, xviii–xix, 67; and accountability, 84, 143, 161; from relationship, 1, 79–80. *See also* rewards and
consequences

no, saying, 138–139

on-line coaching, 15
open questions, 64, 69
"out of balance", 129. *See also* balance
outcomes and goals, discovery of, 19,
21, 22

permission, 18–19, 86, 103
personal growth, 45, 117
perspectives: in balanced life, 127–141;
humor for, 164–165; and the Perspective Game, 136–138; reframing,
107–110
point of view. *See* perspectives
powerful questions: for curiosity,
69–71; dumb questions vs., 72–73;
using, 72, 77, 238–242
Primary Focus exercise, 21, 183
process: and accountability, 143,
155–156; being vs. doing, 143–144;
in model of co-active coaching, 6,
8. *See also* process coaching
process coaching: expanding and
exploring in, 149–150; feelings as
information in, 150–151; finding
resistance in, 145–149; focus of,
143, 144; mirroring clients in,
144–145; pitfalls of, 151–155. *See
also* process
professional coaching, 169, 170–173

reason and intuition, 56
recharging and ruts, 163–164
referrals, 173
reflection, 73
reframing, 107–109
relationship: accountability in, 11, 82,
83, 85; closing the book on,
162–163; description of, xvii–xx, 3,
5; designed alliance in, 13–15,
65–66, 79–80, 167; disconnections
from, 100–102; environment for,
15–18; eye-to-eye, 159–160; and the
Gremlin effect, 25–26; and intake
session, elements of, 18–25; and
intake session, outcomes of, 26–28;
professional ethics and standards
of, 170–172
requesting, 24, 88–89, 92, 165

rewards and consequences, 84–85. *See
also* motivation
risk taking, xx, 7, 79–80, 101–102
ruts and recharging, 163–164

saboteur. *See* Gremlin
safety, in coaching environment, 15–18
Sanderson, Ralph L., "Essay on Professional Ethics," 170
satisfaction, 20, 162–163
schedules and structures, 165–167
self, and fulfillment, 123–124, 216–221
self-analysis, 99, 102–103
self-creation, 161–162
self-discovery, 4, 125, 156
self-management: coaching skills for,
103–112; as control, 95–98; of disconnections with clients, 99,
100–102; of failures, 24, 102–103,
110–111, 148–149; of Gremlin, 99,
102–103, 111; of Level I reactions,
98–100; in model of co-active
coaching, 6, 11–12
senses, 43, 91; intuition through,
50–51, 54–56, 60; listening with,
37, 38. *See also* communication
Shaw, George Bernard, 128–129
simplicity and accountability, 128
SMART acronym, 84, 87
spaciousness, in coaching environment, 17–18
standards. *See* ethics and standards
status quo, and Gremlin effect, 25–26,
122
stress, x, xviii
structures, 91, 249; and schedules,
165–167; for sustaining action/
learning, 91–92, 93, 249–251
styles of coaching, 167–168

Taming Your Gremlin (Carson), 9n
technology and communication, 128
telephone coaching: environment for,
15, 16, 164; tips for, 9, 164, 166, 167
telling and demanding, 165
therapist vs. coach, x, 150, 152, 173
time frame, 157–159, 166, 167
tips and traps, 8; eye-to-eye relationship, 159–160; flow of coaching,
160–163; humor, 151, 164–165;
ruts and recharging, 85, 163–164;
schedules and structures, 165–167;
styles and differences, 167–168;
telling and demanding, 165; time
frames, 157–159, 166, 167

tools of coaching: acknowledging, 44–45, 47, 74, 125, 131, 148–150, 163, 165; articulating, 40–41; blurting, 55, 59, 67; bottom lining, 104; brainstorming, 17, 86, 131; challenging, 90–91, 92, 165; championing, 105, 112; clarifying, 41–42, 82–83, 87, 117–119; clearing, 98–101, 106–107, 112; goal setting and planning, 87; humor, 151, 164–165; inquiry, 73–75, 77, 243–248; interpretations, separating, 109–110; intruding, 24, 57–59, 61, 72, 165; metaphor, 43, 47, 149; meta-view, 42–43, 46–47; permission, asking, 18–19, 86, 103; powerful questions, 69–73, 77, 238–242; reframing, 107–109; requesting, 24, 88–89, 92, 165; structures, 91–92, 93, 165–167, 249–251
traps. See tips and traps

triggers: management of, 96–97, 98–100, 111–112. See also self-management
trust, 16; in intuition, 51, 52, 54, 56; and listening, 31, 100
truth, 40. See also veracity

value: of curiosity, 65–67; of failure, 24, 102–103, 110–111, 148–149; and fulfillment, 119–122; of risk taking and commitments, xx, 7, 79–80, 101–102. See also fulfillment
values clarification, 120–122, 226–236
veracity, 16–17. See also truth
vision statement, 124–125

Wheel of Life exercise: and balanced life, 135, 136, 203; for definition of fulfillment, 118–119; at intake session, 20, 182
Whitmore, John, Coaching for Performance, x

The Coaches Training Institute

Professional Training Since 1992. The Coaches Training Institute (CTI), the largest nonprofit educational institution for the profession of coaching, is headquartered in San Rafael, California, with programs delivered nationwide. CTI welcomes and admits students of any race, gender, and national and ethnic origin to all its rights, privileges, and programs, and it is nondiscriminatory in its administration of the school.

CTI awards Continuing Education Units (CEUs). The CEUs are awarded by training programs that meet the criteria of the International Association for Continuing Education and Training and are recognized by several professional licensing boards.

What Is Unique About CTI? CTI trains coaches to develop their own personal coaching style. Our unique teaching methodology, the quality of our course leaders, and our strong commitment to coaches and coaching foster an environment of individualized learning, innovative thinking, and intuitive interaction. While we provide our students with a strong theoretical background, our emphasis is primarily experiential. Through demonstrations, exercises, and practice, each student receives hands-on experience in developing a full complement of effective coaching skills.

Certification. CTI's Certification Program is both comprehensive and rigorous. Upon successful completion of the program and of written and oral certification examinations administered by a board of practicing professional coaches, participants earn the designation Certified Professional Personal Coach (CPPC).

Vision of the Coaches Training Institute. CTI provides the highest-quality advanced training and continuing education for the profession of coaching. CTI envisions a world in which people of all cultures, ages, and vocations are working with a coach—becoming more skilled at choosing what they want, staying on track with their vision, and realizing fulfillment and balance in their lives.

Contact Information

The Coaches Training Institute
1879 Second Street
San Rafael, CA 94901
Internet: www.thecoaches.com
Telephone: (415) 451-6000
Toll-free: (800) 691-6008
E-mail: CoachTrain@aol.com